THE THINGS OF LIFE

THE THINGS OF LIFE

MATERIALITY IN LATE SOVIET RUSSIA

ALEXEY GOLUBEV

CORNELL UNIVERSITY PRESS
Ithaca and London

Cornell University Press gratefully acknowledges receipt of a grant from the College of Liberal Arts and Social Sciences, University of Houston, which aided in the publication of this book.

First published 2020 by Cornell University Press

Printed in the United States of America

Library of Congress Cataloging-in-Publication Data
Names: Golubev, Alexey, author.
Title: The things of life : materiality in late Soviet Russia / Alexey Golubev.
Description: Ithaca, [New York] : Cornell University Press, 2020. | Includes bibliographical references and index.
Identifiers: LCCN 2020003685 (print) | LCCN 2020003686 (ebook) | ISBN 9781501752889 (hardcover) | ISBN 9781501752896 (ebook) | ISBN 9781501752902 (pdf)
Subjects: LCSH: Material culture—Soviet Union. | Space—Social aspects—Soviet Union. | Soviet Union—Social life and customs.
Classification: LCC DK266.4. G65 2020 (print) | LCC DK266.4 (ebook) | DDC 947.085—dc23
LC record available at https://lccn.loc.gov/2020003685
LC ebook record available at https://lccn.loc.gov/2020003686

To Nastia

Contents

Figures

ACKNOWLEDGMENTS

This book reflects a significant part of my academic biography. It began at the University of British Columbia in 2011, and I am extremely grateful to Anne Gorsuch for her guidance, feedback, and encouragement. I appreciate the guidance provided by other UBC faculty members—Alexei Kojevnikov, Bill French, and Carla Nappi, who directed my attention to social lives of technologies, fueled my interest in visual, material. and affective turns in history, and encouraged me to think about the complexity of the interaction between the natural world, human bodies, and systems of knowledge. Michael David-Fox of Georgetown University provided a constructive and holistic critique of my project that helped me identify key areas for revision. I am also thankful to Michel Ducharme, Courtney Booker, David Morton, Eagle Glassheim, Tadeo Lima, Denis and Katerina Kojevnikov, Dmitry Mordvinov, and Sarah Basham who were an important part of my intellectual and social life during my time there.

This book took its present shape during my time at the University of Toronto and my work at the University of Houston, and I am indebted to my colleagues in both cities for their support and assistance over these years. The Russian *kruzhok* in Toronto provided me with an excellent opportunity to discuss my research, and I received valuable feedback from Lynne Viola, Allison Smith, and Simone Attilio Bellezza, among others. Lynne was an ideal mentor whose advice helped me both during and after the completion of the postdoctoral project. The vibrant intellectual environment at the University of Houston enriched this project in multiple ways, for which I am grateful to David Rainbow, Philip Howard, Abdel Razzaq Takriti, José Angel Hernández, Cihan Yüksel, Igor Alexander, and Luis Oliveira.

This book would have been an entirely different work without the input of Serguei Oushakine. My main argument took its present shape in our numerous debates about Soviet culture and society, affect theory, materiality, subjectivity and selfhood, and the production of knowledge. His feedback helped me refine the concepts and intellectual framework of my research. His critical engagement with the theory and practice of Soviet and post-Soviet studies as well as eagerness to help and generosity in sharing his immense knowledge taught me many important lessons.

The almost decade-long work on this book has been greatly facilitated by the help and encouragement of many people on both sides of the Atlantic. I thank Julia Obertreis, Dietmar Neutatz, Willibald Steinmetz, and Michel Abeßer in Germany; Ekaterina Emeliantseva Koller in Switzerland; Catriona Kelly, Olga Smolyak, and Nick Baron in the UK; Markku Kangaspuro, Simo Mikkonen, Maria Lähteenmäki, and Pia Koivunen in Finland; Lars Elenius and Mats-Olov Olsson in Sweden; and Hallvard Tjelmeland in Norway. Anastasia Fedotova, Anatoly Pinsky, and Zinaida Vasilyeva provided an attentive and constructively critical audience in St. Petersburg. This book drew significantly on my earlier research in the history of North Russia and Northern Europe that I carried out at the Petrozavodsk University, where I thank Irina Takala, Sergey Verigin, Aleksandr Antoshchenko, Ilya Solomeshch, Dmitry Chetvertnoi, Yevgeny Kamenev, and Aleksandr Tolstikov. Special thanks to Alexander Osipov for taking several interviews for me. On various occasions I received invaluable feedback on my research ideas and portions of this text from Dmitry Gromov, Yevgeny Efremkin, Yvonne Howell, Dragan Kujundžić, Alaina Lemon, Aleksei Popov, Tadeo Lima, Marko Dumančić, Benjamin Sutcliffe, Adam Frank, Brian Wilson, and Perry Sherouse. I also want to acknowledge the feedback from two anonymous reviewers and Roger Haydon of Cornell University Press that helped me at the final—and most important—stage of preparing this book.

I appreciate the financial support I have received for this research. At the University of British Columbia I have benefited from funding from the Faculty of Graduate Studies, the Faculty of Arts, the Department of History, and the Margaret A. Ormsby Memorial Scholarship. The Killam Trusts and Gerda Henkel Stiftung were my two major external sources of funding during the graduate studies. My postdoctoral project was supported by a Banting Postdoctoral Fellowship of the Government of Canada. The fact that I could present and discuss different aspects of my argument as conference papers was made possible by the financial support from the Canadian Historical Association, European University at St. Petersburg, Moscow Higher School of Economics, University of Nottingham, Princeton University, Havighurst Center for Russian and Post-Soviet Studies at Miami University, University of Zurich, University of Erlangen-Nuremberg, Winterthur Museum, and University of Houston.

An earlier version of chapter 2 has been published as Alexey Golubev, "Time in 1:72 Scale: Plastic Historicity of Soviet Models," *Kritika: Explorations in Russian and Eurasian History* 17, no. 1 (Winter 2016): 69–94. An earlier version of chapter 4 has been published as "'A Wonderful Song of Wood': Heritage Architecture of North Russia and the Soviet Quest for Historical Authenticity," *Rethinking Marxism* 29.1 (2017): 142–72. I thank these journals and their publishers for the permission to use these materials.

Last but not least, I thank my family and friends. My mother Valentina, father Valery, and brother Anton were always supportive of their only family member who chose a career in humanities instead of the family profession of energy engineering. My children Misha, Masha, and Anya made the writing of this book an occasional intervention between the making of toy cities, farms and sand castles, fighting for candies and other junk food, cleaning and cooking, bike rides, playdates, visits to the doctor, and hospital stays. Finally, I thank my wife Anastasia Rogova. She was the main reason why I decided to exchange an already established career in Russia for the perils of a graduate school in a different hemisphere, a decision that eventually led to this book, and it was primarily her support that helped me write it.

Abbreviations

CPSU	Communist Party of the Soviet Union
d.	*delo*, file
f.	*fond*, collection
GTO	Soviet physical culture training program "Ready for Labour and Defence of the USSR"
Gulag	Main Administration of Corrective Labor Camps
KASSR	Karelian Autonomous Soviet Socialist Republic (1923–40; 1956–91)
KFSSR	Karelian-Finnish Soviet Socialist Republic (1940–56)
Komsomol	All-Union Leninist Young Communist League
l.	*list*, page (ll., *listy*, pages)
NARK	National Archive of the Republic of Karelia
op.	*opis'*, inventory number
RSFSR	Russian Soviet Federated Socialist Republic
TASS	Telegraph Agency of the Soviet Union
TRIZ	Theory of Inventive Problem Solving
TsGA SPb	Central State Archive of St. Petersburg
TsGAIPD	Central State Archive of Historical and Political Documents of St. Petersburg
UFO	Unidentified flying object
UNESCO	United Nations Educational, Scientific and Cultural Organization
USSR	Union of Soviet Socialist Republic
VTsSPS	Central Council of Trade Unions

THE THINGS OF LIFE

Introduction

Elemental Materialism in Soviet Culture and Society

> An instinctive, unconscious materialist standpoint
> [is] adopted by humanity, which regards the external
> world as existing independently of our minds.
>
> —Vladimir Lenin, *Materialism and Empirio-Criticism*

When doing interviews for this book, I asked my respondents to describe a day in their lives back in the Soviet era. It did not have to be any particular day, I suggested. Let it be some winter weekday in the early 1980s. What was your typical daily experience back then?

One respondent told me about her daily bus trips to and from work. She accentuated that it was dark both on her way to work and back home. She went into detail explaining how the small and outdated Soviet-built Liaz was warmer than the more spacious and modern Hungarian-built Ikarus. Her stories about bus trips, mundane as they were, suggested some important insights into the organization of daily life in a northern Soviet town. These stories described its tactile and temperature regimes: the density of people's bodies in public spaces, the rapidly numbing fingers and toes, the difficulty of maintaining one's body temperature when circulating between the freezing cold of the streets, the relative warmth of a Liaz, and the heated indoor spaces. They also included references to the social temporality of late socialism—or, more precisely, its particular forms in this urban community dominated by the sub-Arctic day-night cycle and punctuated by the public transit system and work shifts.

Another respondent told me that he developed a strong fascination for bodybuilding in the early 1980s. One might have trouble imagining bodybuilding as a Soviet phenomenon, but it did exist as a semilegal activity frowned on by most officials and sports managers. My respondent spent many evenings in a bodybuilding gym set up in the basement of a residential apartment block and run by several enthusiasts like him. Yet another, a student at a vocational school, had no particular hobby, and so he spent most of his time loitering with his teenage friends in the streets and stairwells of his neighborhood. Occasionally they broke streetlamps, painted graffiti on the walls, consumed alcohol, and fought with other teenagers—all this out of sheer boredom, as he claimed. These stories reveal some specific historical forms of Soviet spatiality, such as the appropriation of common spaces by teenage groups, the experience of alienation in the socialist urban space, and the practices of its overcoming. They tell us that Soviet space was constructed and lived, hierarchical and flexible—but most of all, heterogeneous and multilayered.

As my respondents narrated their everyday life experiences under late socialism some thirty years later, they often described it through their material conditions and not just in terms of consumption. Sure, consumption was important with its shortages, queues, and networks that formed a large part of most Soviet people's lives. Yet Soviet materiality was something more than just the Soviet commodity. Material objects and spaces navigated people through the socialist city, structured their daily activities, defined their relations with their family, friends and neighbors, and forged communities. Scattered through my interviews were fragments of Soviet historical experience showing how the material structured the social and how socialist practices of selfhood—collective and individual alike—were, in so many cases, object-centered.

Official Soviet documents were attentive to this interaction between the material and the social. Reports, memoranda, and other documents produced by low-level Soviet officials are interesting to read from this perspective. On the one hand, they are highly formulaic: the same phrases about the Communist Party's leading role were reproduced from Vladivostok to Kaliningrad. On the other hand, their authors, Soviet bureaucrats, had to deal with vibrant material—the fabric of Soviet everyday life—that escaped schemas of the official discourse. Their observations and interpretations captured Soviet people in their immediate interactions with their social and material environment, which led to frequent gaps and slippages in otherwise clichéd official narratives. In the language of Soviet bureaucratic reports, this interaction was often complex. Not only were people depicted as agents of socioeconomic processes, but objects of the material world were also interpreted as their active participants. For example, a 1963 report of the Ministry of Finances of Karelia, an autonomous republic in the northwestern USSR, stated that "Motor transport inflicts losses on collective farms. This is caused by the low use factor, falsification of figures and over-expenditure of fuel. [For example,] a tractor Belarus of the state farm Medvezhyegorskii stood idle a whole day while there was a complicated situation with the transportation of the potato harvest and fodder at the farm."[1]

Complaints such as that swampy soils prevented the planned expansions of towns and cultivated lands, that waste products of industrial enterprises piled up and created hazards for people and tangible assets, that inadequate infrastructure interfered in the process of educating and disciplining Soviet teenagers, and that insufficient street lighting encouraged petty crimes are abundant in official Soviet documents. Scholars of Soviet history have long noted that the desire to conquer and exert full control over the material world—natural and man-made alike—was one of the founding pillars of Soviet ideology and culture from 1917 to 1991.[2] Yet Soviet bureaucrats—just like my interviewees—spent much of their time dealing with the surprises, difficulties, and obstacles created by the stubborn resistance of infrastructure, equipment, and natural phenomena to Soviet government planning. And like my interviewees who referred to their material environment when asked to recall their everyday experiences, Soviet officials admitted that the material environment could define the human condition. To explain why all this could happen, the language of official Soviet documents in these and innumerable other instances turned nearly animist; material objects and spaces were represented not simply as the setting for or tools of human actions, but also as coparticipants—sometimes assisting, often resisting—in socio economic processes. For officials dealing with a complicated economic situation at a Soviet collective farm it was important that, at this specific point in time, trucks and tractors stood idle or spent too much fuel. Their colleagues inspecting logging sites were concerned that the piles of wood waste and the overly dense storage of lumber created fire hazards.[3] The inspectors of vocational school dormitories were terrified when they observed how a lack of facilities for extracurricular activities correlated with violent and disorderly behavior among students.[4] The language of these reports implied a certain level of social potency, if not agency, of material objects. This is because the difficulties that Soviet officials dealt with were often caused not just by human incompetence and laziness but also by a material world that resisted the will of the party and the government.

Such explanations can be discarded as naive, and it is easy to build a cause-and-effect relationship that would instead explain the situations described above as derivative of the systemic shortcomings of the Soviet planned economy, such as a lack of competition and motivation. Yet I suggest that it might be equally productive to think of my interviewees and Soviet officials as "situational materialists," for whom such a grand scheme of things was of abstract interest. What was important for them was that equipment broke down and thus affected production plans, and local industrial waste accumulated in and around living areas and created various hazards. Weightlifting equipment transformed one's body, while buses were either cramped but warm, or spacious but cold. Untamed urban landscapes produced social deviations or, from the opposite perspective, provided proper settings to gather together to spend free time, exchange the news, and develop and maintain social bonds.

In other words, there was a reason why in my interviews and historical documents I kept on encountering explanations of social situations that operated not only with people and things taken separately but also with assemblages of humans, material objects, and the natural and man-made landscapes. This reason was that this spontaneous materialism reflected the actual historical complexity of the human-object relations in late Soviet society. When we encounter explanations that defined people through the objects of the material world and interpreted objects as encapsulating social relations and tensions, concepts and emotions, this particular attentiveness to interactions between people and their material environment was not necessarily an artifact of the naivety or ideological bias of their authors. To scholars of Soviet history, these concerns about things and spaces suggest important insights into social life during late socialism. At the same time, the daily, spontaneous, and elemental materialism of Soviet people helps us to better understand the social effects and aspects of materiality in general, outside of the Soviet context. The Soviet attentiveness to human-object relations—a product of particular historical conditions shaped by the planned economy, welfare state, and socialist discourses—bears in itself an implicit challenge of anthropocentric concepts of society. Echoing Bill Brown, the author of "things theory," I ask: "Can't we learn from this materialism instead of taking the trouble to trouble it?"[5] What I want to learn from Soviet officials, journalists, and ordinary citizens, these spontaneous and elemental materialists, is their recognition of the actual ability of objects and material environments to organize social life.

Defining Elemental Materialism

The term "elemental materialism" first appeared in Friedrich Engels's *Anti-Dühring* as "naturwüchsiger Materialismus."[6] Engels's primary motivation was to discredit philosophical idealism and its temptations for the socialist movement that he personified with Eugen Dühring, a notable German critic of Marxism. Tracing philosophical predecessors of Karl Marx's materialist dialectic back to ancient Greece, Engels argued that "the philosophy of antiquity was primitive, spontaneously evolved materialism. As such, it was incapable of clearing up the relation between mind and matter."[7] His drafts preserved a more expanded definition of ancient philosophy as "the whole original spontaneous materialism which at its beginning quite naturally regards the unity of the infinite diversity of natural phenomena as a matter of course, and seeks it in something definitely corporeal, a particular thing, as Thales does in water."[8]

The common English translation of "naturwüchsiger Materialismus" is "spontaneously evolved" or "spontaneous materialism." The canonical Russian translation is *stikhiinyi materializm* (i.e., elemental materialism). This translation includes a reference to the foundational question of pre-Socratic philosophy with its attempt to find the originating principle of nature in one of the classical elements (Engels mentions Thales, who championed water as the primary element). In this form, the term elemental materialism became standard in Soviet histories of philosophy as the earliest stage of materialist thinking.[9]

What Soviet philosophers omitted was that another form of elemental materialism was all around them: a culturally rooted recognition of the power of matter and things to shape human bodies and selves, a prominent feature in the Soviet system of signification which regulated the production of meanings on a daily basis. It was elemental in the sense that it dealt with the experiences of daily life and with the entangled assemblages of bodies, objects, and physical spaces that exercised social agency but did not necessarily originate from the dominant order of ideology. Elemental materialism was a set of spontaneous and situational cultural forms that gave Soviet people ways to make sense of this social agency. It often made them—in Engels's words—"incapable of clearing up the relation between mind and matter." Yet I argue that it was not some form of naivete as Engels's evolutionary model implies, but rather a cultural reaction to "the suddenness with which things seem to assert their presence and power,"[10] as well as to the stubbornness with which they do it.

An important question to clarify pertains to the place of elemental materialism in the ideological landscape of late socialism. Although I borrow this term from the Soviet Marxist history of philosophy, in no way I infer any persistent link between Soviet elemental materialism and communist ideology. Ernst Gombrich suggested that "no lesson of psychology is perhaps more important for the historian to absorb than [a] multiplicity of layers, the peaceful coexistence in a man of incompatible attitudes. There never was a primitive stage of man when all was magic; there never happened an evolution which wiped out the earlier phase."[11] The studies of ideology—both in the general and Soviet contexts—have shown how pervasive its effects are, and how easily it escapes the domain of the official doctrine intruding into social relations, everyday life, and practices of selfhood.[12] Yet not everything happening under the Soviet sky was a socially constructed product of the official ideology. This book examines the situations in which Soviet material objects and spaces asserted themselves as the basic elements of social life, as well as analyzes different cultural forms through which people of late socialism conceptualized and problematized the subject-object relations in their historical conditions. In this sense, elemental materialism was anything but a uniquely Soviet phenomenon, and my focus on the material and spatial makes evident the ways in which the Soviet self was an integral part of the global experience of modernity and modernization, rather than just an outcome of communist discourses, education, and propaganda. Yet the particular manifestations of elemental materialism were specific for the Soviet historical context, and by focusing on them I seek to describe the historical process in the late Soviet Union in such a way that would show inner workings of Soviet society where cultural meanings and social acts often resulted from people's interactions with material objects and spaces. Finally, a focus on things, on their ability to organize society, communities, and human bodies and selves in this particular socialist context can account for a more complex understanding of historical change in modern societies in general.

Writing about the Material as the Social

My research method draws on the rich legacy that critical studies of the body and material culture have created in the social sciences. These studies have challenged scholarly representations of "a world of actors devoid of things" and offered various approaches to conceptualizing and interpreting the role of materiality and material objects in social processes.[13] Examples of such approaches range from the anthropological research of Bronislaw Malinowski and Igor Kopytoff, who described how things become socially active objects animated by their passage through the social fabric, to Pierre Bourdieu's and Daniel Miller's inquiries into the role of things in the objectification of social meanings, to a more recent scholarship of new materialists who argue that things are as social agents in their own right.[14] Particularly influential for my research were the approaches of two notable figures of the Russian avant-garde, Sergei Tretiakov and Viktor Shklovsky.

In 1929, Tretiakov, addressing Soviet writers and journalists in a collection published by the Left Front of the Arts, attacked the persistence of old, pre-revolutionary forms of writing which, he argued, prevented Soviet literature from catching up with the pressing and immediate tasks of socialist trans-formations in the USSR. His main object of attack was the classical novel centered on the life trajectory of its protagonist, a genre so burdened with the novel's roots in the bourgeois social order that its uncritical reproduction in socialist literature petrified and annihilated the transformative potential of the latter:

> The novel based upon the human hero's biography is fundamentally flawed and, currently, the best method for smuggling in the contraband of idealism . . . I came up against this in my own practice when I wrote the bio-interview *Den Shi-khua*, the biography of a real person whom I followed with the highest possible degree of objectivity . . . Despite the fact that a substantial number of objects and production processes have been incorporated into the narrative, the figure of the hero is dis-tended. Thus, this figure, instead of being conditioned by these objects and influences, begins to condition them himself.[15]

Tretiakov notes here that an old literary form imposed on him its own reduc-tionist logic, and he is terrified to discover that he is no longer in control of his text. In a way, he describes "the death of the author," a basic postmodern notion that the form of writing has its own politics that cannot be reduced and sometimes are directly contradictory to the author's intended content.[16] Yet Tretiakov is not interested in deconstruction or critical analysis; he wants to reach "the highest possible degree of objectivity" in his understanding and representation of social change, and so he suggests a radical solution: instead of novels based on biographies of real or fictional characters, Soviet writ-ers had to start producing "biographies of the object": "The compositional structure of the 'biography of the object' is a conveyer belt along which a unit of raw material is moved and transformed into a useful product through human effort . . . The biography of the object has an extraordinary capacity to incorporate human material. People approach the object at a cross-section of the conveyer belt . . . People's individual and distinctive characteristics are no longer relevant here. The tics and epilepsies of the individual go un-perceived. Instead, social neuroses and the professional diseases of a given group are foregrounded."[17]

The focus on the object is, in other words, important because it provides a new perspective that allows people to "appear before us in a new light and in [their] full worth."[18] The biography of the object helps us to better understand human society because objects condition people; ignoring the object would be "smuggling in the contraband of idealism." Tretiakov's approach to writing about the material as the social resonates with Kopytoff's famous text on the "cultural biography of things" that popularized object biography among anthropologists; Bruno Latour's inquiry into the social circulation of objects on par with bodies, texts, and ideas; and Judith Butler's writings on the materiality of the body. Underlying them all is the understanding that society is more than a sum of individuals, institutions, and networks: materiality matters, too.

Even though none of my chapters is a biography of a particular Soviet object in the sense of Tretiakov's factography, I owe to him the idea that writing about Soviet scale models, heritage buildings, or stairwells of apartment blocks can be a productive form of social and cultural history. The focus on Soviet objects helps to avoid easy and often forced schematizations of historical material that might be provoked by the use of even the most productive grand categories of political and social analysis, such as socialism, nation, consumption, citizenship, and others. For example, the history of hallways and basements of Soviet apartment blocks that I discuss in chapters 4 and 5 provides insights into how some of the social divisions and conflicts in the late USSR were linked with the urban landscape of late socialism. These conflicts had a concrete material basis, in addition to more abstract divisive social factors, such as income level, education, or family history. Being a man or a woman of late socialism could require not only body rituals and discursive practices, but also checking in, or conspicuously avoiding, a certain register of places that varied substantially from one social group to another.[19] While recent works on social and cultural history of post-Stalinist society accentuated intergenerational distinctions, including books by Donald Raleigh on the "Sputnik generation," Alexei Yurchak on the "last Soviet generation," and Vladislav Zubok on "Zhivago's children," biographies of things make manifest deep divides along class lines.[20] Another example: a history of scale models of aircraft, ships, and ground vehicles in the USSR (chapter 2) can be written as a history of a particular hobby, but can also suggest the importance of their collections for the organization of the Soviet and post-Soviet historical imagination. Tracing the social trajectories of things is about seeking nuances and details in the grand scheme of economic, social, and political change. Yet for history as a conjectural discipline, to use Carlo Ginzburg's term, it is details—trivial and unimportant as they might seem—that "provide the key to a deeper reality, inaccessible by other methods."[21]

Defamiliarizing Soviet Society through Things

For Sergei Tretiakov and some other representatives of the Soviet avant-garde, such as the documentary filmmaker Dziga Vertov, an interest in the material side of social life translated into attempts to exclude to the maximum extent the authorial presence in their works. But not for all. For example, Viktor Shklovsky, another leading figure from their cohort, was skeptical that Tretiakov's factographic writing or Vertov's cinematographic montages of Soviet everyday life could attain "the highest possible degree of objectivity." Although Shklovsky shared their ideas on the importance of things and matter in the organization of social life, he criticized the representational techniques of his fellow avant-gardists because they ignored the fact that the medium—the written word (Tretiakov) or cinema (Vertov)—was not neutral to the message.[22] "I want to know the [identification] number of the steam locomotive lying on its side in Vertov's film," wrote Shklovsky in one of his works, using the example of a filmed train to demonstrate the artistic conventionality inherent in any representation, even in those claiming absolute objectivity.[23]

Shklovsky's response to the realization that "the medium is the message" was to turn this conventionality from a liability into an asset; to use things in the complexity of their social lives as a way of organizing one's narrative—like a literary device or a technique of writing.[24] His most lasting contribution to the field of literary analysis has been the idea of defamiliarization (*ostranenie*), coined in his early work "Art as Technique" (1917). Defamiliarization is a technique in which an author represents a common thing or a typical situation in a strange way (estrangement is an alternative translation of this term) that challenges its conventional understanding. Using examples from Leo Tolstoy's prose, Shklovsky shows how this technique helps to create a more nuanced and fresher outlook on the world: "Habitualization devours work, clothes, furniture, one's wife, and the fear of war . . . And art exists that one may recover the sensation of life; it exists to make one feel things, to make the stone stony. The purpose of art is to impart the sensation of things as they are perceived and not as they are known."[25]

What Shklovsky writes for art is applicable to social analysis as well. For example, a common experience in many Soviet families in 1989 was watching tele-séances of Soviet psychics Anatoly Kashpirovsky and Alan Chumak, who claimed paranormal abilities to remotely heal their audiences through the TV screen. Many explanations of this phenomenon refer pejoratively to obscurantism and the stupidity of Soviet television audiences. But what if we look at these tele-séances as rituals taking place in the home environment and involving interaction between material objects (e.g., TV sets), people's bodies, and alternative epistemic forms (beliefs in the paranormal)? This act of defamiliarization complicates commonplace interpretations of these sé-ances as a "zombification" of Soviet television audiences and provokes questions as to what degree the Soviet television network exercised social power that cannot be reduced to the directives of the Communist Party and the government (chapter 6). Looking at Soviet things "as if for the first time" can serve as a device to resist the "habitualization" of historical knowledge and to challenge commonplace truths that too often disguise the politics of knowledge, as I show in chapter 4 that discusses Soviet stairwells and their residents. What can come as a result might be a reassessment of the process of historical change in the late USSR.

The specificity of working with historical sources is that often their authors leave out details that seemed unimportant to them. Many of my steam locomotives are without identification numbers. Yet there is another important thing that I learned from both Tretiakov and Shklovsky: that the focus on objects should not be a goal in and of itself. Its goal is to make people "appear before us in a new light and in [their] full worth."[26] For this work, writing about the things of late socialism is a method and a technique to better understand the Soviet people: their selves, their social lives, and their interactions with the state.

Materiality and Soviet Selfhood

Since the turn of the 2000s, materiality has become an increasingly important category of academic research, offering new epistemologies, ontologies, and political agendas. Among historians, the materialist turn has challenged anthropocentric views of historical processes and offered interpretative frameworks in which things and matter are treated as capable of facilitating historical change, rather than being simply passive objects of human will. The history of science and technology was quick to acknowledge that objects were instrumental in the process of scientific and technological change; social and cultural histories soon followed, interpreting humans and objects as coparticipants of the historical process.[27]

The response to this material turn in the field of Soviet history was uneven. Although studies of the early Soviet period produced novel research that inspired materiality studies of other regions and periods, historical inquiries into materiality in the late Soviet sociocultural change were more limited.[28] Studies of consumption and housing in the post-Stalinist era have enriched our knowledge of its material world.[29] At the same time, the focus of these works is primarily on Soviet consumption and housing as state projects with the corresponding competitive and didactic implications—consumption as a measure of socialist progress, housing as enlightenment, and vice versa. Their authors emphasize the international aspects of both Soviet consumption and housing, placing them in the framework of Cold War confrontation. The favorite story regularly repeated in the studies of both Soviet consumption and housing is the so-called 1959 kitchen debate, when U.S. vice president Richard Nixon and Soviet leader Nikita Khrushchev confronted each other at the opening of the American National Exhibition in Moscow and engaged in an argument about whether consumer goods, rather than nuclear weapons, should serve as a measure of progress.

Studies of materiality in the late USSR have thus been an integral part of the much bigger and more traditional scholarly field: studies of official Soviet politics. This is reflected in the titles of works on Soviet consumption and housing, as most of them use the names of Soviet political leaders for purposes of periodization. Overall, these studies have created one of the most dynamically developing fields in the history of the post-Stalinist era: the problem of socialism as a form of modernity. By focusing on the specific ways in which socialist modernity was materialized in its objects and embodied in its subjects, they have immensely contributed to our understanding of state politics in late socialist societies. The reverse side of this tendency is that the scholarship of consumption and housing in the late USSR is only marginally interested in the social autonomy and agency of Soviet things and spaces. The latter are represented as the medium that the Soviet authorities used to shape modern, disciplined, and cultured citizens, and that citizens used to negotiate their understanding of socialism.[30] Yet this medium had its own message that too often interfered with what the Soviet authorities wanted it to deliver.

Writing about and from the perspective of elemental materialism in the late USSR offers an opportunity to trace and describe the social power of things, especially their relationship with Soviet bodies and minds. The representational aspect of Soviet material culture (socialist modernity made manifest) is important for my research. However, this book also contributes to another important field of historiography of the Soviet Union: studies of Soviet subjectivity and selfhood. By subjectivity, I understand the ideological construction of individuality—a subject as an effect of the work of structures of power. By selfhood, I understand the personal and cultural misrecognition of one's bodily, emotional and discursive heterogeneity and fragmentariness—misrecognized as the unity of the self.[31] Starting with Stephen Kotkin's *Magnetic Mountain*, the questions of how the Soviet state fashioned its citizens into subjects, and how Soviet people embraced and questioned the dominant paradigms of selfhood, and designed their own ways of self-fashioning, have been addressed by numerous scholars.[32] Historical studies of subjectivity and selfhood is one of the fields in which the current historiography of the USSR is at the forefront of history as an academic discipline. These studies operate within the general postmodern scheme of a decentered and fragmented subject, recognize that any historical form of selfhood is unstable and always requires work to maintain it, for example, through writing or rituals, and identify subjectivation as a form and effect of power.

Although particular methods, techniques, and objects of research in the scholarship of Soviet selfhood and subjectivity vary from scholar to scholar, the general modus vivendi in this field is logocentrism.[33] In studies of the post-Stalinist period, one particular and influential example is Alexei Yurchak's *Everything Was Forever until It Was No More: The Last Soviet Generation*. Yurchak draws on J. L. Austin and Judith Butler to build a discursive model of the late socialist selfhood, which reproduces itself through the repetition of certain speech acts. His main argument is that the people of late socialism combined the mastery of performance of the Soviet authoritative language with trickster skills to employ official language forms to express new meanings. It was this combination that constituted the historical specificity of "the last Soviet generation."[34]

This book also employs the conceptual model of selfhood as a fragmented, unstable, and performative phenomenon, and the problem of language (as structure) and speech (as performative acts) in constituting Soviet subjects is important for my argument. When I discuss elemental materialism as a cultural recognition of the power of things, I deal with the cultural logic of late socialism that became manifest in its discursive production. But this is where I also divert from many of the studies of Soviet subjectivity and selfhood. I look at the social and cultural landscape of late socialism as a field with multiple and divergent subjectivizing forces. To speak of "one generation," both in the late Soviet context and elsewhere, means to extrapolate the historical experience of one particular social group onto the entire society at the expense of other groups. Different cultural languages (or, in terms of Michel Foucault, discursive formations), ideology, social relations that varied from one community to another, and the material environment offer different models and practices of selfhood. People's selves are a result of material, in addition to linguistic, production. Shklovsky's involvement in the Russian Revolution, when he commanded a squadron of armored cars during the February 1917 overthrow of the tsar, made him particularly sensitive to this fact:

> It is the machine that changes the man more than anything else . . .
> Subways, cranes and cars are human prostheses . . .
> Drivers are measured by the horsepower of the engines they operate.
> An engine of more than forty horsepower annihilates the old morality . . .
> We should not forget the car's contribution to the revolution . . .
> You, cars, sloshed the revolution like foam into the city [of Petrograd].[35]

Shklovsky pioneered the understanding of historical agency as produced through the interaction of humans and material objects. He noted that affect usually acts as the mediator between them. For Shklovsky—and I follow his lead in this book—things do not have agency per se; it is by causing an affective response in people that they enter the historical scene and contribute to the historical change by "annihilate[ing] the old morality," "contribut[ing] to the revolution," and in multiple other ways. Affect is thus an important concept for my book, as my empirical material provides a wealth of evidence that various affects played a key role in how the Soviet people made sense of themselves and the world around them. Drawing on these insights, I reject a historical description of Soviet selfhood as a list of immanently Soviet features or as a phenomenon derived exclusively from language. It is also necessary to take into account repetitive, culturally reproducible, and materially specific situations in which the people of late socialism came into social being as Soviet persons.

The material world of late socialism could repeatedly fail the authorities in their attempts at its rational transformation, and officials and intellectuals could be genuinely scared by assemblages of Soviet bodies and material objects that exercised unexpected and potentially disruptive social agency. Yet Soviet materiality could not provide any space that was continuously autonomous from power structures. In chapter 5, for example, I show how Soviet bodybuilders were excluded from the official sports system and had to occupy the basements of apartment blocks, where they exercised semilegally and were subject to persistent criticism in the Soviet press. Yet in the late 1980s, some of them came out from their basement gyms to perform in international bodybuilding competitions as Team USSR, whereas some others sought to discipline—by force, if necessary—punks, hippies, metalheads, and similar youth who dressed and behaved in conspicuously Western, non-Soviet manners. The marginal location of bodybuilders in the Soviet social space was not translated into social marginality. Quite the opposite, the Soviet basement gym revealed an ability to produce citizens loyal to the regime even in situations where the regime misrecognized this loyalty as a threat and opposed it through its sports officials.

One of the most important questions of my research is why Soviet meanings proved so resistant to the political and cultural changes related to the collapse of the USSR in 1991. Or, put differently: why did post-Soviet social and cultural structures so often resemble their Soviet predecessors? If the succession of economic and sociopolitical changes caused by perestroika, liberalization, and the ultimate collapse of the Soviet state was so radical, then what is it that makes the contemporary Russian society of the 2000s and 2010s reproduce the cultural and political forms that it inherited from its Soviet past?

Maybe this question should be rephrased in a radical way. Perhaps, it is actually the crisis of conventional forms of describing post-Soviet societies that forces both participants and observers of the recent political changes in Russia to interpret it as a reincarnation of the late USSR. After all, Marx's famous saying in *The Eighteenth Brumaire of Louis Napoleon* that "history repeats itself . . . first as tragedy, then as farce" draws from the analysis that shows it is not socioeconomic structures that remained unchanged ("repeated themselves") from the reign of Napoleon Bonaparte to that of his nephew—they actually changed. What lagged behind were political and cultural forms that provided Louis-Napoleon with an interpretative framework to mobilize French public opinion in his favor.[36] Could it be that the persistence of Soviet meanings, in a similar fashion, is not an intrinsic property of modern post-Soviet states and societies, but rather an artifact of politics—including the politics of knowledge and representation? Thinking about it with and through Soviet elemental materialism might provide some insights on the latter question, and I explore it in the concluding sections of the chapters.

Material Coordinates of the Soviet Self

To investigate the tenacious, yet elusive link between Soviet materiality and selfhood, I look at different ways in which things of late socialism came to embody and negotiate different and often contrasting social understandings and techniques of time and space in the final three decades of the Soviet Union. I focus on those material objects which, in the specific late Soviet historical contexts, pushed Soviet people to occupy different positions vis-à-vis historical process and social space. In other words, I am interested in the objects that helped Soviet people make sense of historical time and social landscape of late socialism.

This approach determines the structure and composition of this book. The first three chapters explore the link between material objects and the different temporalities of post-Stalinist Soviet society. In chapter 1, I look at the productivist language of late socialism as a discursive framework that inspired and produced Soviet elemental materialism and was itself inspired and reproduced by it. Productivist language linked a vision of the grand Soviet future with technological objects and sought a rational social organization along industrial production and scientific progress. It abducted the imagery of Soviet factories, machines, vehicles, and space rockets, immersed it into the hermetic space of visual and textual representations, and used it to define, for the Soviet symbolic order, the position of the USSR at the cutting edge of technological progress. In this discourse, technologies and technological objects secured the possession of the present and future of human history for Soviet society, as well as ensured the superiority of the USSR in its competition with the Western bloc. The perceived might and transformative agency of Soviet technological objects made them affective for the Soviet public, and they became translated into distinctive discursive practices—vernaculars of the Soviet techno-utopianism—that sought to transform the Soviet material world but instead represented rigorous forms of self-making. In addition to affect and its politics, chapter 1 introduces several other key themes that I discuss in the following chapters, including the idea of making oneself by making things, which Soviet educators and ideologists understood in terms of the development of creativity, and the performativity of objects.

Chapter 2 explores the scale model hobby in the USSR, focusing on models as objects that made manifest the historical imagination inherent in Soviet technopolitics. Models, especially when assembled in collections, challenged Marxist interpretations of history and helped organize the Soviet historical imagination along national lines. As with their prototypes, scale models were also affective but in a different way, because of their ability to showcase Soviet industrial and technological capabilities and to stand as a synecdoche for historical progress. The miniaturization of history in its particular technocentric and national understanding made models performative, as they organized history into a spectacle for the educated male gaze of Soviet model enthusiasts. This chapter also addresses the themes of the public space, performativity, and visuality.

Chapter 3 turns to other types of material objects that were capable of performing history: timber buildings associated with cultural heritage and historical ship replicas. The last three decades of the Soviet Union evidenced a fast growth in the number of heritage sites related to traditional wooden architecture. This chapter examines the museumification of old architecture as a process that was similar to scale modeling hobby in its politics, but stimulated the nationalist understanding of Soviet history in its Romantic, rather than techno-utopian, interpretation. In particular, I show how wood, a traditional building material, became a symbol that objectified the "deep cultural roots" of Soviet society and served, because of its texture, as a living witness of its authentic history.

The second part of this book moves from the temporal to the spatial coordinates of Soviet selfhood. Here I shift focus from the Soviet educated class and activities requiring specializing skills and taking place in the highly visible public sphere to marginalized social groups who used things and spaces of late socialism to cope with alienation and historical change. In chapter 4, I look at the mass housing program launched by the Soviet leadership in the late 1950s from the perspective of urban planning and management. I am interested in the transit spaces of new socialist neighborhoods, focusing on the stairwells of Soviet apartment blocks. Designed as utilitarian spaces for the fast passage of people from home to work to leisure activities, they revealed an ability to accumulate people and connect them in various ways, which Soviet authorities and intellectuals often interpreted as threatening to the public good. The Soviet stairwell established different affective regimes of Soviet people's interactions with urban space and provoked some of the hidden social conflicts of late socialism that became reflected in socially dominant structures of the Soviet self.

The communities I discuss in chapter 4 were predominantly male. The material and social conditions of late socialism provoked different regimes and forms of masculinity, which is another important topic of this book. In the first three chapters, I examine those forms of masculinity that were more common for the Soviet educated class, while the second part focuses on male homosociality practiced in more marginal settings. Chapter 5 continues the exploration of the marginal urban spaces of late socialism from a slightly different perspective, as it examines the peculiar phenomenon of basement bodybuilding in the late USSR. Driven by the transnational imagery of the cultured male body as hypermuscular, many Soviet teenagers and men turned to weightlifting equipment with its power to help achieve muscle gain and transform their bodies into cultured bodies. At the same time, the failure of Soviet bodybuilding to become part of the official sports system led to its social marginalization, which became visible in social topography. The Soviet press repeatedly denounced basement bodybuilding as a criminal activity. But for most people who engaged in it, it was a form of acquiring strength, health, self-assurance, and—through it—social agency, which many of them interpreted as loyalty to the dominant symbolic and political order.

Finally, chapter 6 investigates how the television set as a material object changed the Soviet domestic space and Soviet selfhood. This chapter brings together most of the topics I discuss in this book. It looks at the social conflict between the educated class and marginalized groups in Soviet society, which found its manifestation in public debates over presumably healing or harmful effects of the television set. I deliberately focus on the material form in addition to the content of television to argue that its inclusion in the Soviet home instigated new forms of identity performances that cannot be reduced to the content of television programs but can rather be traced to the physical nature of television as a medium of mass communication. Focusing on the phenomenon of paranormal séances broadcast on Soviet television in 1989, this chapter explores the various ways in which Soviet television audiences discovered that the television set had power over their bodies and selves, as well as looks at different forms of social reaction that this discovery caused in late Soviet culture.

This book is based on a wide variety of published and unpublished sources. To combine both central and regional perspectives on my subject, I have done archival research in the National Archive of the Republic of Karelia (NARK) and the museum of Kizhi in Petrozavodsk, the Central State Archive of St. Petersburg (TsGA SPb), and the Central State Archive of Historical and Political Documents of St. Petersburg (TsGAIPD SPb). Because of the broad scope of my research, I did not focus on one particular collection but instead examined collections of documents of various official Soviet organizations, including local and regional cells and committees of the Communist Party of the Soviet Union, governmental agencies and ministries, and public organizations such as housing committees and hobby groups based in Palaces of Young Pioneers. Research for this book also included taking multiple interviews; though I used only a few of them in the text, they were helpful in providing me with the general historical background and innumerable details about the Soviet everyday life during late socialism. Other unpublished sources include email correspondence with people who were engaged in the practices that I discuss in this book.

Soviet periodicals are another major source of this work; given my focus on the material side of life in the USSR, I was particularly interested in amateur science and technical magazines such as *Tekhnika—Molodezhi* (Technology to youth), *Modelist-Konstruktor* (Modeler-Designer), and *Nauka i zhizn'* (Science and life). They combined top-down and bottom-up approaches to content creation, as their readers contributed many of the materials appearing in them. In addition, I used many books published by central and regional Soviet presses. The postwar Soviet Union was covered by an extensive publishing network which, in theory, was under the strict control of the communist authorities. In practice, however, the sheer size of this network created a structural disjunction between its official—strategic—mandate to contribute to the socialist cause and the local—tactical—agendas of editors, managers, and authors of numerous Soviet presses who were engaged in their own dialogues and disputes. This was how books on such topics as bodybuilding, romantic nationalism, and even paranormal phenomena were published in the USSR. Treating these texts anthropologically, as sources into Soviet systems of meaning, helped me understand historical forms of interaction between Soviet society and its material world.

The main advantage of following Soviet objects in their passage through social space, their interaction with people, and their representation in texts and visual aesthetics is the opportunity to see society in its spontaneous forms. Some of these forms were influenced by dominant ideological narratives, some of them reflected the global experience of modernity and modernization, and yet others represented—to use Vladimir Lenin's phrase—"the instinctive, unconscious materialist standpoint" adopted by Soviet people to deal with the unpredictable and resisting, but also flexible and manageable, materiality around them. By examining the interaction between Soviet people and things, this book shows how the material world of the late Soviet period shaped and influenced people's habitual choices, social trajectories, and imaginary aspirations.

CHAPTER 1

Techno-Utopian Visions of Soviet Intellectuals after Stalin

> Our path leads through the poetry of machines, from the bungling citizen to the perfect electric man. In revealing the machine's soul, in causing the worker to love his workbench, the peasant his tractor, the engineer his engine—we introduce creative joy into all mechanical labor, we bring people into closer kinship with machines, we foster new people.
>
> —Dziga Vertov, "We: Variant of a Manifesto"

The émigré Soviet historian and philosopher Mikhail Heller titled his 1985 historical inquiry into "the formation of Soviet man" as *Cogs in the Wheel*.[1] This mechanistic metaphor underlined Heller's main argument that the course of Soviet history was shaped by "a planned, concentrated and all-encompassing attack of unparalleled intensity" carried out by the Soviet state to "turn human beings into cogs."[2] Heller argues that the entire communist leadership—from Vladimir Lenin to Konstantin Chernenko, the Soviet leader at the time he wrote *Cogs in the Wheel*—intentionally orchestrated this manufacturing process. It was from this perspective that Heller described "the formation of Soviet man" as a thoroughly designed project, which had been meticulously implemented since the earliest days of the Bolshevik regime. On one occasion, he referred to the communist leadership as "the creator" and Soviet state institutions as its "tools," bringing demiurgic implications into his historical explanation.[3]

The historical imagination in *Cogs in the Wheel* is a good illustration of what Jacques Derrida called a secrecy effect; that is, a cultural tendency to explain political developments as the result of secret planning by the government and, consequently, to emplot and write history as the uncovering of this planning.[4] It is not surprising that this book has produced a negligible influence on Soviet historiography, although it is still cited regularly in non-scholarly works. This conspiratorial form of historical imagination not only disregards historical transformation in Soviet Russia over seventy years but is also counterfactual. Heller manipulated some of his sources when, for example, he attributed to Joseph Stalin a statement that "Soviet man should consider himself a mere 'cog' in the gigantic wheel of the Soviet state," or when he claimed that the term "cogs" was commonly used by another Soviet leader, Nikita Khrushchev.[5] In fact, the metaphor of people as "cogs in the wheel" is almost impossible to find in official Soviet language. The official Soviet writing on the "new Soviet man"—those texts that became the foundations of Soviet pedagogy, cultural policies, or quotidian party work—emphasized that the socialist state "not only provided working masses with an unlimited access to spiritual wealth, but also made them immediate creators of culture."[6] Heller's attempt to prove that Soviet leaders were engaged in an intentional and planned campaign of dehumanizing the Soviet population seems especially fallacious if one considers the theory and practice of Soviet education with its emphasis on the development of creative skills among students and the ultimate rejection of Anton Makarenko's militarized approach to education.[7] Although Soviet ideologists openly acknowledged that the making of the new Soviet person was a vital part of their political agenda, a "cog" is hardly a suitable term to describe the official understanding of an ideal communist personality.

The easiest way to deal with this contradiction would be to dismiss Heller's account as a purely political statement aimed at discrediting the Soviet historical experience. Instead, I want to suggest that *Cogs in the Wheel* represents an interesting entry point to discuss Soviet cultural fantasies of control over the material world. Heller operates with two ostensibly different discursive regimes of Soviet culture, making use of one to criticize the other. His account of Soviet society is framed in concepts and arguments typical for a Marxist critique of capitalist societies in which the machine stood for the highest form of alienation and cogs for people alienated from humanity and which was a standard critique of capitalism in Soviet political philosophy.[8] A graduate of the Faculty of History of Moscow State University, Heller was deeply immersed in this Marxist critique of capitalism. It is therefore hardly surprising that he employed its concepts and imagery to represent the Soviet state as a dehumanizing machine and Soviet people as cogs, thus turning the official Soviet language (with its critique of capitalism) against the source of its production.[9]

The other discursive regime that was targeted for criticism in *Cogs in the Wheel* is what I hereafter call the productivist language of Soviet culture. On many occasions, when Heller claimed to engage with the facts of the Soviet sociopolitical reality, he criticized facts of the language—that is, statements and documents that were produced as meaningful in this discursive regime but did not necessarily translate into social and economic practice. In one case, Heller quotes a slogan of Sergey Tretiakov, who advocated that literature and art should acquire a practical role in social transformation: "The worker in art must stand side by side with the scientist as a psycho-engineer and a psycho-constructor." This, coupled with his quoting of Stalin's famous reference to Soviet writers as "engineers of human souls," gave Heller a rationale to claim that the entire Soviet history, from the moment the Bolsheviks took power in Russia, was an immense project of social engineering aimed at creating a society that would work like a machine and would be accordingly easily manageable.[10] Heller's was an analysis that extrapolated one particular discourse to the entirety of Soviet history. It is by disguising the productivist language of Soviet culture as the Soviet social reality that Heller produced a plausible—despite its ahistoricity and counterfactuality—genealogy of the Soviet man. Heller is undeniably biased and often inaccurate in his interpretations of Soviet history. Yet his account provides one important observation: a widespread tendency of Soviet officials and intelligentsia to define individual and collective selves through things.

This chapter examines the relationship between the productivist language of "the machine and the cogs" (the original Russian title of Heller's book) and the technologies of the self that it invoked in late Soviet society. The focus here is on how this language provided Soviet society with a set of metaphors and concepts to understand the course of human history as the process of technological change as well as provoked and reinforced widely shared cultural fantasies of total control over the material world. This discussion is essential for the understanding of how human-matter interactions were conceptualized and reflected in the cultural logic of late socialism.

The ubiquitous character of the cultural language of productivism was noted by Serguei Oushakine, who suggested that the Soviet economy should be historically characterized as an economy of storage rather than of shortage. The overstocking of commodities—but also of the means of production—was not simply a sign of its ineffectiveness (an assessment that implies that surplus-oriented economic liberalism is taken as a universal economic model), but rather an indication of a different set of socioeconomic rules and principles that produced the Soviet economy as a specific historical phenomenon. These rules and principles can be traced back to early Soviet theorists of industrial production like Aleksei Gastev and Alexander Bogdanov as well as to the avant-gardist ideas of Soviet Productivists such as Boris Arvatov who sought to modernize Soviet everyday life through a new industrial design.[11] Dziga Vertov's writings and documentaries reflected both the ideology and the aesthetics of Soviet Productivism, with machines acting as models for men and factories representing a superior form of the organization for social life. Whereas Fritz Lang's *Metropolis* (1927) or Charlie Chaplin's *Modern Times* (1936) represented machines as dehumanizing and alienating people from society and from themselves, for Vertov machines had to show the "path . . . through the poetry of machines, from the bungling citizen to the perfect electric man."[12] In his *Entuziazm: Simfoniia Donbassa* (Enthusiasm: Symphony of Donbass [1930]), machines orchestrate and choreograph the movement of people, transforming them from scattered individuals into a powerful collective; the factory becomes an art object that creates new, perfectly socialist forms of social life.

The language and imagery of productivism with its tendency to imagine and organize society around machines was engaged in a complex relationship with economic processes and agents: it simultaneously described and constituted them. Despite its seemingly pragmatic and apolitical character, this language produced and was produced by the Soviet ideological order maintaining a specific "representation of the imaginary relationship of individuals to their real condition of existence."[13] As such, it was an authoritative (and officially sanctioned) discursive regime, but unlike the official language of *Pravda* or similar Soviet publications, its production was deregulated and delegated to individuals for whom "speaking productivist" was not a ritualized and petrified activity, but rather provided the means of building and expressing their true ideals and visions of the future.[14] In addition, the productivist language of Soviet culture had no particular centers of production. Examples of productivist speak can be found from Khrushchev's memoir to popular Soviet magazines to specialized technical writing to grassroots pedagogic theories. Its seeming noninvolvement with the language of official Soviet ideology entailed the misrecognition of the fact that productivist language immersed its speakers in fantasies of subdued material reality, ranked Soviet people in accordance to their relationship to the production process and mastery over things, and created moral panic when certain Soviet people engaged in relationships with presumably mean and unworthy objects instead of sublime ones.

Machine as the Essence of Socialism

The mid- and late 1950s in the Soviet Union were a period of a revival of the techno-utopian ideas forged in the 1920s. Soon after Stalin's death, in 1954, leading Soviet nuclear physicists wrote a collective essay to the Soviet government, warning that it was impossible to win a nuclear war and that such a conflict could potentially obliterate life on Earth.[15] Their opinion informed the top-level decision-making process in the USSR: at the Twentieth Congress of the Soviet Communist Party in 1956, Khrushchev ruled out the inevitability of a military conflict between the socialist and capitalist blocs, and instead suggested that socialism would outcompete capitalism peacefully.[16] This placed Soviet technological objects into a different plane of historicity in comparison to late Stalinism with its focus on the applied military use of technologies. For the officials and educational theorists of the post-Stalinist era, inspired by early Soviet techno-utopianism, the national mastery of technology was a way to secure the position of the USSR at the cutting edge of technological progress, a goal that inherently implied the possession of the present and future of human history.[17] Prior to 1953, Stalin and the Communist Party were the key symbols of socialism. From the mid-1950s on, machines and technological development replaced them as the essence of socialist progress for many Soviet intellectuals and their audiences.

The Soviet space program that triumphantly burst into the Soviet public consciousness with the launch of Sputnik-1 in October 1957 made rockets and other space technologies the most prominent objects for encapsulating the long historical time of socialism. The first Soviet passenger hydrofoil boats launched in 1957 and notable for their ultra-modernist design were promptly named Raketa (Rocket), as was a premium watch brand introduced in 1961 at the Petrodvorets Watch Factory in Leningrad. The conquest of the outer space became a prominent theme for Soviet mass media, as well as for the writers, artists, and film directors working in the genres of popular science and science fiction, including Ivan Yefremov, Aleksander Deineka, and Pavel Klushantsev.[18] Real and imaginary space technologies provided the Soviet public with a new understanding of the relationship between humans and technological objects. Shiny satellites and interplanetary probes, crewed spacecraft with intricate mechanisms, sophisticated computers, and cosmonauts in high-tech spacesuits suggested an intimacy of bodies and machines, their amalgamation as a necessary precondition of both technological and social development. During the following decades, Soviet space imagination acted as a testing ground for negotiating, probing, and defining the cultural boundary between the human and the technological.[19]

This renewed fascination with machines was not limited to space technologies. Beginning in the mid-1950s, the socialist realist canon in visual arts—with its focus on static compositions and "varnishing of reality," a term that was widely used in the Khrushchev-era critique of this canon—became increasingly challenged by a partial and cautious revival of the politics and aesthetics of Soviet avant-garde. This revival was most prominent in photography, where a new generation of Soviet photographers turned to productivist motifs to catch a techno-utopian atmosphere that characterized post-Stalinist Soviet society. The national photography magazine *Sovetskoe foto* (Soviet photo), initially established in 1926 and discontinued in 1942, was revived in 1957 by the USSR Ministry of Culture under pressure from Soviet professional photojournalists. Its editors and contributors immediately launched a campaign against Stalin-era genres, typical compositions, and techniques.[20] Lev Sherstennikov, a member of this generation, later described this change in his memoir as a conscious search of new forms and compositions that defied the "formulaic" and "staged" Stalinist aesthetics.[21] Photojournalism, with its attentiveness to the "labor routine of workers and kolkhoz farmers" as well as "everyday life of Soviet people," was declared a method that was best suited to reflect, inspire, and accelerate the building of a socialist society.[22]

The new aesthetics and politics of Soviet photography were, in a way, a reiteration of Vertov's writings on and practice of filmmaking that called for "filming life unawares" make "the invisible visible, the unclear clear . . . making falsehood into truth."[23] It was this agenda that led Vertov to film "the poetry of machines" to find a new socialist man in the human-machine assemblages. In a similar way, at the turn of the 1950s Soviet photographers turned to industrial photography to catch life "unaware" in its supposed sincerity. In the launch issue of *Sovetskoe foto*, Yakov Gik, an editor at *Ogoniok* (Little flame) and *Literaturnaia gazeta* (Literary newspaper), lambasted "certain photojournalists [who] prefer not to observe life, not to catch it in all its manifestations, but rather to "stage" these manifestations."[24] A contributor to the next issue of *Sovetskoe photo* referred to Vertov in the title of his piece, "What Photo-Eye Failed to See at the Factory," and demanded that Soviet photographers "broadened the assortment of industrial photographs" in order to catch the true selves of Soviet people in their interaction with tools, machines, and products of their labor.[25] Over the next years, Semyon Fridlyand, Vsevolod Tarasevich, Yuri Krivonosov, Nikolai Rakhmanov, and other photographers who collaborated with Soviet illustrated and specialized journals, such as *Ogoniok*, *Iunost'* (Youth), *Smena* (Next generation), and *Sovetskoe foto*, greatly expanded techniques, compositions, perspectives, and angles of their photography, offering a new vision of socialism as a complex fusion of collectives, individual bodies, machines, and the natural world. Fridlyand (1905–64), a prominent figure of Soviet photography during the 1920s and 1930s, who became a photo editor at *Ogoniok* in the mid-1950s and joined the editorial board of *Sovetskoe foto* in 1959, was one of the leaders of this fundamental shift in Soviet photography. His photograph published in the July 15,

1956 issue of *Ogoniok* exemplifies this new cultural logic that defined Soviet people through their relationship with machines (figure 1.1).

Fridlyand took this photo for a special issue of *Ogoniok* that focused on the industrial transformation of Siberia during the Soviet era. To illustrate the "face of modern, Soviet Siberia," he created a set of industrial landscapes, including this photograph featuring two workers at a Novosibirsk factory that produced equipment for power stations in Siberia.[26] A critic of avantgarde photography during the 1920s and early 1930s, Fridlyand here appropriates some of its techniques, such as an unusual perspective, angle and light pattern, placing the workers inside a frame created by the silhouette of a turbogenerator rotor. This technical object acts as a lens that highlights their working-class identities. What is more important is that it hints at the biopolitics of post-Stalinism with its focus on combinations of bodies and machines for the transformation of nature into a socialist landscape.

This understanding of labor as a process in which machines helped Soviet people find their true selves was an important part of the Soviet cultural logic in the post-Stalinist period. Redeploying rhetorical figures of the First Five-Year Plan, which had been downplayed in the first decade after World War II, official Soviet publications announced from the mid-1950s on that technical literacy was a new cultural front where socialist development was at stake. "Machine is your friend!," "Master your equipment!," and other similar slogans became common in Soviet propaganda activities and didactic texts.[27] Emerging as a reaction to numerous party and government resolutions aimed to facilitate technical progress in the USSR and build "the material basis of socialism," this propaganda and related didactic discourse saturated Soviet cultural space with productivist ideas. Writing in June 1956, several months after Khrushchev's de-Stalinization speech, a director of one Moscow's technical colleges appealed to Soviet youth: "Immense goals are set for the Soviet people in the Sixth Five-Year Plan [1956960]. In these years, new types of machines, lathes, presses, devices and equipment will appear. Our factories will require thousands of highly qualified metal workers, millers, turners, engineers, and specialists of many other qualifications."[28]

Both rhetorically and ideologically, this appeal equated Sovietness ("for the Soviet people") with the mastery of technologies and called on *Smena*'s readers to define their future professional selves as derivative of machines in order to secure uninterrupted socialist development (a reference to the Sixth Five-Year Plan). It was through this world of modern technological objects that official discourses created an image of Soviet society as a progressive, technocratic, and industrialized nation comprised of rational

FIGURE 1.1. Semyon Fridlyand, "Turbogenerator manufacturing plant in Novosibirsk: Turbogenerator rotor windings," 1956. Courtesy of the Dalbey Photographic Collection at the University of Denver.

socialist subjects. School education, mass media, and the state network of hobby groups (*kruzhki*) promoted an obsession with these objects as a characteristic feature of the Soviet person. Popular scientific and technical writing mounted a discursive support of it, as in the following example from a technical magazine for amateur engineering and model design: "If you are seriously interested in space engineering and exploration, if you have chosen your life path from a model rocket to a spaceship—remember that this is a long and demanding path."[29] The author of this quote, Yuri Stoliarov, was an enthusiast of intensive technical education of school-age children, an author of multiple books and journal articles on STEM education, and the founder of the specialized journal *Modelist-Konstruktor* (Modeler-designer), and its editor-in-chief from 1962 to 1992. He points at material objects—"a model rocket" and "a spaceship"—as the reference points between which Soviet teenagers were encouraged to build their biographies as well as the building blocks from which socialism was to be constructed. Characteristic of the Soviet cultural language of productivism, these examples reveal its persistent tendency to imagine society around machines. This form of social imagination—a reiteration of Vertov's *Enthusiasm: Symphony of Donbass* with its workers dancing around their machines—was immensely important in late Soviet society mobilizing grassroots initiative of people who sincerely believed in socialism and wanted to achieve it through mastery of friendly machines.[30]

Stoliarov's writing also bring to the surface a certain ethos inherent in the productivist language of Soviet culture regarding the interaction between Soviet people and their material environment. This ethos represented the Soviet person as a creative subject, a representative of the species *homo creativus*. Soviet ideology interpreted creativity as a necessary trait for a socialist personality. Starting with Lenin, who argued that "vital, creative socialism is a creation of the popular masses themselves," Soviet philosophers, political writers and activists amassed writing in which they argued that an ability to create new meanings and new things was a characteristic feature of people living in a socialist society.[31] Meanwhile, the Soviet press characterized manual labor with the same terms used to describe the creative activities of artists, poets, and composers.[32] This ideological definition of the Soviet subject as a "creative" personality implied human mastery over the material world, and Soviet technical magazines—one of the primary sites where the productivist language was reproduced—appealed to their readers as the generation of "creators and explorers."[33]

"Creation" in the Soviet context implied a Promethean vision of the transformative human role in a world waiting to be transformed.[34] This vision referred to a particular version of the normative Soviet person as a self-aware, rational, and free actor capable of manipulating and reconfiguring matter. The technocratic, productivist language of Soviet culture found expression in the cultural fantasies of Soviet intellectuals who dreamed of various fusions of human bodies and machines as a necessary precondition for an advanced communist society. Perhaps its most perfect example was Genrikh Altshuller's grand attempt at creating a system of technical innovation to accelerate both technological and societal evolution.

TRIZ: Genrikh Altshuller's Vernacular of Soviet Techno-Utopianism

Genrikh Altshuller (1926–98) was a prominent Soviet inventor who is best known in the former USSR as the author of the Theory of Inventive Problem Solving (TRIZ). Altshuller, who dropped out of the Industrial Institute of Azerbaijan in 1944 to enlist in the Red Army, started working on a universal algorithm that would simplify technical inventions in the late 1940s. In late 1948, he and his collaborator, Rafael Shapiro, wrote a letter to Stalin, where they criticized the sluggishness and inertia of Soviet industry in regards to technical innovation and suggested that a statewide introduction of Altshuller's algorithm might lead to a much-needed transformation of the Soviet system of innovation management.[35] In July 1950, Altshuller and Shapiro were arrested; most histories of TRIZ refer to their letter to Stalin as the cause of the arrest, although one of their friends later claimed that it was an ordinary denunciation that was related to the widespread anti-Jewish sentiment of the late Stalinist era.[36]

Altshuller was released in 1954; like many of other Soviet intellectuals of the Thaw generation, his Gulag experience made him anti-Stalinist, but not anti-Soviet. Altshuller continued working on his algorithm with a firm conviction that its popularization and application would accelerate the cause of socialism and thus prevent injustices committed under Stalinism. He published early works on it the mid-1950s, and developed it into a comprehensive theory of invention with a methodological apparatus and a growing number of enthusiasts in the 1960s.[37] He was also a theorist of pedagogy and a science fiction writer. Altshuller founded his theory of invention on the premise that to solve a technical problem (that is, to make an invention), an inventor should first identify an internal contradiction inherently present in any technical object or system. The ideal solution to the problem would then be to reformat the technical system so that the contradiction is removed, but without adding other mechanisms or parts.[38] In other words,

TRIZ approached technical objects and the material world as "infinitely flexible," as possessing a hidden potential for their more effective usage, and as fully subordinate to the human will, given that people had the necessary skills to see technical contradictions and find solutions to them.[39]

In 1964, Altshuller had a lengthy correspondence with the brothers Strugatsky, whose works would soon become part of the Soviet literary canon. In one of his letters he claimed: "Since my childhood, at all stages [of my biography], science fiction determined my life. It is a kind of religion. Of course, I am not a fanatic and admit that one temple can serve to worship different gods. As for myself, I prefer prognostic science fiction, when it is used not as a literary device, but to look into the future, as precisely and as far as possible."[40] For Altshuller, himself a prolific science fiction author under the pen name G. Altov, science fiction was inseparable from his theory of invention. One of its postulates was that technological inventions and consequently human progress were hampered by the psychological inability of people to see solutions to technical problems, or even to perceive technical problems as an obstacle to be overcome. Science fiction was, in his theory, necessary to develop the professional vision of an inventor—a vision that could easily identify problems and find solutions to them. As one of his regular coauthors and another practitioner of TRIZ claimed, "It is impossible for an inventor to acquire advanced professional thinking without reading science fiction regularly."[41]

Beginning in the late 1960s, regional schools started appearing all over the USSR, and by the early 1980s TRIZ transformed into such a recognizable brand that Altshuller had to deal with an unexpected trend, namely, fake and self-appointed instructors exploiting the popularity of the movement, as well as with a former student who claimed that he was the actual developer of this theory.[42] The expansion of the movement also required a unification of teaching curriculum, and in the mid-1970s the leading proponents of TRIZ came up with a set of teaching recommendations, materials, and instructions that have gone through several editions before Altshuller's death in 1998. Writing and reading science fiction hold a prominent place in the curriculum so that students would learn to see technological things in their potential flexibility and changeability.[43] One such group in Petrozavodsk had regular training sessions during the 1980s at a local factory club; watching science fiction films, imagining fantastic objects and creatures, and enacting scenes from the communist future were regular activities for its students.[44] For the theorists of TRIZ, science fiction was important because it showed their audiences that better things could create a better society and vice versa. In a creative take on Soviet Constructivist fascination with objects as friends, rather than servants, the corpus of TRIZ texts suggested that the main goal of technical intelligentsia was to improve things, and through better things construct a better future.[45] Science fiction allowed for the visualization of an intimate relationship between people and machines that lay at the basis of TRIZ and was, in essence, symbiotic. People relied on technologies to pave the way to communism, but to do so they had to change themselves into creative, technologically literate citizens. Soviet productivist language provided Altshuller and his audience, mostly Soviet scholars and engineers, with the necessary symbolic vocabulary to express and perceive the idea that the path to building a communist society is charted through the creation of machines and tools that would extend the capabilities of human bodies and selves.

By the 1980s, Altshuller's quest for more inventive means to accelerate technical progress led him to develop another theory called the Theory of Creative Personality Development.[46] Dissatisfied with the perceived rigidness and lack of inventiveness among the Soviet engineering cadre, Altshuller argued that to build the material basis of the communist future, the Soviet engineering cadre and, ideally, all Soviet people should be trained in creative thinking. In other words, be trained to treat the world as flexible and subordinate to human imagination: "We know that developed socialism would be unimaginable without universal literacy. More years will pass, and a society will emerge in which every person will be able to solve the most complicated intellectual tasks. This will probably be regarded as an obvious necessity: after all, is it possible that under communism the summits of intellectual creativity would be available only to a small group of people?"[47]

Having emerged in the 1950s as an algorithm for solving industrial production tasks, by the 1980s TRIZ had transformed into a didactic system that sought to remodel first Soviet people, and only then machines. TRIZ encapsulated and expressed cultural fantasies of flexible materiality and demanded vigorous self-fashioning from its followers in pursuit of these fantasies. Practical courses of TRIZ were framed in the rhetoric of technological invention, but structurally they were built as psychological training aimed to teach students to "overcome a psychological inertia and a fear to think creatively."[48] The promise of mastery over the material world acted as bait to lure Soviet people into imagining themselves as creative socialist subjects and investing their personal time in techniques of self-making.

Altshuller summarized this logic in a 1976 edition of his "Recommendations of how to teach TRIZ classes." According to this publication, new students came to TRIZ classes with a simplistic understanding of technical problems. As they progressed through the course, students learned to treat objects, technologies, and technological systems as infinitely flexible, possessing powerful qualities and abilities that were invisible to an untrained eye. The final outcome was a rational and systematic way of thinking about materiality and technology.[49] Even though TRIZ was created by a former Gulag inmate, and its practitioners regularly criticized Soviet authorities for their inability to modernize the nation, they did not resort to resistance or even attempts to find spaces "outside" of the dominant ideology. Instead, they engaged in a very materialist project to retrofit socialism from below and sought to produce proper socialist subjects by teaching them how to imagine, design, and build better things.

TRIZ was a prominent vernacular of Soviet techno-utopianism that defined socialist selfhood through its relationship with the material world. One's belonging to the collective of Soviet people was relatively marginal for this definition; what really mattered was one's skills to see technical systems and objects as flexible and ready to subdue themselves to their creator's will. Since its vocabulary was based on the understanding of technological objects as encapsulating long historical time, mastery of technologies became a key factor for socialism to occupy its place as the next, more progressive, stage of human history. Training sessions in the Petrozavodsk school of TRIZ took place under a large poster reading, "The history of human civilization is the history of inventions!"[50] This understanding of technological progress as the essence of personal and social development pushed enthusiasts of TRIZ to argue in the late 1980s and early 1990s, as the socialist economy was gradually collapsing around them, that a national adaptation of TRIZ in education and industry would allow for a rapid and effective reinvigoration of state socialism.[51] While they continued speaking their dialect of Soviet productivist language, other less rational forms of interaction with the material world captivated audiences around them. Following the Baku pogrom in January 1990, Altshuller, a Jew, fled with his family from Azerbaijan to Petrozavodsk where the local TRIZ group helped him obtain an apartment during the dying gasp of the Soviet system of housing distribution. In the post-Soviet period, TRIZ associations and schools gradually moved to position themselves primarily as personal and career counseling services, and only secondarily as technical consulting services.[52]

Flexible Materiality in Soviet Do-It-Yourself Magazines

The story of TRIZ is not much different from what happened with another vernacular of the Soviet productivist language—the discourse of Soviet technical do-it-yourself magazines. These magazines were immensely popular in the late socialist era, although the peak of their popularity coincided with perestroika. One of them, *Modelist-Konstruktor*, had an impressive circulation which grew from 140,000 copies in 1966, its launch year, to 850,000 copies in 1982, to 1,800,000 copies in 1989, its peak year. As for similar do-it-yourself magazines, in 1989 their figures for monthly circulation were 1,777,000 copies for *Iunyi tekhnik* (Young technical designer) and 1,555,000 copies for *Tekhnika—Molodezhi* (Technology to youth). Other journals with prominent do-it-yourself content included *Katera i yakhty* (Motorboats and yachts), *Radio*, and a Russian edition of the Polish *Horyzonty techniki dla dzieci* (Horizons of technology for children). A significant share of their circulation was distributed through individual subscription, but these magazines were also available through libraries, schools, and hobby groups (see chapter 2), and thus had a multimillion-strong audience of Soviet technical enthusiasts. In addition, it was possible to occasionally purchase Eastern European journals in newsstands or from Soviet tourists after trips abroad, such as Polish *Mały modelarz* (Young modeler), Czechoslovak *Modelar* (Modeler), and East German *Technicus* and *Jugend und Technik* (Youth and technology).

The first issue of *Modelist-Konstruktor*, a cult magazine of Soviet amateur engineering, appeared in January 1966. Its first editorial address promised to the magazine's readers that "the magazine will tell you how to build . . . real small airplanes, helicopters, motor gliders, which will take you to the sky. As for future conquerors of the ocean, *Modelist-Konstruktor* will . . . supply them with the blueprints and technical characteristics of yachts, catamarans, motorboats . . . Car and bike fans will find on the magazine's pages detailed materials about amateur designs of sport models and personal cars."[53] The magazine fulfilled its promises. In the following decades it published hundreds of blueprints and instructions on how to produce virtually everything with one's own hands, ranging from light aircraft with motorcycle engines to holiday rafts made of truck tires.

Modelist-Konstruktor was not the only cultural venue that popularized amateur engineering in the USSR. Launched in 1963, *Katera i yakhty*, a specialized periodical for amateur boat- and yacht-building, published hundreds of designs ranging from small riverboats to ocean-worthy yachts. Beginning in the 1960s, another widely circulated technical magazine, *Tekhnika—Molodezhi*, started popularizing homebuilt cars. In 1966, its editorial board organized the first Soviet exhibition of homebuilt cars, an event that became regular during the 1970s and 1980s.[54] *Radio* published electronic circuits and blueprints that could be used to assemble sophisticated electronic devices or to repair virtually everything produced by the Soviet radio-electronic industry. Apart from periodicals, from the 1960s to the 1980s books were printed by hundreds of thousands that advised how to build summer cottages (*dachas*), cars, boats, and electronic appliances.[55] From the early 1970s until 1991, the central Soviet television broadcast a TV show called *Eto vy mozhete* (You can make it), which introduced to a multimillion television audience different amateur designs ranging from kitchen appliances to cars and small aircraft.

An immense popularity of amateur engineering magazines and books was, at least partially, due to the shortage of consumer commodities in the eastern bloc. For example, the Soviet industry did not produce subcompact utility tractors, as routine work at collective farms required larger vehicles, while private households were not supposed to engage in large-scale for-profit agricultural production. However, plenty of advice was offered on how to use spare parts of motorcycles, cars, and even gas chainsaw to manufacture a mini-tractor. In an effort to compensate for a poorly developed system of after sale service, *Za rulem* (Behind the wheel), a journal for auto enthusiasts, published instructions on how to fix and tweak nearly everything in one's car. Finally, they publicized innumerable designs of home appliances such as innovative vacuum cleaners, automatic lighting, security systems, heaters—all those appliances that one had trouble finding in the Soviet retail trade.

Despite their seeming pragmatism, these journals did have their ideology. Like TRIZ, Soviet technical magazines aimed to shape the Soviet subject as a master of the material world. They published blueprints of a car to be made of plywood and an electric generator mounted on a kite to provide electricity during tourist trips; the combination of bearings, metal pipes, and plastic could be used to make virtually anything ranging from a bicycle car to boat engines to gliders to tractors to all-terrain vehicles to snowmobiles.[56] There was virtually no technical equipment or home appliances that Soviet amateur engineers could not theoretically assemble using the innumerable circuits and instructions published in Soviet technical magazines and the basic radio components sold in Soviet stores. The list included computers and even, albeit humorously, a time machine.[57]

Soviet materiality as it was represented through this discourse was flexible; in late Soviet culture, any given thing could become anything else, and thus a priori performed the function of raw material or assembly kit even if it was brand new. The first editorial of *Katera i yakhty* explained why the magazine would publicize do-it-yourself practices by appealing to its audience: "We are far from believing that everyone involved in sailing as tourism or sport should build a yacht or a motorboat by himself. One can use an [industrially] produced vessel. But what enthusiast [of sailing] would refuse the pleasure of remaking [*peredelat'*] it in his taste?"[58] This discourse suggested that an exemplary Soviet subject was able to overcome the attraction of passive consumerism (a feature Soviet ideologists and intelligentsia alike associated with the threats of the petty bourgeois lifestyle)[59] by changing the material form of an industrially produced commodity, and so becoming its co-producer. After all, since the building of socialism included the overcoming of alienation, amateur engineering offered a possible solution to people's losing part of their identity with the products of their work, even though pragmatically it implied a partial return to the artisanal mode of production.

The politics of Soviet amateur engineering logically pushed its advocates to develop educational theories that fostered "the formation of Soviet man," to use the subtitle of Heller's work, although this imaginary Soviet man was in no way submissive and passive. Instead, the spirit of Soviet do-it-yourself culture emphasized human ingenuity and implied that, if properly applied, it would not be limited by the scarce material resources at hand. Just like the TRIZ publications, Soviet technical journals offered different methods to "develop" and "stimulate" imagination on their pages.[60] Some activists of amateur engineering went further and from sporadic advice moved to develop more coherent pedagogic theories of personal development through extracurricular technical education. One of them was Yuri Stoliarov.

In addition to being one of the most influential figures in Soviet amateur engineering, Stoliarov was an important theorist of education whose works appeared as monographs and articles in leading educational research journals such as *Sovetskaia pedagogika* (Soviet pedagogy), *Shkola i proizvodstvo* (School and industry), and *Fizika v shkole* (Physics in school). He was one of the coauthors of the article on "Child Creativity" in the third edition of *The Great Soviet Encyclopedia*—a mark of prominence in the Soviet hierarchy of academic capital.[61] In his works, Stoliarov advocated a nationwide adoption of technical education as early as middle school, arguing that "the material-technical basis of communist society will comprise large and deeply mechanized industrial production based on full electrification and automatization. This means that we should start training our youth to be qualified to work in highly mechanized and automatized production . . . Creative work [in extracurricular classes of technical design] will greatly assist schoolchildren in appropriating the latest scientific and technological advances in the industry, and prepare them to be active participants of the rationalization and invention process."[62]

Stoliarov follows a productivist logic when he argues that industrial development should define the career choices of Soviet students and that the earlier students start getting training in technology, the better citizens they will eventually become.[63] But Stoliarov's ideal of Soviet society organized around machines was very far from its dystopian interpretations by Heller and some other scholars.[64] Like Altshuller, Stoliarov, and other Soviet theorists of early technical education believed that technical literacy was a solution to the problem of social alienation in the age of machines. A nationwide network of extracurricular hobby groups—a phenomenon that I discuss in more detail in chapter 2—had to immerse Soviet students in the do-it-yourself culture, and make them in this process self-aware, rational, and free actors capable of manipulating and reconfiguring matter, and of creating new, modern, and friendly socialist things.[65]

The mastery over materiality suggested by the discourse of amateur engineering was a cultural fantasy, just as it was in Altshuller's writings. Publications on how to make complex things with one's own hands acted as traps that lured people into established patterns of subjectivation due to their seemingly pragmatic, apolitical, and de-ideologized character. In addition, amateur engineering (both as an actual practice of making things and reading about it in technical magazines) was an important way of performing Soviet masculinity in its educated, technocentric version—a version of gender as constitutive of certain skills in do-it-yourself culture. The emphasis by Soviet technical magazines on the conquest of Soviet space with the help of homebuilt cars, yachts, motorboats, and planes is symptomatic in this respect. As I argued elsewhere, Soviet cultural fantasies of spatial conquest exploited the traditional gender divide men as active users and women as their passive passengers.[66] Like in other modern cultures, mastery of space was a male prerogative in Soviet culture, and do-it-yourself magazines enticed their male audiences to imagine themselves as travelers in homebuilt cars, boats, or planes, joining the ranks of mythologized Soviet explorers who rose to social prominence in the 1930s and who made the conquest of nature a Soviet affair.[67]

Although thousands of people read about such means of personal transportations, few actually ventured to build them, judging by the fact that even national exhibitions of homebuilt cars or planes never gathered more than several dozens of vehicles, a minuscule quantity compared to the scale of the Soviet Union.[68] Amateur engineering could not overcome the problem of infrastructure, especially when it came to airfields or ports, which were ill-suited for private aircraft or yachts; besides, their owners were often forbidden to use these state-owned facilities.[69] Enthusiasts of homebuilt cars had to struggle with a shortage of spare parts, a situation that plagued the Soviet car market during its entire existence.[70] As a result, homebuilt yachts and cars were something more typical of the Soviet collective imaginary than the real Soviet landscape. The extensive circulation of Soviet technical magazines and the popularity of *Eto vy mozhete* secured a wide distribution of images of modern-looking garage-built vehicles, aircraft, and ships.

Amateur engineering was something to be looked at and read about; that is, it was a discursive field that turned the materiality of self-made things into a spectacle and that totalized the scattered experiences of their producers into a governing text with a dominant idea, that of human mastery over space. "Sometimes we receive questions asking why the magazine *Tekhnika—Molodezhi* organizes collective trips of amateur cars through dozens of Soviet cities. Does [Soviet] industry produce cars of poor quality? This is not the case. The romantic aspirations of young masters to build a car of their own using plastic and aluminum, an amphibious car capable not only of driving, but also of sailing, should be supported. This is also a search for new discoveries."[71]

This quote from an article by Vasilii Zakharchenko, editor-in-chief of *Tekhnika—Molodezhi*, highlights several key points of the techno-utopian vernacular of Soviet technical magazines. It associated amateur engineering with the romanticism of exploration—or, if put in Michel Foucault's terms, with the will to knowledge[72]—that gnostic drive that defined people involved in this culture as subjects of knowledge, as explorers who would fashion themselves into conquerors of land (homebuilt cars), water (yachts and motorboats), and air (small aircraft).[73] The discourse of amateur engineering worked all the more effectively since in most cases, this conquest of the elements was imaginary; to use a metaphor, Soviet technical magazines "abducted" the actual practice of building vehicles in garage conditions and traveling in them. This was then represented to their readers as texts and images, constructing them as one large male audience joining this effort to conquer nature and to transform it with travel from a wilderness into a landscape.[74] The discourse of amateur engineering worked by seducing readers into imagining themselves at the steering wheel of a motorboat or a car reaching into an otherwise inaccessible wilderness, driving a propeller sleigh through Arctic plains, observing the landscape from a light aircraft, or touring the countryside in a motorhome. In many ways it resembled the socialist realist canon with its focus on the world "depicted . . . as it should be according to theory" rather than real life.[75] This discourse needed the actual practices of building cars, boats, or planes only inasmuch as they provided examples to be incorporated into its corpus to make it more convincing and tempting; in other words, to create a desire to make things with one's own hands.

Given the bottom-up approach to content creation in Soviet technical magazines (nearly all of their designs were initially developed by readers for themselves and then successful solutions were shared through the journal), it is not surprising that the producers of the Soviet discourse of amateur engineering misrecognized the cultural fantasy of subdued materiality for reality. In the late 1980s, enthusiasts of do-it-yourself culture unsuccessfully argued—in a logic similar to that of the advocates of TRIZ—that amateur engineering could become a nationwide basis for small businesses that would reinvigorate the socialist economy.[76] As the Soviet socioeconomic model collapsed, the audience of this particular vernacular of the Soviet techno-utopianism shrank to the actual number of amateur engineers in Russia. The monthly circulation of *Modelist-Konstruktor* fell from 1,800,000 copies in 1989 to 5,150 in 2010, while *Katera i yakhty* transformed into a modern illustrated magazine focused on consumption. Yet their discourse has its post-Soviet afterlife, as can be recognized in statements claiming that the technological advances of modern industrial states have been achieved via the application of methods or technologies borrowed from TRIZ or amateur engineering magazines.[77] One typical statement argues that "in the Soviet era, the Japanese subscribed to Soviet journals such as *Modelist-Konstruktor*, *Tekhnika—Molodezhi*, *Iunyi tekhnik*, and patented all our ideas and inventions. This is how they built their prosperity."[78]

Since Japan is routinely perceived in Russia as a model state in terms of economic development achieved through technological progress, the people who associate themselves with the Soviet discourse of amateur engineering naturally interpret its present as the desirable, but failed, Soviet future. What Japan represents now is how the USSR could have looked if their discourse had been taken seriously by the state authorities. Similarly, enthusiasts of TRIZ associated the technological and social progress of the West and the stagnation of late Soviet society with the application and nonapplication, respectively, of TRIZ methods.[79] Aleksandr Seliutskii, the leader of the TRIZ movement in Petrozavodsk (he helped Altshuller to move there from Baku in 1990), claimed in an interview that at least some of the recent technological breakthroughs in South Korea were a result of the adaptation and widespread use of Altshuller's theory: "You see, we live in Russia, that is why this idea [TRIZ] failed to get national recognition . . . but in [South] Korea it is part of corporate training. You cannot get a promotion above a certain level without a TRIZ certificate . . . Samsung issued a corporate order: its employees need to pass a TRIZ exam for a promotion . . . And we were [a] closed [society], the country was closed . . . The [Soviet] system was not interested in a transformation, even though we offered that, with TRIZ, we could take the current state of affairs and immediately, at once, upgrade it to the next level."[80] These beliefs are a logical outcome of a common misrecognition that various dialects of techno-utopianism were more effective in producing Soviet subjects than marketable commodities.

TRIZ and amateur engineering demonstrate the importance of material objects for the cultural definition of proper Sovietness, both in terms of individual and collective selves. At the center of this definition stood mastery over space achieved through technological objects; through this mastery these objects were key to the national possession of the future, which endowed them with their own historicity. Victor Shklovsky wrote in 1922 that "subways, cranes and cars are human prostheses;"[81] mastery over these and other technological objects brought with them a promise of the spatial and temporal extension of Soviet selves. In post-Soviet political discourses, this historicity turned grand technological objects associated with Soviet techno-utopian visions into nostalgic objects.

On July 2, 2013, a Russian rocket Proton-M carrying three satellites for the Russian navigation system GLONASS burst into flames in the first seconds after the launch. The leading opposition newspaper *Novaya gazeta* (New newspaper) responded to this event in its next issue by placing a caricature by Pyotr Sarukhanov showing a group of primitive people dancing with spears in a circle around a rocket (figure 1.2).

Sarukhanov's image plays on the contrast between two incompatible historicities: one archaic, embodied in the black figures that, in an undeniably racist metaphor, personify the Russian engineering cadre, and another progressive, encapsulated in the slim silhouette of a space rocket. For the Russian public, with its cultural expertise in Soviet texts and imagery, this image represents a reference to the visual aesthetic of the post-Stalinist era with its emphasis on body-machine assemblages. But whereas Soviet bodies and selves lived up to the challenges of their technological objects, the irony of Sarukhanov's image capitalizes on the perceived inability of post-Soviet bodies and selves to enter into affective assemblages with the grand technological objects of the Soviet era. In public debates, these objects regularly become a measure of contemporary Russian people, society, and the state, usually to emphasize their inadequacy and pettiness in comparison to ambitious visions of the conquest of space and time embedded in Soviet-era technologies. Following the 2009 accident at the Sayano—Shushenskaya hydroelectric power station (built in the 1970s and still the largest power plant in Russia), when seventy-five people died and the national power supply was disrupted, *Novaya gazeta* reported: "[This disaster] has brought to the surface the most vital lesson for us, so vital that there is nothing more important. For a nation that still launches rockets into space, the most vital task is to revive the following reflex: at the sight of an unfastened bolt to put a screw on it and then regularly check and secure it with a wrench."[82]

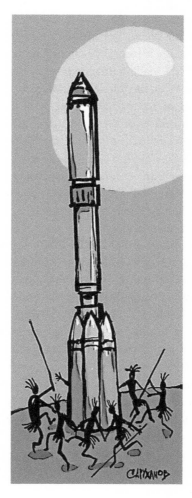

FIGURE 1.2.   Pyotr Sarukhanov, a caricature on the current state of the Russian space program, 2013. Courtesy of Pyotr Sarukhanov.

The author of this article openly claims that Russia as a nation has a future only if it masters anew the skills demanded by its technological objects. This statement is informed by productivist language, now in its post-Soviet variation influenced by the Chernobyl disaster, the collapse of the USSR, and the secondary position of post-Soviet Russia in the global quest for progress. According to its logic, the revival of the national body is only possible through a restored mastery over the advanced infrastructure and vehicles that would allow for the control of Russian national space and, consequently, time. In fact, productivist language can be recognized in much of the political criticism of the current leadership of Russia. Yulia Latynina, one of the most vocal liberal critics of Vladimir Putin's government (except when it comes to climate change denial and the measures restricting immigration to Russia), described her 2010 trip to the leading Russian producer of rocket engines, NPO Energomash, in terms of an incredible technological progress that abruptly stopped in 1991. She then attacked the ruling government, claiming that it did not live up to the promises of these technologies, left their potential unrealized, and thus betrayed the future of the Russian nation: "I was watching these absolutely fantastic engines. I was present during an engine test. I was looking at the engineers who were testing them, and I saw that all of these engineers were older than 60. In the meantime, young [specialists] keep on leaving [Russia]. And then you understand that this is, in fact, our last chance [to remain competitive internationally]."[83]

Latynina as well as many critics of the Russian government from both right and left deploy Soviet-era visions of technological grandeur to define the Russian national body (emphasized by the obligatory use of the first person plural "we") as losing or already lacking vital connections to the material world of advanced technologies. This is why the Russian public sphere, both on the left and right, is so anxious about the developments in the private spaceflight (mainly U.S.-based) that have marginalized the Russian space program. Whereas for Heller, a humanist, the main fault of the Soviet regime was in its desire to turn people into "cogs" of the Soviet system-as-machine, contemporary critics of Russian authorities routinely employ productivist language to accuse them of unwillingness or inability to adapt Russian society to the challenges and potential of machines that it inherited from the Soviet past.

CHAPTER 2

Time in 1:72 Scale

The Plastic Historicity of Soviet Models

> It is a grand attempt to overcome the wholly
> irrational character of the object's mere presence at
> hand through its integration into a new, expressly
> devised historical system: the collection.
>
> —Walter Benjamin, *The Arcades Project*

When the Soviet government ordered the construction of the national exhibition center in Moscow in 1935, it was conceived as a showcase of Soviet agriculture and was named, accordingly, the All-Union Agricultural Exhibition. Two decades later, with the dawn of the space era and the rapid industrialization and urbanization of Soviet society, this focus on agriculture no longer seemed relevant and, in 1959, the exhibition center was renamed the Exhibition of Achievements of the National Economy. As part of this reorientation of the Soviet national exhibition, a pavilion that had previously been devoted to bog peat was renamed Iunye tekhniki (Young technical designers) and started featuring the craftsmanship produced by schoolchildren's extracurricular hobby groups (*kruzhki*) and centers of young technical designers (*stantsii* and *kluby iunykh tekhnikov*), such as hand-built vehicles and agricultural equipment, scale models of ships and planes, and designs of existing and future space crafts.

The allocation of a special pavilion at the Soviet national exhibition to young technical designers highlighted the importance that Soviet education officials gave to the extracurricular activities of school-age children. The Department of Extracurricular Education was established within the People's Commissariat of Education of Soviet Russia in November 1917, and in 1952, the Council of Ministers of the USSR passed a resolution that introduced common organizational and teaching standards for extracurricular clubs and centers. Over the course of the following decades palaces and houses of Young Pioneers, centers of young technical designers, school hobby groups, and other forms of extracurricular activities sprang up all over the Soviet Union.[1] In 1988, 464,384 extracurricular clubs and centers existed in the Soviet Union, or roughly four times the number compared to 1950. The official statistics claimed that 7,500,000 schoolchildren attended them, with technology-related clubs and groups being the most popular (2,132,659 children).[2] According to the 1989 Soviet census, the number of schoolchildren between the ages seven and seventeen in the USSR exceeded 45,000,000,[3] which means that approximately one in every six Soviet school-age children attended extracurricular activities at any given time. Given the high turnover rates in them, the proportion of Soviet students who at some point in their education enrolled in hobby groups was likely to be even higher.

The development of extracurricular technical activities was driven by the productivist discourse, and it pursued a pragmatic function: the incorporation of their labor into the productive forces of the Soviet economy. The idea to spread technological literacy among schoolchildren was borrowed from late imperial pedagogy; in particular, from the works of Evgenii Medynskii, a prominent theorist of extracurricular education who continued to work under the new authorities.[4] During the 1920s and especially the 1930s, it became increasingly associated with one's civil obligation to serve the national cause, whether in peace or wartime.[5] The Young Technical Designers pavilion reflected a further, post-Stalinist development in the political fantasy of schoolchildren's contribution to the national economy, which was also prominently featured in educational theory[6] and Soviet teen science fiction.[7]

The dreams of Soviet enthusiasts of extracurricular technological activities did not come true. As later publications bitterly noted, nearly all of their technical innovations were wasted through inefficient bureaucratic management.[8] Yet, because of their inclusion in the Soviet politics of technology and hence the political process, schoolchildren's hobby groups and centers were also engaged in symbolic production, which had a more profound effect on Soviet society. The official stance behind extracurricular activities promoting science and engineering to children was not only pragmatic but also pedagogical and disciplinary. By engaging technologies both in theory and practice, Soviet children were expected to use their leisure time as an investment not only in their future but also in the socialist progress of their state.[9] For example, a panegyric article published in a Soviet technical magazine and dedicated to an enthusiast of extracurricular technical education said that his "deserved reputation" came from his persistent effort to turn "mischievous boys into socially useful people."[10] A theorist of school education argued in an article in the flagship journal *Sovetskaia pedagogika* (Soviet pedagogy) that engaging technology-related extracurricular activities helped schoolchildren become responsible persons with "serious interests" in working and engineering occupations; it eventually led to "the formation of moral consciousness" and "proper" adulthood.[11] Linking national and personal development, extracurricular hobby groups were part of Soviet technopolitics, a concept that Gabrielle Hecht developed in order to conceptualize "hybrid forms of power embedded in technological artefacts, systems, and practices."[12] In Soviet education theory, extracurricular activities were meant to bolster the technological and industrial progress in the USSR and to ensure that children were raised as disciplined and patriotic Soviet citizens. The link between Soviet technopolitics and extracurricular activities made young Soviet hobbyists subjects to the ideological process. What is particularly important for this chapter is that it also transformed the material objects of these activities into ideological objects endowed with political and historical meanings.

The most common activity in technology centers and clubs was the construction of models of historical and contemporary ships, planes, and vehicles. This focus on modeling existing vehicles in the extracurricular activities of the late socialist era marked an important difference with similar activities of the Stalinist era. From the 1920s to the 1950s, Young Pioneers mainly built flying, sailing, or driving machines, albeit in miniature. The resemblance with actual vehicles was optional.[13] Late socialist hobbyists built those, too, but their focus was increasingly on miniature replicas that were designed exclusively for display. This transition was facilitated by the postwar development of plastics technologies, as their use allowed Soviet manufacturers to organize industrial production of scale model kits. But the transition was not only a technological one, as the materiality of models was closely tied to discourse and ideology. The shift of focus to static replica models immersed late Soviet enthusiasts of modeling into a historicity that stressed divisions and hierarchies on the basis of nation rather than class. It suggested that the Bolshevik Revolution was not so much a rupture as a continuity and established a genealogical succession from the medieval East Slavic states to Muscovite Russia, the Russian Empire, and the Soviet state. Finally, the making of historical models was premised on explanations of history that favored great men at the expense of the toiling masses, thus prioritizing an elitist perspective over an egalitarian one.

The argument that historical knowledge in the Soviet Union employed national, if not nationalist, discourses alongside internationalist and class-based ones is anything but new. David Brandenberger and Kevin M. F. Platt traced the turn to nationalist interpretations of Soviet history to the late

1930s when the Soviet leadership searched for new models of popular mobilization in a complicated international context and with a European war looming on the horizon,[14] and Richard Stites showed how this tendency intensified multifold during World War II.[15] What this chapter adds to this discussion is an exploration of some of the quotidian and materialist mechanisms through which this national perspective of Soviet history departed from the framework of official cultural production, obtained a broader audience, and became encapsulated in material objects and their collections.

The incorporation of this national perspective of history in the activities of children's technology groups and centers made it particularly convincing since it was marketed to its audience as a by-product of the seemingly pragmatic activity of obtaining new skills in handicraft and engineering. If one examines school and university textbook and curricula—the main medium through which the Soviet state authorities sought to disseminate the dominant forms of historical knowledge among the population of the USSR—throughout the entire Soviet era they remained committed to the Marxist interpretations of history as a process of class struggle and change of social formations. The undergraduate history curriculum in Soviet universities was organized along the Marxist theory of social formations. It was a peculiar feature of the late Soviet society that the understanding of history in nationalist terms became so prominent through relatively marginal epistemic genres and forms, such as state-funded hobby activities. This was the sphere in which Soviet schoolchildren encountered material assemblages and mastered historical narratives that prioritized nations over classes and great personalities over masses.

The affectivity of models and their collections—their ability to showcase Soviet industrial and technological capabilities and to stand as a synecdoche for historical progress—was important in the production and circulation of the Soviet Union's national historical imagination at the grassroots level. Reemerging in various locations in the USSR, this historical knowledge was all the more persuasive, since it was produced in a decentralized way: Soviet schoolchildren acquired it from enthusiasts of modeling and engineering, older peers, and technical literature, as well as produced it themselves, literally with their own hands. As I discuss in chapter 1, Soviet culture interpreted machines and technologies as symbols of historical progress;[16] and their scale models—planes and ships small enough to fit on bookshelves and on tables—allowed for miniaturization and domestication of this symbolism. This process was even more complex since historicities were performed by scale model collections themselves, which organized history into a spectacle for the educated and the quintessentially male gaze of Soviet model enthusiasts.

Censoring Objects of Modeling

There are two principal ways of making a scale model: from an industrially produced kit or from scratch, using blueprints, historical descriptions, and photographs.[17] The first way is labor-saving, but the variety of models is limited by what the market offers. The second way requires much more labor, time, and skill, and the making of such a model by children is usually possible only under the supervision of an experienced hobbyist. However, the variety of vehicles that can be imitated is virtually unlimited. As a result, plastic models made from kits formed the bulk of private collections in the Soviet Union, both among children and adult hobbyists, whereas custom-built models were made and then exhibited in school hobby groups, centers of young technical designers, and Palaces of Young Pioneers.

"Not only people are part of history; machines and vehicles are, too," wrote the Soviet technical journal *Modelist-Konstruktor* in 1969 in one of its numerous articles that called on Soviet teenagers to immerse themselves in the hobby of model making.[18] This logic, in which the making of models was understood as part of historical knowledge, made the assortment of scale model kits in stores or blueprints in journals subject to tacit censorship. The USSR-designed model kits featured exclusively Russian and Soviet ships, aircraft, and vehicles, such as the battleship *Potemkin* and the cruiser *Avrora*, various makes of such aircraft as the MiG or *Tupolev*, as well as Soviet battle tanks. It was possible to buy kits from East German, Czechoslovakian, or Polish manufacturers, but their range of products was dominated by models of Soviet vehicles, and the absolute majority of the blueprints for scale models in *Modelist-Konstruktor* were those of Russian or Soviet vehicles. Finally, the activities in state-sponsored clubs and hobby groups for children were focused almost exclusively on custom-built models of Soviet ships and aircraft.[19]

This apparent exclusion of non-Soviet technological objects from the activities of Soviet modelers was somewhat shattered in 1977, when Soviet factories started producing kits designed in England. This story provides a particularly good illustration of the importance with which Soviet ideologists endowed scale models as objects of historical knowledge. In the mid-1970s, the British model kit manufacturer Frog (famous, among other things, for making 1:72 one of the standard scales for aircraft modeling) was going out of business, and the USSR Ministry of Light Industry entered into negotiations with its parent company, Dunbee-Combex-Marx, to purchase the injection molds used for industrial production of plastic model kits. From the beginning, Soviet negotiators refused to buy models of those aircraft or vessels that belonged to the Central Powers (World War I) or the Axis Powers

(World War II).[20] This decision reduced their choice to 120 models which, beginning in the late 1970s, were produced in various locations in the USSR, from Moscow to Tashkent. Most were models of British and U.S. aircraft and ships of the interwar and World War II periods.[21]

The Soviet side insisted on a barter deal to repay the cost of purchased equipment with manufactured model kits. Dunbee-Combex-Marx established Novo, a UK-based company that packaged and distributed kits supplied from the USSR. The international marketing of Soviet-built model kits was similar to products made by Western manufacturers: pseudorealistic representations of battle scenes involving the model's prototype on the cover, its full name and basic technical specifications, brief development and operational history, and detailed assembly instructions. The marketing of the same model kits domestically for Soviet consumers followed a different, much more simplistic and utilitarian pattern, as figures 2.1 and 2.2 demonstrate.

With rare exceptions, ex-Frog model kits of Western planes and ships were sold in the USSR in an anonymous form, without information about the specifications or history of their prototypes. For example, the World War II–era Barracuda bomber was marketed as an "aircraft model kit" (figure 2.2[22]), and under the same generic name of an "aircraft model kit" the Soviet retail trade offered dozens of other models of British and U.S. planes. The famous World War II–era British Supermarine Spitfire and Hawker Hurricane fighters were sold as a "frontline fighter plane" and a "fighter plane," respectively. HMS *Hero* was sold as a "destroyer," HMS *Torquay* as an "antisubmarine ship," and HMS *Royal Sovereign* as a "battleship." In addition, the UK-designed kits available in Soviet stores provided neither historical notes about their prototypes nor decals (pictures imitating national identification marks) nor painting schemes.

FIGURE 2.1.   Box cover design of the Fairey Barracuda produced in the USSR for Western European markets under the Novo Brand, ca. late 1970s.

СБОРНАЯ МОДЕЛЬ САМОЛЕТА   Ф 161

Для технического творчества детей от 10 лет и старше.

FIGURE 2.2. Box cover design of the Fairey Barracuda produced in the USSR for the domestic market, ca. late 1970s and 1980s.

In other words, many models of foreign ships and aircraft were stripped of their identity and historical background and marketed as objects of purely functional value, which was emphasized by the obligatory phrase, "Designed for the technical creativity of children aged 10 and up," and generic box cover images without national colors. An assembled model represented a piece of unpainted plastic with no identification signs and no name: an object of technical design, not of history. What could sometimes pierce the silence about a model's historical prototype was its operational history in the Soviet armed forces. Model kits of U.S. Curtis P-40 and Bell P-39 fighter planes, which were supplied to the USSR during World War II under the Lend-Lease Act, included both names and a brief description of their service with the Soviet air force. The assembly instructions for the P-39 started with a short historical reference to the Soviet ace Aleksandr Pokryshkin, who flew this aircraft, his rank and awards, and his official score of fifty-nine enemy planes. It also provided decals and advice on a painting scheme for it.[23]

Even when made anonymous, the ability of models to encapsulate historical and ideological meanings led to several cases in which production was suspended or stopped altogether. The *Daily Telegraph* mentioned in one of its April 1985 issues that the Soviet newspaper *Komsomolskaya pravda* had launched a campaign against the production and sale of Soviet models of British Harrier jets and Vulcan bombers used by NATO forces, even though they were produced without identification marks and in unnamed boxes.

The campaign resulted in suspended production.[24] One of my informants shared similar stories that circulated among Soviet enthusiasts of scale modeling. For example, production of the model of the F-4 Phantom in Minsk was suspended after an article in a local newspaper decried the use of this plane by the U.S. Army in Vietnam and asked how its model could be produced in the USSR. In another case, the head of a toy factory in Sukhumi, a World War II veteran, allegedly attempted to destroy the mold for a model of the British DH Sea Venom, which he mistook for the World War II German Focke-Wulf 189.[25] Although these stories are hard to verify, their widespread circulation among Soviet hobbyists is symptomatic; they revealed the materialist logic that associated models with historicities that could be appropriate or inappropriate in the Soviet cultural context. Scale models made manifest the historical imagination inherent in Soviet technopolitics. This imagination demanded that the national perspective of technological progress—which, for some, meant downplaying its other, "foreign," histories—be highlighted to inculcate a sense of national pride in Soviet youth. An examination of the fetishism given to detail in Soviet scale modeling as a hobby provides another vantage point on the historical meanings that models offered for appropriation and internalization by their enthusiasts.

The Fetishism of Detail

While Soviet officials and managers sought to strip models of Western machines and vehicles of their historicity, the historicity of Soviet and Russian models was thoroughly praised. Scale modeling, whether it was practiced individually or in hobby groups, was always accompanied by advice on how to assemble models of Russian or Soviet ships, planes, or ground vehicles, which strongly encouraged modelers to immerse themselves in the history of the model's prototype, to gather as much historical information about it as possible, and to build it in complete accordance with the original design and coloring scheme. The fetishization of detail dominated the activities of young Soviet hobbyists. The standard guide for model ship hobby groups, Sergey Luchininov's *Iunyi korablestroitel'* (Young shipbuilder), demanded that its participants should learn how to "make in the precise scale important equipment such as bitts, mooring chocks, anchors, capstans, portholes, steering wheels, lights, [as well as] to sew sails if the model represents a sailing ship."[26] Among model aircraft hobbyists it was not unusual that students thoroughly and in detail reproduced the interior of the pilot's cabin, which in many cases remained invisible once the construction of the model was completed. The painting scheme and decals were also supposed to represent a particular moment in the prototype's history—not a generic plane but, ideally, a plane with the tail number of a prominent pilot, in the colors and camouflage of his regiment. Advocates of modeling as a hobby argued that such a model makes history palpable and bridges the gap between famous historical figures and school-age kids. This logic was explicated by a prominent Soviet enthusiast of modeling in his report of the 1975 All-Russian competition of school-age modelers: "Most of the models which participated in the competition copied Soviet planes. It is excellent that school-age modelers are encouraged to build [such models]. When building a replica model, a schoolboy nearly touches its designers and the aces who shot down enemy planes."[27]

It was details that transformed models from objects of technological design into objects of history, and in the process immersed Soviet hobbyists into the national historical discourse. After all, any model is primarily a sign, with its prototype serving as the signified. In semiotic theory it would belong to icons, a category of signs introduced by Charles Peirce in which the relationship between a signifier and signified is based on visual likeness. When stripped of details, like most models built between the 1920s to the 1950s as small flying or sailing machines or like the anonymous copies of Western planes and ships sold in the USSR, their signified was abstract planes and abstract ships, the products of technological progress par excellence. By contrast, details located a model in a concrete point in history, thus endowing it with a particular historicity. In Luchininov's book, the appeal to make models in precise detail to achieve the utmost likeness to their originals was placed next to a requirement that young shipbuilders should also master firm knowledge in history when building models of Russian or Soviet ships.[28] All Soviet guides and books on model shipbuilding started with extensive sections on the history of Russian and Soviet seafaring.[29] This link between detail and history was repeated in other modeling hobbies. The following advice from the authoritative 1989 aircraft modeling guide, A Plane on the Table, features the same logic that linked historical knowledge with the fetishism of detail,[30] so encouraged among young modelers:

When you are choosing a plane for modeling, it is desirable to have, in addition to detailed blueprints, as much information as possible: the name of the chief designer and of the production facility, technical specifications, characteristic features, the period in production, what changes were implemented during its years of service, and so forth. The most complete information can be found in specialized [modeling and aviation] journals, such as Modelist-Konstruktor or Krylia Rodiny

[Wings of the Motherland] . . . They often publish feature articles about certain types of planes with detailed blueprints. If the plane is military, they also describe its operational history, famous pilots who flew it and their achievements. Yet as a rule, in order to make this picture complete other sources should also be consulted, including magazines, photographs from newspapers, books, and memoirs. All materials related to the chosen plane should be stored in one folder.[31]

The fetishism of detail—thoroughly nourished in hobby groups—called for the creation of an archive of historical knowledge at home. In the quotation above, this advice is neatly visualized through the didactic suggestion to use separate folders for the storage of materials related to each model. Short historical notes on the prototype's service in the Russian or Soviet armed forces, which were supplied with assembly instructions in kits, served as entry points to this archive, but they provoked only a desire for knowledge about everything related to the history of the model's real prototype. To satisfy this desire, modelers were advised to turn to "specialized journals . . . magazines, photographs from newspapers, books, memoirs, etc.," and to copy relevant materials to "one folder," thus reproducing in their apartments a particular section of the grand historical archive. The structural elements of this archive were neither classes nor productive relations, as would have been implied by historical materialism, but technological objects, their designers, and prominent users and operators.

There were different means by which modelers were expected to further explore this archive. Supervisors of modeling groups in the Palaces of Young Pioneers and centers of young technical designers organized trips to airports, seaports, or military bases, where their students encountered real technological objects and their operators. Meetings with World War II veterans and historical lectures by supervisors were also obligatory activities in state-run modeling clubs. Several such events were typically held in the course of an academic year.[32] Modelers were also advised to read specialized and popular technical magazines and literature. In the quote above, Lagutin referred his readers, in particular, to *Modelist-Konstruktor*, which provided accurate blueprints for models, but always supplemented them with patriotic or at least didactic episodes from their operational histories. For example, in 1982, *Modelist-Konstruktor* started publishing a series of blueprints of models of historical fighter planes, which continued into 1983 and 1984, and covered the period from World War I to the Vietnam War. The articles provided a comparative overview of major national designs produced in a certain period showing how technological innovations introduced by one manufacturer provoked a wave of changes among all air powers. However, the detailed blueprints were provided only for the aircraft designed or at least used by the Russian or Soviet air forces; the articles provided episodes from their operational histories featuring prominent aces and the plane's contribution to the national war effort. The first article in this series discussed early fighters of World War I. Since the Russian Empire had failed to develop a national fighter aircraft by its outbreak, the author focused on the French Morane-Saulnier G, which had been supplied to the Russian army before the war. The article opened with a story of the aerial ramming—the first in history—of an enemy plane by the Russian aviator Petr Nesterov flying a Morane-Saulnier G, which made it possible to include this plane in the pantheon of Soviet aviation history.

The modelers who aspired to build this plane were given only one painting scheme and one set of identification signs—those of the plane that was flown by Nesterov on his last flight. To supplement the young hobbyists' archive of historical knowledge, the article quoted praise from imperial Russian newspapers: "So the fight in the air has commenced. And the person who blazed this trail was the Russian hero, the owner of the wreath of glory for the [first in history] loop, Pyotr Nikolayevich Nesterov." The article took for granted that its hero, Nesterov, was an imperial officer and a noble, a representative of the class toward which the Bolshevik Revolution was most hostile and that his attitude to the "First World Imperialist War" was that of dignity and patriotism determined by his class origins. He is quoted as allegedly giving a vow: "I give you the word of honor of a Russian officer that this Austrian will cease flying." Such an attitude could hardly be farther from the Bolsheviks' "revolutionary defeatism" and "struggle for the transformation of the imperialist war into a civil war" as represented in Soviet history textbooks.[33] This was the first article in a series that traced the evolution of fighter aviation to the third-generation jet fighters. It also created a historical continuity between the Russian Empire and the Soviet Union by tracing the genealogy of contemporary Soviet aviation to its imperial Russian predecessor, thus implicitly undermining the idea of the Bolshevik Revolution as a radical rupture with the prerevolutionary era.

This tendency was even more visible in ship modeling: numerous publications on models of ships of Kievan or Muscovite Russia and the Russian Empire emphasized the inventiveness of Russian shipbuilders, their use of cutting-edge technologies and innovations, the valor of Russian sailors in all of Russia's wars at sea and the preeminence of Russian seafarers in the exploration of the world's oceans. The same emphasis can be observed in the activities of state-run hobby groups: there was a compulsory requirement for their supervisors to lecture the students on the history of the Russian navy from "ancient times."[34] This emphasis on historical continuity lured Soviet hobbyists into imagining Soviet history in de facto primordialist terms in which Soviet equaled Russian, and national history was explained as a linear and progressive development from the Middle Ages on. In at least two cases the authors of books on model shipbuilding mentioned to their multiethnic Soviet audience that the Slavs of Kievan Rus were "our ancestors."[35] The box of the model kit of the Russian frigate *Oryol* (the model was produced throughout the 1980s) had the following text:

> The history of shipbuilding dates back to ancient times. The naval craft of the Slavs had many original features that distinguished them from the shipbuilders of the Mediterranean. Slavs built ladyas which were equally fit for river and sea journeys. They were steady on waves and had good maneuverability. Ladyas served for many centuries as the largest commercial and naval ships. In the seventeenth century Russia started building warships. In 1668, in the village of Dedinovo at the influx of the Moscow River into the Oka, a double-decked, three-masted sailing vessel was built. It was 25 meters long (similar to a ladya) and 6.5 meters wide. The ship was named the *Oryol* [eagle]. It was armed with six-pound and three-pound guns. It was the first Russian warship.[36]

The reference to Slavic ladyas, which occupied half of this short historical note, was quite out of place in pragmatic terms, on the box of a model of a different vessel; instead, its message was a symbolic creation of a continuous linkage from the "ancient times" through the seventeenth century to the 1980s, when the model became available for Soviet hobbyists. The silences of this text are also symptomatic as this note, while emphasizing the technical details of the *Oryol*, failed to mention that Dutch shipbuilders played an important role in its design and construction.[37] As insignificant and short as this historical note on the box of a model kit was, it encapsulated and reproduced a historical narrative that operated in terms of nations and accompanying concepts such as national pride, which was reflected in praise of ladyas' seafaring qualities. The ubiquity of such texts in the activities of modeling enthusiasts created a many million-strong army of Soviet citizens who learned, in a casual and noncentralized manner, to envision and interpret Soviet history as a continuation of the Russian nation-building project.

In the Soviet context, the roots of this phenomenon to "praise all things Russian" dated back to the mid-1930s, when Soviet leaders adopted a Russocentric stance in their interpretations of scientific progress—a change which itself had its genealogy in the late imperial era.[38] In the post-Stalinist period, this tendency became independently produced and reproduced at the grassroots level owing to the general decentralization of Soviet society. Articles in technical journals, specialized literature on modeling, and supervisors of modeling hobby groups alike encouraged young and adult modelers to acquire books about the histories of prominent ships, aircraft, and ground vehicles. These were published in runs of hundreds of thousands of copies by such presses as Voenizdat, which specialized in military histories, and Sudostroenie, which specialized in naval histories. State modeling clubs also purchased such literature to lend books to their students.[39] The urge to construct their models to the tiniest and most authentic detail lured modelers into the consumption of historical narratives that glorified the Russian and Soviet war effort and celebrated technological progress. The discourse on modeling created, as part of its archive of historical knowledge, a library on the history of technology, which placed technological objects and their famous designers and operators at the heart of the historical process.

In military histories and histories of ships or aircraft, which were strongly associated with modeling, the fetishism of detail reached its apogee. Authors provided maximum information on their development history, technical specifications, and modifications; compared them with similar designs of their time; and meticulously described their operational histories, including minute-by-minute battle accounts.[40] The fetishization of a model's detail entailed fetishization of historical detail; both lured enthusiasts of modeling into imagining the historical process as a progressive development driven by the genius of engineers and the valor of military commanders, sailors, or pilots—in other words, the users and operators of technological objects.[41] Models captured their prototypes not in the relations of production but at some moment of "consumption" (hence the advice to paint model fighter aircraft in the colors and identification marks of famous aces). Their representations in the popular Soviet archive of historical knowledge reflected them not in their circulation through social space, but rather frozen at some, presumably most glorious, episode of biography. Scale models thus confirmed and reinforced the historical alienation of labor in the production of technological objects by emphasizing the process of their consumption. The explanatory logic they brought to the Soviet historical imagination was conspicuously nationalist and non-Marxist, which is particularly evident if one looks further at the historicities that scale models produced when accumulated in collections.

Historicities of Scale Model Collections

Among the characters in Walter Benjamin's *The Arcades Project*, both the flâneur and the collector are engaged in a never-ending search for rare, curious, and decaying objects. Yet they have different, if not divergent, interests. The flâneur is seeking things that were denied a place in history; his curiosity is provoked by historicities forgotten and discarded. By contrast, the collector is interested in objects that belong to a particular historical system, which is the collection itself. This is how the collector participates in cultural production, for the collections are the sites in which historicities are materialized and thus preserved and transmitted through generations. Together with narratives, collections are the cultural forms through which history—both past and future—is imagined and controlled.[42]

Collections of scale models were less common in the Soviet Union than collections of stamps, postcards, or coins, but they still enjoyed enormous popularity. Palaces of Young Pioneers and clubs of young technical designers boasted large collections built by several cohorts of schoolchildren. Most home collections represented a dozen or two amateurishly assembled plastic models, usually unpainted, without decals, and with visible traces of glue. But there were also plenty of enthusiasts who created extensive and elaborate collections of models showing an extreme level of resemblance to their originals.[43] Unlike beginner modelers who were satisfied with whatever assortment of model kits they found in stores, these hobbyists engaged in searches for rare kits. Their demand created lively gray markets around Soviet toy stores in major Soviet cities, where one could buy model kits unavailable in the Soviet retail trade, including kits of foreign manufacturers imported by tourists, diplomats, or sailors.[44] When no kits were available, such modelers turned to wood, plastic, textile, cardboard, and other basic materials, and plunged into original or reconstructed blueprints, historical photographs, and textual descriptions.[45] Because building models from scratch required an intimate knowledge of the prototype's tiniest details, as well as advanced building skills and special tools, they often formed amateur modeling clubs to share knowledge and instruments. Such clubs operated during evening hours on the premises of state-funded children's clubs.[46] They also posted classified ads in newspapers and journals offering to exchange blueprints and other data on models' prototypes with modelers from other Soviet regions.[47]

Such a level of engagement in the modeling hobby changed the relationship between the enthusiast and his objects. An engaged enthusiast did not seek just "any" model. This was because the creation of a model that resembles its original in the tiniest detail was an incredibly time-consuming and labor-intensive process, which sometimes included a search of archival materials and interviews with former designers and operators.[48] Any collection, private or public alike, follows a certain classificatory scheme.[49] A rare modeler, however, started compiling a collection with a preconceived classification in his head. As a rule, models suggested the scheme. In 1989, *Modelist-Konstruktor* published an interview with the supervisor of a technical center for schoolchildren in Kotelnich, a small town in central Russia, that praised the center's collection of models and explicated its logic:

> At first, boys produced single models, such as a dreadnought or a moon rover, a walking excavator or a dredge. So much labor invested in each of them! . . . But how to preserve the materialized products of children's labor? . . . This is when the supervisor had the idea to use these models to create a children's museum. Yet would it be correct if this collection would have a model of an eighteenth-century metallurgical plant, but would not reflect the development of Soviet metallurgy nowadays? Or a model of the first electric engine in the world without a story about the history of electricity?[50] This is why [the supervisor] decided that they should address a certain branch of Soviet industry or a type of Soviet military technology only as an assemblage in historical progression.[51]

The move from an object to a collection is represented here as driven by historicities inherently present in the objects of collecting. In the article, the modeling enthusiast describes his drive to create a museum of scale models as quite literally caused by their longing not to be exhibited alone.[52] A model, when taken alone, was a "materialized product of children's labor," but as an object of display in a "children's museum" it abhorred a vacuum around itself and demanded a collection. Due to the semiotic nature of a scale model, their collections stood for a fragment of the real world ("a certain branch of Soviet industry or a type of Soviet military technology"), but their incorporation into a collection created a different system of signification in which it was possible for models of World War I planes to stand next to jets of the Cold War era, or for the *Sputnik* to be placed alongside not-yet-existent, but already modeled space probes and crafts of the future.

The inclusion of an object in a collection comprises two actions: first, the object is decontextualized from its original environment and, second, it is recontextualized in a collection. Most collections exist as systems in which meanings are produced internally, through the interplay of differences between objects of collecting. It is more complicated with scale models since they, unlike most other objects of collecting, have no prior circulation as commodities or technological objects, but are intentionally created as representations of real, usually historical, objects. In this respect, scale models exist on the border territory between Saussure's and Peirce's semiotics. They are incomplete without other models, that is, without a collection, which can be described as a Saussurean paradigm.[53] The most typical story among modeling enthusiasts about how they got into this hobby starts with an accidental purchase or present of a model, which triggered the interest in modeling and led to the purchase of new model kits and the creation of their first collection.[54] To put it in Jean Baudrillard's words, "the need to possess the love object can be satisfied only by a succession of objects, by repetition."[55]

Yet the lack of their own history prior to inclusion in a collection prevents models from creating a hermetic world, in which objects of collecting acquire their meanings exclusively through interaction with each other. Without biographies of their own, models abduct the biographies of their prototypes and stand as icons—in Peirce's typology of signs—of them. In addition, unlike with most other types of collections, the classification scheme of a scale model collection is not based on the properties of models. Instead, they are arranged according to the properties and specifications that their prototypes possessed, such as country of origin, operational history, type of hull, or propulsion. The decontextualization process, thus, cannot be completed as the work of a model collector is that of a shuttle, perpetually moving between the object he is manufacturing or possesses and historical information about the actual vehicle. That is why a scale model is not an ideal or completed object. As a hobbyist acquires new knowledge and the skills of his discipline, old models are often remade in better detail, replaced with new ones that are deemed more authentic, or just removed from the collection.

In this sense, scale models are not passive objects with a "subjective status," of which Baudrillard speaks in his analysis of "the system of collecting."[56] They urge modeling enthusiasts to embark on a never-ending search for historical details pertaining to military and technological history, which is understood in national terms, since the country of origin and operation is a major classification rubric in the hobby of modeling. Models simultaneously encapsulated and generated the imagination of Soviet history as a continuous development from the early East Slavic states to the USSR and further into the communist future (models of nonexistent space crafts), and their collections added a performative aspect to it. With sailing vessels standing next to steamships and piston aircraft next to jets on the same shelf, scale model collections demonstrated historical progress by showing technological change for the eyes of modeling enthusiasts and their audience, both predominantly male, educated and willing to comprehend history as a process of nation-building. Tony Bennett in "The Exhibitionary Complex" pointed out how architectural scale models—"the miniature ideal cities"— subordinated urban space to the "white, bourgeois, and . . . male eye of the metropolitan powers."[57] In a similar manner, collections of scale model

vehicles established a visual dominance over history interpreted as a historical continuum driven by technological progress and the struggles of major
world powers, among which Russia/Soviet Union was thought of as occupying a leading position. This is how, for example, a Soviet writer, Mark Kabakov, described his visit to the museum of the S.M. Kirov Submarine School
in Leningrad where he was deeply impressed by the museum's collection of
scale models: "[The museum was located] in a long red brick building which
had served as naval barracks before the [Bolshevik] revolution. Every submariner dreams of visiting its rooms. For they contain not only the history
of the submarine school, but of the entire [Soviet] submarine fleet. Model
submarines—from the very first one built in the Baltic Shipyard in 1866 to
modern nuclear submarines, unique historical documents."[58]

Kabakov continues this paragraph by mentioning the Russian submarine *Tiulen*, which sank four and captured two enemy ships in 1916, and the
Soviet submarine *Volk* of the early 1920s, before discussing the heroism of
Soviet sailors in World War II. The collection performed this historical continuity by bringing together imperial Russian and Soviet submarines before
the eyes of the author-as-spectator; model submarines as displayed objects
suggested a difference in details, but the similarity in substance, which was
"the history . . . of the entire [Soviet] submarine fleet." In this case, scale
models were assisted in the making of this continuity by another material
object—the prerevolutionary building of the barracks of the Imperial Russian Navy, in which the museum was located. To describe the collections
as mere assemblages of historical copies would be a mistake because they
are performative in J.L. Austin's understanding of this term: they materialize and transform into a spectacle the epistemological and political categories of historical time. The collections also call their audience into social
being. When Kabakov wrote that "every submariner dreams of visiting [the]
rooms" of the museum with its scale model collection, he was not referring to the mental state of all Soviet sailors; he described the effect that this
collection exerted on him. Appreciating the power of the collection after it
had called him into being, he represented that exemplary Soviet submarine
sailor, always male, most likely of Slavic origins, well trained and educated to
operate complex machinery, aware of his historical roots going back through
the flames of the Civil War and World War II to the Imperial Russian Navy.

James Clifford linked the collection and modern selfhood, speaking of collections as "the assemblage of a material 'world,' the marking-off of a subjective domain that is not 'other.'"[59] Because he was preoccupied with the genealogy of collecting, he interpreted it as mainly a reflection of the modern

self, an artifact of subjectivation forces. Yet if we look at scale models and their collections synchronically, the effect is bilateral: they not only objectify ontologies and classifications for any given culture but also produce responsible citizens by performing history as national and progressive. The understanding of responsible citizenship provoked by Soviet scale models, their collections, and practices of their enthusiasts had few things in common with the officially projected Marxist-Leninist narrative of internationalism, solidarity, and anti-imperialism. In this respect, the scale modeling hobby was not a mere artifact of Soviet technopolitics: scale models were its active producers and participants materializing the Soviet techno-utopian historical imagination and luring people into understanding history as a linear process reduced to scientific and technological progress.

The obsession with detail moved scale models from the domain of private possession into the domain of the spectacular and hence the public. In the Soviet Union, the exemplary manifestation of this process was regional and national competitions of scale models among schoolchildren attending extracurricular hobby groups. The winners were determined by the authenticity of their models, and the authenticity was interpreted as whether a scale model was constructed in accurate detail or not. Moreover, the winning models from all over the USSR were often exhibited in the Iunye tekhniki pavilion at the Exhibition of Achievements of the National Economy in Moscow or in other central spots of the Soviet exhibitionary complex, such as the Moscow Palace of Young Pioneers or even the Kremlin,[60] an ultimate move from someone's private possession into the public visual domain. Any model was, from its earliest stage of existence as a kit or a set of blueprints, a potential object for display. This potentiality found its realization in collections of scale models, thus preventing them from becoming merely objects of possession. Scale models consumed the private time of their enthusiasts to produce social perceptions of historical time and a spectacle of history. The fetishization of detail—a necessary condition for models to become objects of display—interpellated a modeler—in Clifford's gloss—as a "good," rather than "obsessive," collector, the one whose relationship to the object was regulated by social rules and socially acceptable emotions.[61]

Following the collapse of the USSR, modeling as a hobby blossomed now that its enthusiasts finally received unrestricted access to the products of Western manufacturers and new private manufacturers emerged all over the ex-USSR. Modelers acquired a voice which was no longer mediated by Komsomol censors. At first, it was in the form of the magazine *M-Hobbi*, founded, published, and read by enthusiasts of the scale modeling hobby, and later in internet forums and social networks. Around them, critical perspectives of

Soviet history dominated the post-Soviet cultural space. Yet surrounded by collections of Russian and Soviet planes, ships, and ground vehicles, modelers produced nostalgic narratives, where the object of nostalgia was the Soviet-era visions of historical continuity and progress—or, in Reinhart Koselleck's term, "a past future," which was betrayed by the collapse of the USSR. A 1996 editorial in *M-Hobbi* argued that "products of Ukrainian [scale model] companies arouse an equal (if not greater) interest in the Russian market than products of their more renowned Western counterparts. This is hardly surprising: after all, Ukrainian companies choose Soviet vehicles as the prototypes of their models. The vehicles that were designed, produced and operated in combat by our ancestors who at that time were not yet ordered to divide themselves into Russians and Ukrainians."[62]

The referential function of models turns out to be capable of overcoming not only a temporal rupture but also the territorial dismembering of the USSR. Models heal a lost geographic unity by embodying an imagined historical community and continuity (a reference to Soviet prototypes built and operated "by our ancestors"). For post-Soviet modeling enthusiasts, collections became a medium that materialized this historical imagination and rendered the territorial collapse and temporal rupture of 1991 as nonnatural and contrary to the logic of historical development that found its manifestations in scale model collections.

The 1990s were a decade of unprecedented historical pluralism in Russia, with critical assessments of Soviet history by Russian liberal historians and organizations, such as the human rights organization Memorial, publication of works that advanced totalitarian interpretations of Soviet history, and widely publicized revisionism of Viktor Suvorov. With national pride under fire from many sides, scale modeling turned out to be one of the forms of historical imagination in which this emotion found its refuge. To use Slavoj Žižek's insightful observation, in a culture characterized by the absence of one dominant master narrative, where a set of narratives coexisted as counternarratives to each other, "the things . . . themselves believe in [people's] place."[63] Enthusiasts of scale modeling organized regular competitions and hosted permanent exhibitions in their clubs, which often shared space with local military and patriotic clubs, teams of diggers searching for the remains of missing Soviet soldiers and wartime equipment (*poiskoviki*), and clubs of historical reenactment. For example, the museum of the Petrozavodsk Palace no. 2 of Children's Arts and Crafts has an exposition, which has been on display and added to since the early 1990s and which combines World War II–era weapons and military equipment found by local diggers, wax figures in historical uniforms of the Imperial Russian and Soviet Army, and

FIGURE 2.3.   Scale models of historical armored vehicles and a fragment of a World War II–era themed diorama. Military history museum of the Petrozavodsk Palace no. 2 of Children's Arts and Crafts. Photo by Sergei Rogov, 2019.

collections of models of historical vehicles ranging from the early twentieth to the turn of the twenty-first century (figure 2.3).

The ontologies and classifications encapsulated in this and numerous other collections reproduce the historical logic that emerged in the Soviet cultural context. In a similar way, although modeling magazines and guides are no longer published by state-run presses, they follow the same principles of exclusion as their Soviet predecessors did, with non-Russian/Soviet models largely marginalized unless they had a strong connection to Russian military history, as in the case of Nazi Germany's armored vehicles or NATO aircraft.[64] Since the mid-2000s, after having been largely neglected for over a decade, the modeling hobby as an organized state-sponsored activity has experienced steady growth.[65] The recent revival of patriotism as a dominant social discourse requires objectification, and scale model of Soviet ships, aircraft, and vehicles are a perfect medium for performing patriotism and historical continuity, both in public and private space. One can argue that, in fact, they had not stopped performing this continuity and foreshadowed— among other factors—national reassertion as a pressing social demand in early twenty-first-century Russian society.

CHAPTER 3

History in Wood

The Search for Historical Authenticity in North Russia

> The architecture of peasants' houses, as well as their
> tools, everyday objects, design, and other forms of
> folk art, have preserved much of what emerged in
> far more remote times, what is rooted in the deep
> foundations of feudalism, what goes back to the cradle
> of the ancient ethnic cultures of the [Soviet] people.
>
> —Aleksandr Opolovnikov, *Museums of Wooden
> Architecture*

Superficially, two of the UNESCO heritage
monuments in Russia—the Narkomfin Communal House in Moscow and
Kizhi Pogost in the Republic of Karelia—are the absolute opposite of each
other. The Narkomfin House (figure 3.1) epitomizes the early Soviet approach to architectural planning. For Soviet Marxist architects and urban
planners of the 1920s and 1930s, the city was a space intended to organize a
new social life. Their writing and practice sought to transform urban space in
ways that would allow for new social relations to emerge. Moisei Ginzburg
(1892–1946), a theorist of Soviet Constructivist architecture, reflected this
transformative social approach to architecture in the design of the Narkomfin House (1930). With its minimized private space and in-built service facilities, including daycare and a canteen, the Narkomfin House had to act as a
"social condenser" (a term coined by Ginzburg in 1928), that is, as a material
form that aggregated people into collectives and forged new forms of communal life.[1] By contrast, Kizhi Pogost (figure 3.2) is an architectural complex
consisting of two eighteenth-century wooden churches and an octagonal
bell tower built in 1862. It is also the core exhibit of an open-air museum
of wooden architecture that was established after World War II to collect,
preserve, and display objects of North Russian village architecture. Whereas
the Narkomfin House embodied the understanding of history as a vibrant,
present, and active process, the museum of Kizhi represented an attempt to

FIGURE 3.1. The Narkomfin Building, November 2019. Photo by Svetlana Yakovleva.

FIGURE 3.2. Kizhi Pogost, October 2019. Photo by Ilya Timin.

capture and freeze it in a historic landscape. The Narkomfin House sought to materialize the socialist future in concrete and glass. Kizhi Pogost objectified the national past in wood. Yet a deep connection exists between these two objects. The architectural preservation effort in the postwar USSR encapsulated in the open-air museum of Kizhi drew extensively on the theory of early Soviet Constructivist architecture. Its main ideologist, the restoration expert of Kizhi Pogost and the first designer of the museum of Kizhi, Aleksandr Opolovnikov (1911–94), was Ginzburg's student.

As the Soviet leadership turned to nationalist interpretations of Soviet history, this change required objectification in architecture. As a result, the postwar period saw a growing effort on behalf of architectural preservation. The foundation for a changed state politics of architectural preservation was laid with decrees in 1947 and 1948 that expanded the list of heritage objects in the USSR and imposed a legal responsibility for their proper maintenance on regional authorities. The de-Stalinization reforms also greatly intensified the scale of museumification of old buildings and other structures. In 1960, the Russian Soviet Federative Socialist Republic Council of Ministers passed a resolution establishing a national register of buildings and structures, recognizing designated buildings and structures as officially protected monuments and further expanding the practice and coverage of architectural preservation.[2] Titled "On the further improvement of the protection of monuments of culture in the Russian Soviet Federative Socialist Republic" (No. 1327 of August 30, 1960), it included a list of several thousand buildings and structures, mostly churches.[3] The list grew almost every year, and in the course of the last three decades of the Soviet Union, the landscape of late socialism became punctuated with tens of thousands of buildings, including churches, that became officially recognized as objects of historical and cultural heritage.[4] This was followed by a related process where old buildings and structures from abandoned villages were disassembled, moved, and restored in specially designated areas to create open-air museums of heritage (usually wooden) architecture; according to a Polish museologist, by 1990, their total number had grown to fifty-eight.[5]

This chapter examines the museumification of old architecture in the post–World War II USSR as a process that reflected and stimulated the nationalist understanding of Soviet history in its Romantic interpretation. Focusing on North Russia, where vernacular architecture survived better than elsewhere in the USSR due to late modernization, I show how wood, a traditional building material in local communities, became a symbol of the "deep cultural roots" of Soviet society. Recent scholarship in the studies of socialist materiality has enriched our knowledge of how socialist regimes sought to objectify their understanding of modernity and visions of historical progress in such materials as plastic, concrete, iron, and glass.[6] This chapter seeks to add wood to this register of materials that was instrumental in the objectification of socialism; as a material, wood, due to its very texture, could serve as a living witness of its authentic history.

Whereas the Soviet Marxist architecture of the 1920s and 1930s understood history as a vibrant process and sought to contribute to its making with new material forms, the postwar architectural preservation movement sought to transform history into visual pleasure through curating historical landscapes and heritage buildings. What made this situation paradoxical is the fact that Soviet preservationists borrowed the rhetoric and methodology of Soviet Constructivist architecture. For both, the search for authentic architectural forms was the essence of their activities. Soviet Marxist architects argued that architectural forms had to serve a new function; namely, the organization of the material conditions of social life (hence his call to Soviet architects to "realize [their] design from the inside out"). Yet for Soviet enthusiasts of architectural preservation the forms with which they worked were devoid of any functions other than performing history.[7] In an epigraph to this chapter, Aleksandr Opolovnikov argued that traditional wooden architecture "preserved much of what . . . goes back to the cradle of the ancient ethnic cultures of the [Soviet] people."[8] This understanding of the heritage architecture translated into an effort to find the primordial, ideal aesthetic system allegedly inherent in wooden vernacular architecture and cleanse surviving objects of any later accretions.

The architectural preservation movement, which existed both in the Soviet center and the periphery, was intrinsically connected to the struggle for social power in post–World War II Soviet society. Stephen Bittner and Catriona Kelly showed in their research on architectural preservation in Moscow and Leningrad, respectively, how heritage architecture gave Soviet urban intelligentsia the social power to define the historical imagination by appealing to national memory as an essential, materialized phenomenon. Many Soviet urban planners and officials were still eager to produce new socialist forms of social organization through architecture. However, growing preservation activism among Soviet intellectuals after World War II, and especially beginning in the mid-1950s, complicated any large-scale reconstruction or demolition of heritage architecture. Using the postwar legislation on architectural preservation, as well as diverse institutional opportunities such as letters to newspapers or public hearings, heritage architecture enthusiasts became a force to be reckoned with in late Soviet architectural planning.[9]

The campaigns in Moscow and Leningrad were spearheaded by "old intelligentsia"—people whose families had lived in these cities for several generations. At stake for them was their immediate lived space. It was different in the Soviet provinces where an architectural preservation movement also sprouted up in the late 1940s and further developed in the post-Stalinist era. The people whose work lay in the foundation of open-air museums of

wooden architecture, including Aleksandr Opolovnikov and Vyacheslav Orfinsky in North Russia or Sergei Balandin in Siberia, came from regional urban centers, such as Petrozavodsk and Irkutsk, or other Soviet regions. Their
desire to protect heritage architecture, driven by romantic nationalist forms
of historical imagination, led them to extrapolate the perceived historical
authenticity from buildings to their residents. The focus on the authentic
architectural form translated into the artificial archaization and exoticization
of North Russian communities.

The geographic focus of this chapter is the Republic of Karelia, a region
in the northwest of Russia. Karelia appeared on the political map of Russia
only in 1920; although as a historical region populated by the ethnic group
of Karelians it has been known in Europe since the Middle Ages. Located on
the periphery of Europe, Karelia saw a rise of its nationalist movement only
in the early twentieth century, considerably later than many other regions
of Central or Eastern Europe. The Bolshevik Revolution, the independence
of Finland, and the Russian Civil War have resulted in a short upsurge of
the nationalist movement in northern parts of Karelia. Karelian nationalists
controlled northern areas of Karelia during 1919 and early 1920; however,
by the summer of 1920 the Red Army reestablished Bolshevik control over
most of Karelia. Yet this prominent national sentiment coupled with Finnish
appeals to the international community to support the right of Karelians
for self-determination pushed the Soviet government to create Karelia, in
June 1920, as an autonomous region within Soviet Russia. Between 1940 and
1956, it was officially known as the Karelian-Finnish Soviet Socialist Republic
(SSR) and was a full member of the Soviet Union on a par with Ukraine, Es-
tonia, and other Soviet republics. Unlike in the other members of the Union,
its title nation was an ethnic minority in the republic; in 1937, the share of
Karelians in its population was 29.3 percent, a percentage that has only fallen
since then.[10] As a result, its leaders were concerned with the search for national symbols that could represent Karelia on the national stage and justify
its quasi-statehood. The historical landscape of North Russia was one re-
source to which they resorted, empowering in the process Soviet enthusiasts
of architectural preservation.

Lyrical Landscapes of Socialism

"Longing and Form" essay in György Lukács's *Soul and Form* (1911) begins
with a discussion of the persistent link between German, French, and Italian
landscapes, on the one hand, and different forms of longing that dominated
in their respective national literatures, on the other. In trying to describe

this connection, Lukács engaged with the complex issue of the relationship between landscape and literary production. German landscapes, he claimed, "have something nostalgic, something melancholy and sad about them; yet they are homely and inviting." In the context of the history of German literature, such landscapes informed the writing of "poetic songs of longing." It was different, he argued, from the landscape of Southern Europe:

> The landscape of the South is hard and resistant . . . A painter once said: "It has already been composed before you ever get into it." And you cannot enter into a "composition," you cannot come to terms with it, nor will it ever give an answer to tentative questions. Our relationship to a composition—to something that has already taken form—is clear and unambiguous, even if it is enigmatic and difficult to explain: it is that feeling of being both near and far which comes with great understanding, that profound sense of union which yet is eternally a being-separate, a standing outside. It is a state of longing. In such landscapes the great Romance poets of longing were born, they grew up in it and they became like it themselves: hard and violent, reticent and form-creating.[11]

For Lukács the relationship between a landscape and literary production is mediated by affects that vary from one national geography and cultural tradition to another. Recent scholarship has extensively discussed how landscape is not merely an object of social construction, but is itself an important factor of social change—not least by providing forms of a symbolic response to the modernization processes of the last two centuries.[12] Lukács makes another observation, which he applies to Southern Europe but which can be extrapolated to many other cases, including North Russia. He notes that a landscape might offer its observers a persistent composition: a combination of elements accepted as inherent for this landscape. It is a well-known argument that landscape is constructed by the observer's gaze.[13] Lukács suggests that a landscape, in turn, can provoke a certain gaze by providing a combination of formal elements—an inherently present composition.

If conceptualized in terms of a visual effect, North Russia confronted observers with a landscape that had resisted late imperial and Soviet attempts at modernization. For the tsarist authorities of the late imperial period, North Russia remained a low-priority area until World War I when the Murmansk Railway providing a connection between central Russia and the Arctic coast was hastily built.[14] In 1920, when Karelia attained a degree of self-government, its leadership, which was composed mainly of Finnish émigré communists, tried to justify its autonomy by offering it as a model of balanced regional modernization. When their effort failed to achieve rapid industrialization, Karelia became a testing ground for the use of Gulag labor with the construction of the White Sea-Baltic Canal.[15] Yet all these modernization efforts remained rather superficial in terms of their visible impact on the North Russian landscape. North Russia's scarce population was scattered over vast swaths of territory in a large number of small villages; for example, in Karelia, according to the 1933 census, the rural population of some 250,000 people was distributed among 2,700 villages over an area of 147,000 square kilometers.[16] The geographic and economic marginality of local communities meant that wooden vernacular architecture was predominant in the region except for a few local urban centers, most prominently its capital, Petrozavodsk, a city with a population of 70,000 in 1939 that grew to 200,000 by the mid-1970s. As for the natural landscape, most of North Russia is covered by the taiga and has many lakes, rivers, and bogs that formed during the retreat of glaciers at the end of the last Ice Age, with Karelia alone having over 60,000 lakes and 20,000 rivers.

To many observers, the North Russian landscape suggested a persistent composition that linked together tender northern vegetation, omnipresent water surfaces, and wooden buildings of local vernacular designs, such as churches, chapels, and log cabins. This composition became the dominant theme of local artists; in the postwar era, landscape painting became the staple product of artists of the Petrozavodsk art school, such as Boris Pomortsev, Sulo Juntunen, Tamara Yufa, and many others. A 1973 survey of art in the autonomous republics of the Russian Federation singled out "lyrical landscapes" as the dominant genre of Karelian artists. When describing Boris Pomortsev's landscapes (figure 3.3), Viktor Vanslov, a prominent Soviet theorist of aesthetics, wrote that "Karelia reveals itself before the spectators' eyes as a wonderful land of silence and poetry."[17]

Pomortsev's *Saturday* (figure 3.3) depicts an old wooden sauna on the shore of a tranquil lake surrounded by a coniferous forest, with a boat moored at a worn and shabby pier. This and his other landscapes reflected the lyrical gaze provoked by the North Russian landscape. Further, Vanslov's inclusion of Pomortsev and his fellow Karelian landscape painters in the encyclopedia of Soviet Russian art heralded the cultural acceptance of this landscape that blended natural and allegedly archaic architectural elements as a socialist landscape. The framework of northern nature, water, as well as wooden architecture and boats became recognized as the dominant form of the visual portrayal of Karelia, in particular, and North Russia, in general. The landscape paintings of Soviet artists made the North Russian resistance to modernization into a virtue rather than a fault. Karelia was portrayed as

FIGURE 3.3.   Boris Pomortsev, *Subbotnii den'* [Saturday], 1961. Museum of Fine Art of the Republic of Karelia, ZhK-87 KP-1365, reproduced by permission.

a place in which local communities had preserved authentic folk traditions that had been lost in more urbanized regions ("Karelia . . . as a land of . . . poetry"). The lyricism of the landscape became synonymous with the historical authenticity of its people. In contrast to the narratives of the prewar accelerated industrialization, archaic elements in architecture, as well as in social relations, were no longer something to struggle against.

The double movement from the inherent composition of the North Russian landscape to persistent forms of its cultural representations and back to the cultural production of local communities, now understood as an extension and a natural part of this landscape, was reflected in a documentary film commissioned in 1968 by the Radio and Television Broadcasting Commission of Karelia as a "calling card" for the republic. The film, titled *Zemlia karel'skaia* (The Land of Karelia), was based on a screenplay by Vladimir Danilov and directed by Yuri Rogozhin, both from Petrozavodsk. The official annotation described it as a "film about the past and future of Karelia" that shows it "through the eyes of a man who was born and raised here."[18] The film's narrative revolved around a small village in Karelia (it remained unclear, perhaps intentionally, if it was Russian or Karelian) on the shores of an unnamed lake. Its plotline follows the boat trip of two local residents who departed at dawn as a ten-year-old boy and girl, were shown halfway through the film at midday as a young couple, and returned home at dusk as an old man and woman. Short scenes with major landmarks of the republic—including wooden churches, Stone Age rock carvings, the Kondopoga Pulp and Paper plant, and one of the local hydropower stations—served as brief interruptions in this plotline that also included detailed scenes of traditional crafts with a particular focus on boat building.

Zemlia karel'skaia features several allusions to Alexander Dovzhenko's 1930 masterpiece *Zemlia* (Earth), beginning with the title, as well as with a celebration of a new harmonious unity between people and nature and a particular attention to the material foundations of national character.[19] Yet Dovzhenko's film brought together the old and the new to show how the latter supersedes the former in an inevitable class conflict; Rogozhin's film, in contrast, lauded the historical succession of traditions and praised cultural continuity. *Zemlia* is based on the materialist understanding of history as social struggle; *Zemlia karel'skaia* documented the petrification of history and its monumentalization in an archaic landscape. An internal review by the Radio and Television Broadcasting Commission, which was part of the formal approval process and thus reflected the intentions of the Karelian government rather than the actual content of the film, emphasized the film's focus on the organic connection between the archaic history of Karelia and its more industrial present: "The beauty of this place stems from its certain patriarchal character and nicely matches with features of Soviet Karelia's today."[20] Yet, as the editorial script of *The Land of Karelia* shows, "features of Soviet Karelia's today" occupied less than 10 percent of the entire film with the rest devoted to the filming of Karelian nature, lakes, traditional crafts, old wooden buildings and structures, as well as local residents who were portrayed in an intimate unity with this idyllic landscape:

> Early morning. The camera is located on a hilltop from which we can see a lake sparkling in the sun's rays. A small village is visible on a far shore. Waves are washing on rocks. A boy is sitting on a rock. A small sauna on the lakeshore with a little quay leading into the water. [Cf. Boris Pomortsev's *Saturday* in figure 3.3.] The boy pushes a boat with a fair-haired girl off the quay. The boat is moving through the lake. The

boy is sitting on the stern with a steering ore in his hands. The girl is rowing.[21]

Industrial scenes were only a disguise for a film that claimed that the specificity and identity of the region and its people were more about a close connection to an unspecified (and hence mythological) past than to the allegedly foreseeable communist future or even the socialist now. Only two minutes of the film were devoted to industrial and urban scenes and landscapes, even though the urban population of the republic (490,516 people) substantially prevailed over the rural (222,935 people).[22] The director was only partially honest when he claimed that *The Land of Karelia* represented the region "through the eyes of a man who was born and raised here." Instead, the film incorporated the modern gaze with its tendency to dominate the landscape, to employ aerial perspectives through frequent scenes shot from hilltops—the kind of vision generally associated with the quintessentially male occupation of a pilot.[23] Rather than belonging to a native of these shores, this gaze was a product of Soviet urban modernity, just like the fantasy of travel through national space in homebuilt vehicles discussed in chapter 1. The search for historical authenticity in this film, and elsewhere in post–World War II Soviet cultural production, was part of what William Connolly calls a modern "drive to mastery" over nature and populations, a peculiar form of domination that seeks to transform a natural landscape into "a set of vistas for aesthetic appreciation"[24]—even as forms of aesthetic appreciation and appropriation could be suggested by the landscape. After all, for local residents "a small sauna" is a utilitarian rather than aesthetic object. The aestheticization as well as museumification of wooden vernacular architecture were products of the metropolitan claims for finding historical authenticity in the local landscape to establish symbolic control over the northern Soviet regions as a vast lyrical landscape, a mythological past of the Soviet people—disregarding its heterogeneous ethnic composition, a controversial history of forced labor, harsh climate, vast distances, and rocky terrain that resisted acculturation.[25]

The lyricism of the North Russian landscape, with its persistent combination of taiga nature, lakes, and old wooden buildings, informed the restoration efforts and writing of the architectural preservation movement enthusiasts who consistently emphasized "the organic connection" between local nature and traditional architecture.[26] Soviet architectural preservation developed over the postwar period into a process of maintenance and construction of lyrical landscapes for the aesthetic pleasure of urban audiences.

Aleksandr Opolovnikov's Making of Kizhi

The island of Kizhi on Lake Onega is home to one of Russia's largest and most famous open-air museums of wooden architecture. The museum's center is Kizhi Pogost, which acquired the status of a protected "cultural and historical monument" in 1920, although the local parish was allowed to use its churches for religious services until 1936. Although the churches avoided any damage during World War II, immediately after its end, in 1945, the government of the Karelian-Finnish SSR decided to fund large-scale reconstruction work to secure the survival of the site. Motivating the postwar restoration effort was the desire of regional authorities to transform Kizhi into a museum open to the public. As a notable and well-known architectural monument, Kizhi was deemed the most suitable object to embody and perform Karelian locality as well as to use it educationally to foster the formation of a regional identity among the local population.[27] In 1946, the Karelian-Finnish government committed to a long-term plan according to which the island of Kizhi would, in the future, accommodate "a collection of monuments to local autochthonous architecture." According to this conception, notable objects of wooden architecture would have to be relocated to Kizhi from all over Karelia.[28]

Apart from didactic considerations, the regional quest for historical authenticity included an important political component. As mentioned earlier, after World War II, the authorities of Soviet Karelia were seeking ways to legitimize their republic's status as a full member of the Soviet Union even though Russians were an ethnic majority there. As one of the measures, they lobbied the Soviet government to allow the resettlement of Ingrian Finns, who had been forcibly deported from the Leningrad region to Siberia and Kazakhstan during the 1930s. Thanks to this effort, some 21,000 Ingrians moved to Karelia during 1948–49 before the campaign was shut down during the Leningrad Affair, the largest post–World War II political cleansing.[29]

Architectural objects were just as important as people for the making of regional specificity because they could act, if conceptualized in proper terms, as material evidence of Karelia's primordial history. In 1947, the Karelian-Finnish government hired two Moscow architects to take a tour of Karelian villages "in order to survey, register, measure, and photograph monuments of architecture and objects of folk design [narodnoe tvorchestvo], so that urgent measures could be taken for their preservation."[30] One of them was Aleksandr Opolovnikov. Born into a noble family in the Ryazan Governorate, Opolovnikov received a degree cum laude from the Moscow Architectural

Institute in 1939. He defended his graduation work under the supervision of Moisei Ginzburg.

Opolovnikov's career went in a different direction from that of Ginzburg. He became one of the leading practitioners and theorists of the Soviet architectural preservation movement, engaging in numerous preservation and restoration projects in North Russia. After his expedition to Karelian villages in 1947, Opolovnikov was hired by the government of the Karelian-Finnish SSR to carry out its program of preservation, restoration, and collection of heritage wooden buildings. His first assignment was the restoration of the Assumption Church in Kondopoga during the summer of 1948. The next year, Opolovnikov was appointed the chief restoration expert in Kizhi and became responsible for its development into an open-air museum of wooden architecture. In 1951, he supervised the relocation to Kizhi of a nineteenth-century house and a barn, the first two objects in the museum's collection. In 1955, in the atmosphere of post-Stalinist liberalization, he developed a large-scale expansion project of the museum and personally supervised the relocation of twenty-four objects from various locations in Karelia.[31]

The historical landscape of North Russia, perceived aesthetically (as lyrical) rather than socially (as archaic), obviously informed Opolovnikov's politics of restoration. The materials from his field trips to villages in Karelia include not only schemes and plans of surviving heritage buildings but also general plans of the surrounding landscape. For example, his 1954 plan of the former Muromsky Monastery on Lake Onega, from which the fourteenth-century Church of the Resurrection of Lazarus was moved to Kizhi island, shows (apart from the church itself) surrounding log buildings, trees, a lakeshore and even boats moored to a pier.[32] His planning of the open-air museum in Kizhi emphasized an aesthetic unity of architecture and landscape. He reiterated that

> an architectural monument is not just the building itself standing in isolation of its surroundings. The concept of an "architectural monument" also includes its landscape: both natural and man-made. The landscape is an integral part of the aesthetic impression of the monument and *shapes our perception of it* in one way or another. This leads to the conclusion that when we plan restoration works on [an architectural] monument, we should somehow preserve and in individual cases even restore its surroundings. And one more important conclusion . . . Any restoration project should include . . . a protective zone and a landscaping zone restricted for new construction.[33]

To satisfy the political demand of the Karelian-Finnish SSR authorities for primordialist narratives and objects, Opolovnikov developed his theory of architectural preservation as the museumification of a historical landscape. His basic definition of an open-air museum was "a collection of architectural monuments that are exhibited in the background of a typical [for this region] natural landscape."[34] His conception of the Kizhi museum consequently developed into the creation of such a landscape so that its didactic and political potential would be readily available to local audiences (regular ferry trips between Kizhi and Petrozavodsk, the capital of Karelia, had been established by 1948).[35] The use value of vernacular architecture was nullified as it became primarily a sign of history designated for visual consumption. The lyricism of the northern landscape underwent a political translation that turned local communities into exotic reservations of the traditional primordial culture of the Russian and Karelian people. "The Russian North [in general] and Karelia [in particular] are a huge and unique sanctuary of the people's wooden architecture that has emerged historically in a natural way," wrote Opolovnikov in his volume on the Kizhi museum.[36] This artificial approach, which conflated history and nature and treated architecture in aesthetic terms as part of the natural landscape, inevitably brought Opolovnikov's making of Kizhi into conflict with practices of North Russian vernacular architecture.

By the late 1940s, the churches of Kizhi represented an architectural palimpsest: in the 1820s, their eighteenth-century log walls had been covered with planking and domes sheathed with iron; in the 1880s, they were also painted.[37] These changes reflected both the regional architectural fashion as well as the desire of parishioners to distinguish their churches visually from the surrounding landscape. When Opolovnikov designed his restoration program of Kizhi Pogost he discarded these changes as "eclectic" and "ahistorical" and prepared an ambitious project that included their removal to "restore" the original look of the church.[38] These measures unavoidably lead to dramatic changes in the appearance of Kizhi Pogost undoing late tsarist-era renovations that Opolovnikov argued reflected the class oppression of the genuine people's culture:

> Local "do-gooder" nobility and clergy dressed the Church of the Transfiguration in a then-fashionable attire of planking painted in garish bright yellow, while the wood shingles of the domes were replaced with cold and lifeless iron . . . And a wonderful song of wood—eternal, gentle and exciting—was shut down; the texture and beauty of log walls was completely erased; the charm of wooden shingle domes was gone. A unique creation of Onega Lake architects lost its genuine

magic character and became similar to ordinary village churches of the later age.[39]

Opolovnikov's argument played on a perceived contrast between the authentic nature of the monument as "genuine architecture" of the common people[40] and the attempts of nineteenth-century bourgeoisie and clergy to strip the Kizhi Pogost of its authentic character and subdue it to their class interests. Opolovnikov's hostility to architectural ornamentation as something disguising the authentic architectural forms was borrowed from the Constructivist theories of his teacher, whose *Style and Epoch* (1923) famously called for the cleansing of excessive architectural ornamentation: "Architectural monuments laid bare and cleansed of their glittering and superficial attire appeared with all the fascination and unexpected sharpness of an artistic asceticism, with all the power of a rough and austere language of simple, uncluttered architectural forms."[41]

The cleansing of wooden architecture of both natural and man-made accretions became the main focus of Opolovnikov's activities (figure 3.4), and through his published works became part of the theory and practice of architectural restoration in the USSR.[42] His 1975 work on the restoration of wooden architecture emphasized the restoration of buildings to their

FIGURE 3.4. Restoration works of the Church of the Transfiguration, between 1956 and 1959. The upper side of the image shows restored parts of the church with wooden shingles and unpainted log walls; the lower side of the image shows the pre-restoration interior of the church with iron-covered domes and painted planking. Courtesy of the Museum of Kizhi.

original form as the fundamental task of his discipline, an approach that interpreted all later changes as "distortions": "The first and most important task in developing the theoretical foundations of restoration [as a scholarly discipline] is the analysis and complex understanding of the nature, essence and specificity of later distortions to monuments of people's architecture. The problem of distortions and accretions is thus the key and main problem in the methodology of restoration and at the same time remains the most notable stumbling block on the pathway to the reconstruction of genuine masterpieces of wooden architecture."[43]

Yet Ginzburg's and Opolovnikov's similar rhetoric in regard to form should not be misinterpreted as a similarity in their politics. Ginzburg sought to build new communalism and called on his fellow architects to be "not a decorator of life, but its organizer." Form was important for him as long as it reflected a certain function; his *Style and Epoch* draws extensively on industrial design as exemplary in this respect.[44] By contrast, Opolovnikov, an expert responsible for the production of a historical landscape through the creation of an open-air museum, worked with very different functions of architecture. Churches and houses of the Kizhi Museum had to perform the historical authenticity of the Karelian-Finnish republic.

The fact that these churches and houses, as objects of vernacular architecture, were designed and redesigned to perform their particular functions was disregarded since the official ideology was extremely hostile to religion and strove to reform the patriarchal organization of life in rural communities. Opolovnikov appealed to wooden architecture as a medium that had preserved the cultural forms originating in Russia's pre-capitalist period. In his interpretation, these forms embodied an alleged past communalism of the Russian people that had fallen prey to the capitalist development and class oppression of nineteenth-century tsarism. Whereas Ginzburg wanted socialist architecture to overcome social alienation, for Opolovnikov old, wooden architecture served to overcome historical alienation by bridging the gap between the past and present community of the Russian/Soviet people. This belief can be seen in the curious combination of his reverence for the eighteenth-century churches of Kizhi Pogost with a mixed, if not straightforwardly negative, attitude toward its third object, the 1874 bell tower. "The bell tower was built not in the traditions of the people's architecture, but according to a project designed "in an artificial style" by an eparchial engineer . . . It means that its architecture is not only subdued to the petrifying canon of the official conservative Orthodoxy, but also embodies general aesthetic norms of that time's dominant culture: eclecticism and a pseudonational ethos. The decline of architecture is seen in every single detail [of the bell tower]."[45] After two pages of harsh criticism Opolovnikov condescended to grant the bell tower the right to exist: "an integral part of the [Kizhi] architectural ensemble . . . that reminds us, even if very approximately, of the silhouette and general appearance of the original [eighteenth-century] bell tower."[46] In other words, for him the only value of the current bell tower was mimetic, owing to its resemblance to the original bell tower that had been demolished in 1872 due to its dilapidated condition.

The Karelian-Finnish government hired Opolovnikov as an intellectual from the Soviet metropole whose professional expertise could add weight to its claims for regional specificity. This positionality gave him the power to determine what the authentic architecture of North Russian communities was and was not. Yet this power was contested. Opolovnikov and other enthusiasts of North Russian historical heritage started a campaign for its preservation and restoration. This campaign—supported and funded by the government of the Karelian-Finnish SSR—included a struggle against low-level bureaucrats who had prioritized rationality over historical heritage and who were often tempted to demolish old buildings to cut the financial burdens that the latter incurred.[47] The situation became more complicated after the Twentieth Party Congress in 1956, when Nikita Khrushchev denounced Stalin's "personality cult," and the post-Stalinist leadership revived early Soviet techno-utopian visions of rationally built socialist spaces that implied the demolition of old structures. As Steven Bittner noted in his study of Moscow's Arbat neighborhood, "Khrushchev saw [in the heritage architecture of Moscow] remnants of old Russia that were incompatible with the stature of the new."[48] The dominant discourse of socialist construction routinely implied the purge of the old prerevolutionary meanings and structures, and the perceived value of "national antiquities" did not necessarily provide immunity for heritage buildings from persecution by local bureaucrats, as well as from sheer neglect.[49] Last but not least, in July 1956 the status of Karelia was downgraded from a full member of the USSR to an autonomous republic of the Russian Federation.

At the same time, Khrushchev-era liberalization of cultural life in the Soviet Union provided heritage architecture enthusiasts with opportunities to defend their de facto romantic nationalist understandings of Soviet history and challenge—albeit implicitly—the modernist approach to urban development adopted by the Soviet government beginning in the mid-1950s. To justify their claims for the power to define the Soviet historical imagination, Soviet preservation experts appealed to the very material of their objects, wood, as a witness to the authentic history of Russia.

Accretions of History

In justifying his main thesis that the essence of preservation and restoration activities lay in the removal of all later accretions, Aleksandr Opolovnikov repeatedly appealed to the aesthetic qualities of wood. His 1974 textbook of architectural preservation includes a lengthy discussion about the properties of wood that goes beyond its physical qualities and focuses instead on its ability to organize "the rhythm" and "tectonics" of architecture: "The unity of [architectural functionality and aesthetic properties of] wood is particularly outstanding in the tectonics of a log building—in a steady rhythm, as in epic songs, of heavyweight log tails . . . in slim and soft vertical lines of axe-cut corners that trim the building's silhouette; in the plastic structure of walls enlivened with small windows; in the overall color composition of the building with its picturesque palette of half-tints and shades."[50]

Both "rhythm" and "tectonics," as used in this fragment, are borrowed from the theory of Soviet Constructivist architecture. The term "rhythm" is another tribute to Moisei Ginzburg,[51] while the term "tectonics" is borrowed from Alexei Gan, whose writings mentioned tectonics as one of three basic elements of the new social architecture. Understood as a dialectic relationship between people and their material world, tectonics implied the interrelatedness of social and material forms that Constructivist architects, artists, and designers were supposed to embody in their works and thus to contribute to social progress.[52] "Tectonics is . . . an explosion of the [material's] internal essence," wrote Gan in his 1922 manifesto, concluding: "Constructivism without tectonics is like painting without color."[53]

The use of Constructivism's vocabulary had several important implications for the Soviet architectural preservation movement. It provided them with a conceptual apparatus to justify their preservation activities. Dealing with buildings that had lost their original functions, such as churches, houses for extended peasant families, sheds and mills, Opolovnikov had to build a model that explained their historical importance through an aesthetic system allegedly inherent in North Russian vernacular architecture. His analysis of numerous heritage buildings in Karelia and elsewhere in North Russia led him to the conclusion that, by the early nineteenth century, local masters had created and consciously employed a "system of artistic methods" that fully realized the expressive potential of wood as a construction material.[54] Moreover, the borrowing of Constructivist vocabulary with its focus on the dialectic of material and social forms allowed Opolovnikov to link this system to a society free of social conflicts that allegedly had existed in North Russia thanks to its geographic and political marginality before the tsarist oppression of the nineteenth century: "The tsunami of the Mongol invasion that enveloped almost all of Russia missed the North. Here, the fire of Russian statehood and national culture was never extinguished. While the succession of the original traditions of Russian culture dating back to Kievan Rus was interrupted, if not destroyed [elsewhere], in the North this culture and its traditions survived in their purity."[55]

In this logic, the heritage architecture of Karelia was a witness to an authentic and genuine people's history of Russia in its entirety. The historical importance of the churches of Kizhi Pogost was that they represented an exemplary expression of this aesthetic system, a kind of glossary that could be used to understand the original language of Russian culture. The texture of wood offered, in turn, the basic structural elements of this language that, when combined, merged into "a wonderful song of wood." This approach to architectural preservation was understandably hostile to later accretions, prioritizing the antiquity and authenticity (be they real or imagined) of old wooden buildings over the meanings and contexts of their use in local communities. The product of an aesthetic and political position of Soviet metropolitan intellectuals, it valued indigenous architectural forms if they blended into the landscape with the unpainted gray and brown colors of their log walls. To put it in another way, for Soviet restoration experts—and for Soviet authorities and their public via the authoritative discourse of these experts—old buildings were important if they performed authenticity and traditionalism, thus objectifying the much-sought-for historical depth of modern Soviet society. Any "nonnatural" and "nonauthentic" elements, such as plaster, paint, iron, and wallpaper, as well as exquisitely carved ornamentations that local residents had increasingly used since the nineteenth century, were interpreted as annoying interruptions into this performance of Russian authentic historical culture: something like the darkened layers on Old Russian icons that concealed original paintings and had to be removed.

In fact, the restoration of Kizhi Pogost to its original state was accompanied by the restoration of icons that had been confiscated by the Soviet authorities from Karelian churches in the interwar period.[56] In 1945, the same year that the government of the Karelian-Finnish SSR passed a resolution to restore Kizhi Pogost and transform it into a museum, it hired two experts of the Tretyakov Gallery in Moscow to inspect and evaluate the republic's collection of icons.[57] One of them, Vera Briusova (Svetlichnaia), was later invited to prepare a detailed plan and budget for their restoration. When submitting her funding application in 1948 to the Karelian government, she justified the historical importance of this work: "These monuments [icons] are products of the richest creative imagination and the supreme mastery of artists of the local independent school. Their restoration will reveal an immense picture of autochthonous art . . . Adding any elements during restoration is completely prohibited, because every monument [icon] represents a genuine masterpiece that has its own artistic value."[58]

Briusova's emphasis on locality (expressed in three synonymous adjectives— "local," "independent," and "autochthonous") was a direct reference to the political demands of local authorities. As such, it represented an artificial historicization of Soviet local and regional identities that translated into an ever more rigorous search for the historical authenticity of the Soviet-era administrative structures, such as the Karelian-Finnish SSR.[59] It positioned icon painting in the domain of regional folk culture as opposed to religious or national high culture. It also justified the return of some of the icons to the churches of Kizhi Pogost as objects of "autochthonous art" rather than sacred objects. As with the painted planking of the churches in Kizhi that were stripped to reveal the texture of their log walls, later layers were removed from icons to recreate their authentic aesthetic form. Briusova described this process in technical terms as "the removal of old darkened varnish from icons and their re-varnishing."[60] This authenticity of icon painting had never been important in religious worship; just the reverse, icons were regularly renovated by adding new layers on top of previous ones or repainted. It was the Soviet search of historical authenticity that reinterpreted these layers as the dirt of time that concealed primordial Russian culture.[61]

The borrowing of Constructivist vocabulary in architectural preservation politics had one more implication that became increasingly visible in the post-Stalinist period. Constructivist theory reflected the active social program of its authors such as Ginzburg and Gan, and their desire to reform society; the terms "rhythm," "tectonics," and "texture" all implied the transformative character of the new social architecture. As a result, the application of these terms to the vernacular architecture of North Russia could not remain purely academic and descriptive. Opolovnikov and other experts of heritage architecture argued that only the uncovered texture of wood could express the authentic character of Russian culture preserved through the local historical landscape. However, these claims clashed with local meanings and practices related to housing. In the postwar communities of Russian Karelia, it was quite typical to use painted planking for the external walls of log houses, and plaster, wallpaper, and modern furniture for their interiors.[62] On the one hand, this was an obvious borrowing of new tendencies in urban housing. On the other, it was a particular indigenous form of working with landscape, as painted planking offsets a building from its surroundings, while interiors with modern wallpaper and factory-built furniture represent an optical intervention into the everyday visual experience of rural communities that are dominated by the persistent combination of water, northern vegetation, and the bleak colors of unpainted wooden surfaces. Yet for Soviet architects, local residents of Karelian communities had to be saved from their perceived loss of historical authenticity, a task all the more important as they designated North Russia "a sanctuary" of traditional folk culture. In a logic that originated from the theory of Constructivist architecture, yet had nothing in common with its emancipatory moment, architectural preservation experts called on Karelian villagers to cleanse their houses of these eclectic elements that provoked the misrecognition of one's true authentic self. Opolovnikov's 1981 book *Wooden Russia*, for example, condemned the use of wallpaper in contemporary North Russian houses by appealing to the aesthetic system that he allegedly uncovered in pre-nineteenth-century wooden architecture:

> Earlier, people never hung wallpaper in their houses: Russian peasants always had an acute and expert sense about the natural beauty of wood as an architectural material, the beauty of the most common, simple things. And what wallpaper can match the natural texture of unpainted wood, with the dark stripes of its core, the rhythm of knots, the smooth yet slightly coarse surface! A floor assembled from broad half beams, the powerful, non-disguised setting of log walls, plank benches along the walls . . . this all creates a stalwart, steady rhythm of accentuated horizontal lines.[63]

Aesthetic elements of traditional architecture—"natural texture of unpainted wood," "dark stripes of its core," and "rhythm of knots"—are represented here as an interface between the materiality of architecture and genuine selves. From this perspective, the use of wallpaper leads to a loss of physical contact between people and wood, with its affective texture, a situation regarded as highly undesirable. Another preservation expert, Petrozavodsk architect Vyacheslav Orfinsky, wrote in 1972, "The early twentieth century saw the decline of [North Russian] folk architecture, when its genuine beauty escaped again and again from the ornamental nets of small architectural details that imitated fashionable forms of urban architectural styles of that time . . . Isn't it a genuine, although never recognized, the tragedy of an entire generation of folk architects? . . . Having lost the Ariadne's thread of century-long traditions, folk masters wandered off the road and got lost."[64]

A native of Petrozavodsk, Orfinsky grieves here not only the loss of authentic architectural traditions in Karelian communities but also the alleged inability of their inhabitants to comprehend this loss and realize how their neglect of "century-long traditions" damages the historical succession of Soviet society. It is, however, most harmful for themselves ("a genuine tragedy of an entire generation").[65] His authoritative discourse denied local communities the right to assign their meanings to domestic and communal space and pushed him to create in the 1980s a separate academic discipline: *etnoarkhitekturovedenie* (studies of ethnic architecture). Its aims combined scholarship and activism, including the production of a full register of wooden heritage buildings in North Russia, the development of theoretical foundations for the use of folk architectural traditions in modern architecture, and public outreach to local communities.[66] In 1997, it became institutionalized with the establishment of the Research Institute of Theoretical Problems of Folk Architecture, which received a double affiliation at the Petrozavodsk State University and Research Institute of Architectural and Urban Theory (Moscow), with Orfinsky as its head.[67]

Identities under Sail

In addition to vernacular architecture, the documentary *Zemlia karel'skaia* focused on another material example of archaic historical time that was allegedly preserved in the lyrical landscape of Karelia: wooden boats. In the region with approximately 60,000 lakes, including the two largest in Europe (Lakes Ladoga and Onega), as well as a long White Sea coast, water has been the center of economic life. Until recently, locally caught fish have been a staple food for Karelians and North Russians.[68] As a result, boats have been an integral part of the North Russian historical landscape. In the documentary, the sailing of a boat around an unnamed lake—with its unnamed passengers gradually aging throughout the film—is used to tie together various episodes from the life of the republic. The boat was more than just a narrative device, however. One of the lengthiest episodes in the film shows, in detail, the process of boat building. The voice-over narration reads:

> There is no town or village in Karelia that is not located on a lakeshore. And every single one of them has its own boat builder with his unique pattern and secrets . . . And every master passes his skill to someone who comes to succeed him. Isn't this the source of the workmanship embodied in the monuments of wooden architecture of recent centuries that have survived to our age? Looking at the perfectly shaped

domes of wooden churches, one cannot help marveling at the supreme skills of their anonymous architects.[69]

As the narrator read this text, the footage showed close-ups of the boat building process. Images of an axe, a saw, and a plane turned into pictures of logs and planks, then into a delicate silhouette of a boat, and, finally, into the domes of the Church of St. Paul and St. Peter in the village of Virma on the White Sea coast. In the film's logic, the succession of historical traditions acquired a particular material dimension in woodwork. Wood was the medium that secured the succession of traditions and established a physical connection between the people's true, authentic past and the socialist present. Moreover, as history became embodied in the lyrical landscape, the cultural understanding of wood in late socialism made it a mediator between people and their "authentic" historical past.

Modern urban cultures often appeal to wood as an affective material because of its texture and correspondent haptic experience. For example, it is common for contemporary home design to use wood with its "nostalgic" structures and narratives to help urban dwellers overcome their alienation from nature. Krisztina Fehérváry, who writes about the politics of various construction materials in socialist Hungary, noted that beginning in the 1970s, many Hungarian families turned to the use of wood for apartment interiors (a feature inspired by vernacular architecture) to create "heterotopic spaces" in prefabricated concrete apartment blocks that invoked the feelings of national belonging and closeness to nature. "Wood was highly prized for its ability to humanize and warm the interior of concrete panel apartments," she writes.[70] The same period saw the increased popularity of organicist architecture in Western Europe, North America, and Japan with its emphasis on the use of wood. One of its primary advocates, the Japanese architect Tadao Ando, stressed the ability of wood to link the old and the new as well as invoke the feeling of one's authenticity: "In these times of appreciation over the crisis of our earthy environment and the deterioration of our spiritual culture, it is important that we seek a new beginning—through new understanding of our environment and in a new appreciation of forests and the culture of wood."[71]

In the specific historical conditions of North Russia, the ability of wood to perform historical continuity and authenticity through its haptic qualities reinforced a historical imagination in which archaicness was the genius loci of the region. The architectural preservation movement, with its ideological center in the museum of Kizhi, was one manifestation of this imagination. A revival of wooden boat and shipbuilding was another example of how people in the late socialist period used wood to position themselves vis-à-vis national historical time as its worthy successors. In Karelia, this revival has been associated with the club Polar Odysseus.

Polar Odysseus was established in 1978 in Petrozavodsk by a group of amateur yachtsmen who initially wanted to pool together their financial and labor resources to repair and redesign a factory-produced fishing boat, turning it into a leisure vessel.[72] This was a common practice in late socialism, and in chapter 1 I discussed how the state-published amateur shipbuilding journal *Katera i yakhty* (Motorboats and yachts) widely publicized imagery of Soviet people using homebuilt boats to travel. Yet in the case of Polar Odysseus, this gnostic drive to master space through travel acquired a historical dimension when, during one of their voyages in the White and Barents seas in 1982, members of the club encountered the wrecks of old Pomor ships.[73] Over the next two years, yachtsmen from Petrozavodsk used sailing expeditions in the White Sea to examine technologies of vernacular boatbuilding in local Pomor communities (figure 3.5).[74]

In 1987, Polar Odysseus transformed from an amateur yacht club into a heritage shipbuilding club with the construction of the *Pomor* (figure 3.6), a replica of the *koch*, a type of ship that Pomor communities used along the Arctic coast during the Early Modern period. In the summer of 1989, members of the club sailed on the *Pomor* to the Svalbard archipelago, a frequent

FIGURE 3.5.   Members of the club Polar Odysseus examining a Pomor fishing boat in the village of Niukhcha in Karelia, 1984. Courtesy of Polar Odysseus.

FIGURE 3.6. The *Pomor* on its way back to Petrozavodsk from a voyage to the Barents Sea, September 1990. Photo by Boris Semenov.

destination of Pomor hunting expeditions between the late seventeenth and early nineteenth centuries. The following winter, they built three more replicas of historical ships, this time medieval Russian ladyas: the *Vera* (Faith), the *Nadezhda* (Hope), and the *Liubov* (Love). In the summer of next year, these replica ships sailed from Petrozavodsk through the Volga–Baltic Waterway to the Black Sea and then through the Mediterranean Sea to Jerusalem. In the summer of 1991, another ladya, the *Sviatitel Nikolai* (St. Nicholas), built the previous winter, sailed around Scandinavia to the North Sea. Meanwhile, the *Pomor* was transported by steamships along the Arctic coast to the Chukchi Sea, from where its team sailed to Alaska in a symbolic gesture that retraced an old trading route to Russian America.[75] As of the late 2010s, Polar Odysseus had a fleet of twenty-four replicas of various historical designs.

In 2014, when I interviewed Viktor Dmitriev, the current president and one of the founders of the club, wood was one of the central topics of our conversation. For Dmitriev, wood was a medium that connected him with the maritime traditions of North Russia; it allowed for the reconstruction of both regional and national history. Yet historical reconstruction was more than a goal in itself; to travel along the historical routes of North Russian merchants, hunters, and pilgrims was just as important. Born in 1946 and a physicist by education, Dmitriev's original hobby was a technical invention, which included arms and space technologies. Fully employed as a plasma physics engineer, he initially treated yachting as just another way to spend summer vacations. But as his sailing took him to various historical places in North Russia, Dmitriev felt an increasing urge to archaize his ships to fit the historical landscape around him. In 1980, with other club members, he remade a standardized fishing boat into a schooner and then spent several years studying the vernacular shipbuilding of Pomor communities.[76]

Dmitriev's work on wooden ships was a form of self-making as vigorous as autobiographic writing was for the Stalinist subjects studied by Igal Halfin and Jochen Hellbeck, but with an axe and other woodworking tools instead of a pen. His appropriation of the Pomor identity is symptomatic in this respect, as his family came to Karelia after the Bolshevik Revolution. Though lacking a direct genealogical linkage with the Pomors, Dmitriev created material objects that forged this linkage and made him an heir of their maritime culture. His transformation into "one of the last Pomor shipbuilders of the twentieth century," as the official website of Polar Odysseus represents him,[77] was a complex self-fashioning, in which interaction with wood and North Russian landscapes in their materiality was important. A 1989 publication about the *Pomor* in the popular geographic journal *Vokrug sveta* (Around the world) quoted Dmitriev saying "wood itself will suggest how to build [the ship],"[78] a reflection on the vernacular shipbuilding practices that, in the absence of blueprints, relied on an interaction between a shipbuilder and his material. This interaction transformed logs and boards into a vessel. In a dialectical way, it also transformed a Soviet professional physicist who designed spaceships, even if as a hobby, into an enthusiast of heritage shipbuilding who, in 1990, well before the disintegration of the USSR, undertook a pilgrimage to Jerusalem on a replica of a medieval Russian vessel. It was the texture of wood that preserved and demonstrated the essence of authentic architecture for Opolovnikov and of shipbuilding for Dmitriev ("wood itself will suggest how to build"). The work of a preservation expert or a shipbuilder was, consequently, in helping wood to reveal its inherent abilities to perform historical authenticity and continuity. To hide it behind other surfaces, as residents in local communities did with their houses, was to break this continuity.

Architectural preservation and historical shipbuilding represented, both in writing and practice, two instances of Soviet elemental materialism. Their enthusiasts appealed to the very texture of wood to maintain and perform historical continuity. Wooden buildings and structures transformed North Russia into a lyrical landscape in a kind of a symbolic acceptance of the failure of modernization in the region. They allowed for its inclusion in the pantheon of socialist spaces as a landscape of the ancient, uninterrupted, and authentic history of the Russian people. At the same time, the resistance of this landscape to modernization informed a political agenda of historical architecture and shipbuilding. Their enthusiasts sought to preserve and revive wooden structures and technologies to perpetuate the allegedly authentic historic character of the region. By the turn of the 1990s, wood became the main symbol of North Russia as a mythological place that had allegedly preserved the old folk culture of the Russian people.

In June 2013, mass media in the Republic of Karelia circulated photos of eighty-four-year-old Orfinsky, by then a full member of the Russian Academy of Architecture and Construction Sciences, running in formal wear to stop the demolition of a 1936 wooden building in Petrozavodsk. During World War II, Petrozavodsk experienced massive destruction of its prewar architecture and civil infrastructure, and this building located on the central city street (Lenin Avenue) was one of a few survivors of the prewar age. Built during a short-term revival of northern romanticism in Soviet Karelia of the mid-1930s, it was distinguished from the postwar Stalinist architecture that dominated the center of Petrozavodsk and had housed a children's clinic from 1960 to April 2001, when the building was partially destroyed by fire (figure 3.7).

FIGURE 3.7.   The 1936 building of a children's clinic in the center of Petrozavodsk, spring 1997. Photo by Boris Semenov.

Reconstruction was stalled because of a lack of funding, and there were two more fires in 2003 and 2006. Despite the pitiable state of the building, the republican and municipal authorities insisted that, as an architectural monument (official status had been granted to the building in 2000), it had to be restored to its authentic form. In June 2013, the building's owner, desperate to turn it from a liability into an asset, brought an excavator and started illegal demolition works. When news reached Orfinsky, he rushed to stop the destruction of the building.[79]

Orfinsky's interference and, perhaps more important, of then minister of culture of the Republic of Karelia, Elena Bogdanova, stopped the demolition. For the following five years, until early 2018, the former building of the Karelian-Finnish People's Commissariat of Foreign Affairs had remained in its half-destroyed state in the very center of the city, its charcoaled walls covered with tarpaulins. It was only in 2018, seventeen years after the first fire, that the owners of the building finally found common ground with the city authorities and architectural preservation experts. According to the restoration plans, the original logs that survived the fire and almost two decades of neglect should be integrated into the frame of the new building, which will be a replica of the original design. This fetishization of the historical authenticity deploys Soviet-era understandings of old wooden architecture as the core foundation of a regional identity. More important, it demonstrates an absolute priority of architectural form over function in the heritage preservation politics in Russia. While still employing the rhetoric of Soviet Constructivist architecture, the post-Soviet preservation movement was unable to suggest any other justification for its activities than that of the historical authenticity of forms. Devoid of any social content, its politics are more concerned with hollow walls than with their use in social life. The same happened with Constructivist ideas over time. When post-Stalinist Soviet designers turned to Constructivism in search of inspiration and started borrowing some of its ideas for consumer product design since the late 1950s, they capitalized on aesthetic principles developed by Varvara Stepanova, Boris Arvatov, Aleksandr Rodchenko, and other early Soviet Constructivists, but largely discarded their social agenda.[80] The ongoing debate about the restoration of the Narkomfin House is focused on its preservation as part of the Moscow architectural landscape, as a monument to the history of Soviet architecture, just like the wooden churches and buildings of North Russia.

Soviet and post-Soviet architectural preservation discourse sought to reinvent local communities, but eventually it exerted a much greater influence on its producers than on the target audience. The failure of recent measures to revive traditional ways of life and architectural forms in Karelian villages is a particularly illustrative example. Since 1995, a team of Russian and Finnish architects and ethnographers has been working on an ambitious project to preserve the Northern Karelian village of Panozero as an architectural monument and as a living community devoted to traditional ways of life. Funding from the Juminkeko Foundation (Finland) was used to revive domestic weaving, boatbuilding, and sauna building. Trained by Finnish and Petrozavodsk specialists and working on newly imported equipment, the residents of Panozero were paid for performing traditional crafts for tourist groups.[81] In a 2006 interview for the local TV channel GTRK Karelia, Orfinsky argued that "what is happening in Panozero is not only the restoration of exemplars of traditional architecture, but also the maintenance of the centuries-long lifestyle of northern Karelians," revealing that the drive for the museumification of the North Russian landscape, when applied consistently, is capable of transforming into objects not only buildings but also people.[82]

Yet these measures could not stop out-migration from the village and, between 2002 and 2013, the population of Panozero dropped from eighty-nine people to fifty-two, reflecting the rural flight also experienced elsewhere in North Russia. Orfinsky could not conceal his disappointment that local residents were much less enthusiastic about the preservation of their village than were urban enthusiasts from Petrozavodsk and Finland, and called on "the [Russian] state and society" in order to "help Panozero residents to preserve life in this ancient Karelian land."[83] A Petrozavodsk journalist expressed this disappointment in a more straightforward way, writing that "[external] connoisseurs of traditional culture and ancient lifestyle find in Panozero indigenous beauty and charm, which, unfortunately, most local residents fail to see."[84] The project to revive Panozero created new cross-border connections between heritage enthusiasts in Karelia and Finland but did not manage to connect their visions with the practices of local populations. This indifference was also true in the Soviet era when local residents often set abandoned houses and entire villages on fire, destroying the North Russian historical landscape and subverting preservation discourses that sought to transform them into natural extensions to this landscape.[85] Arson, as well as accidental fires in abandoned heritage buildings, has occasionally occurred in the post-Soviet era as well, most notably at the former building of the Karelian-Finnish People's Commissariat of Foreign Affairs.[86]

Having failed to revive rural communities per their supposedly traditional lifestyle and architecture, the conservation movement in contemporary Russia was more successful in mobilizing its own ranks—that is, the educated urban class. Every year, several dozen people from Petrozavodsk travel to the museum of Kizhi and stay for the entire tourist season from May to

October, dressing up in traditional peasant dress from the Onega Lake region and performing traditional crafts. By contrast, residents of surrounding villages largely ignore this practice unless it implies monetary rewards.[87] The wooden shipbuilding school at Polar Odysseus attracts young urbanites from Petrozavodsk and St. Petersburg, most of them university students, but hardly any contemporary Pomors from the still surviving villages along the White Sea coast.[88]

Two nongovernmental organizations in Moscow and St. Petersburg— Obshchee delo (A Common Goal) and Verenitsa (Cavalcade)—pool the financial contributions, labor, and equipment of educated metropolitan residents willing to travel to North Russia in the summertime to participate in the restoration of its wooden churches. Both nongovernmental organizations actively publicize their activities through social media, public conferences, and documentaries. In Aleksandr Pasechnik's 2014 documentary *Kovcheg* (The Arc), produced by Obshchee delo, one of its activists explains the rationale behind his efforts: "If the [North Russian] village keeps on living, then the state [of Russia] will keep on living."[89] The restoration of old wooden churches is thus interpreted as a revival of local communities and, through them, the healing of the national body. The Soviet quest for historical authenticity has produced persistent forms of identification that became influential among the educated urban population as nostalgia for ancient architectural forms, for affective interaction with wood, and for lost cultural traditions.

CHAPTER 4

When Spaces of Transit Fail Their Designers

Social Antagonisms of Soviet Stairwells and Streets

For a Soviet person, an entranceway door [into a hallway of an apartment block] is something fouled, scratched, painted with disgusting red in towns or withered light blue in villages, and oftentimes entirely rotten.

—Andrei Konchalovsky, *Sublime Deception*

I believe that political power also exercises itself through the mediation of a certain number of institutions which look as if they have nothing in common with the political power, and as if they are independent of it, while they are not . . . All teaching systems, which appear simply to disseminate knowledge, are made to maintain a certain social class in power; and to exclude the instruments of power of another social class.

—Michel Foucault, *The Chomsky-Foucault Debate*

Scholars of Soviet history confront a significant imbalance in the ways various segments of Soviet urban space are covered in the primary and secondary literature. The personal accounts of people who lived in the late socialist era provide us with a wealth of information about communal and one-family apartments in Soviet urban centers, the main streets and squares of Soviet cities, sites that attracted intellectual or nonconformist publics (such as the café Saigon in Leningrad), as well as heritage and modern neighborhoods. Studies of late socialist urban space have largely focused on the same objects of Soviet urban space.[1] At the same time, many essential spaces of late socialism have been omitted from this picture. For example, little research has been done on the Soviet dormitories, workers' barracks, or multiapartment wooden houses that were extensively built from the 1910s to the 1950s as "temporary" housing, but are still in use today. These types of housing were far from marginal. In 1990, after more than three decades of a large-scale housing campaign in the USSR, 7,000,000 people still lived in dormitories, 2,000,000 in barracks, and 16,000,000 in "temporary" housing without basic utilities.[2] Small provincial towns and so-called urban settlements (*poselki gorodskogo tipa*), as well as Soviet garrison towns in the USSR, Eastern Europe, and Mongolia are other examples of missing sites in our understanding of late Soviet urban space.[3] Even such urban spaces as post-Stalinist residential apartment blocks and neighborhoods that have been extensively depicted and discussed in primary accounts and the secondary literature have their blind spots—most important, stairwells (*pod'ezd*) and basements (*podval*), as well as their adjacent spaces and infrastructure, including yards, garages, and city parks.

This bias has a social nature. We know about those segments of Soviet urban space that were planned, built, and populated by people who possessed a cultural voice. In other words, the Soviet urban world that we know is the world of Soviet officials and intellectuals. The door of a private apartment, for example, is tacitly present in all current debates about public and private spheres in the post-Stalinist USSR as the default border on which the state has encroached to expand its surveillance and control over citizens' lives.[4] Yet, although this dichotomizing function of the apartment door was characteristic of the Soviet educated class, it was not socially universal. The stairwells and basements of Soviet apartment blocks, as well as their adjacent territories and related infrastructure (such as parks and garages), were colonized by people, mostly of working-class backgrounds, who regarded them as spaces of their own. They were important sites of social interaction and conflicts, community building, and premarital and extramarital sex. That they are disregarded in primary accounts and scholarly narratives is a result of the marginality of their populations in terms of cultural voice.

For the famous Russian film director, Andrei Konchalovsky, for example, the entranceway door of a Soviet apartment block was "something fouled . . . and often entirely rotten," because his social position as a post-Soviet intellectual entailed a certain politics of aesthetics that expressed itself in this disgust of Soviet spaces of transit.[5] Soviet stairwells, yards, and streets provoked different affective responses among different social groups. For Soviet and post-Soviet intelligentsia, negative affects such as disgust and fear were caused by the incapacity of these spaces to act in a strictly functionalist manner, by their failure to provide the unobstructed passage of bodies in Soviet urban space. Stairwell landings and dark archways attracted diverse groups of people. By spending their leisure time in these spaces, these groups challenged attempts by the state bureaucracy and intellectual elite to rationally organize Soviet society both in spatial (urban planning) and temporal (leisure activities) terms. In turn, the people who occupied Soviet spaces of transit developed very different emotional bonds to them. I argue that on the cultural level this situation was reflected in the different affective regimes in which people coexisted with Soviet stairwells, yards, streets, and similar spaces. Konchalovsky's inclusion as a prominent Russian intellectual in the production of cultural knowledge allowed for a universalist claim ("for a Soviet person") that disguised social antagonisms generated by Soviet spaces of transit and extrapolated from one particular affective regime—that of disgust and fear—to the "common knowledge" of Russian culture.[6] Here, I follow one of Michel Foucault's main theses in his famous debate with Noam Chomsky; namely, that all systems of knowledge have their politics that serve to "maintain a certain social class in power; and to exclude the instruments of power of another social class."[7] The archeology of Soviet stairwells and streets that I undertake by looking at their traces in written and visual sources shows the politics of Soviet spaces of transit and their involvement in the production of Soviet bodies and selves.

Exposition: The Soviet Stairwell

In November 1955, the Central Committee of the Soviet Communist Party and the USSR Council of Ministers passed a joint resolution. Titled "On the elimination of excesses in design and construction," the measure marked a radical shift in Soviet housing policies. Instead of Stalinist empire style, which was characterized by a focus on the exterior luxury of a small number of new buildings at the expense of mass housing, the state now reoriented its urban policies toward the large-scale industrial production of apartment blocks. In the next few years, a uniform design of five-story apartment blocks was introduced, tested, and declared standard for the pan-Union construction program. Within the next several decades, the USSR was covered with tens of thousands of new apartment blocks of the same modernist and utilitarian design, known informally as *khrushchevki* after Nikita Khrushchev, initiator of this mass housing program. New designs soon followed. By the turn of the 1970s, apartment blocks of nine stories and higher displaced *khrushchevki* from the housing programs in larger Soviet cities. However, five-story apartment buildings of various designs, including modified *khrushchevki*, remained the staple architectural product in small Soviet towns until the end of the Soviet Union.[8] Thanks to this program of large-scale housing construction, between 1956 and 1966, nearly half of the Soviet population moved to better housing at the state's expense.[9] The state-funded construction program continued at similarly impressive rates in the following years:

between 1966 and 1980, an additional 162,000,000 people, or three-fifths of the Soviet population, moved to better housing.[10]

The various modernist designs of residential apartment blocks in the USSR had one principal feature in common—to maximize the share of residential space, Soviet architects reduced to a minimum the area of their public zones including stairwells, corridors, and landings. For example, khrushchevki were five floors high, with four or more entrances, each leading to a stairwell. The stairwell led residents and visitors to five small landings (roughly two meters wide and slightly over one meter long) with four entrances to individual apartments. There were also landings between every two floors; these served to connect two flights of stairs between floors (figure 4.1). The stairwells divided new Soviet apartment blocks into horizontal sections that were connected only through the yard. Later apartment block designs in the USSR had slightly more spacious public places and apartments but kept this general tendency of dividing them into narrow non-interconnected stairwells.

The ostensibly utilitarian nature of public spaces in the new apartment blocks was a remarkable feature of post-Stalinist mass housing and a conscious choice of Soviet officials and architects. Professional and public debates of the 1950s and 1960s on the mass housing program explicitly rejected (or, more precisely, indefinitely delayed to the communist future) the Constructivist idea of "commune houses," which implied the communal use of facilities for cooking, dining, and leisure time and reduced private space to individual bedrooms.[11] Instead, new apartment blocks were designed to accommodate as many individual apartments as possible at the expense of corridors, stairwells, and other public spaces. This did not herald the rejection of communalist values and ideals in the planning of Soviet cities. Although discarded at the scale of separate apartment blocks, these ideals became projected to larger city units known as microdistricts (*microraion*). Microdistricts had been the primary structural elements of Soviet urban planning since the late 1950s, combining residential dwellings and public service buildings. Reflecting a rationalist approach to the planning of Soviet people's leisure time, the microdistrict as a concept of urban planning was a commune-house expanded to the size of a neighborhood.[12] In Soviet urban theory, its libraries, cinemas, clubs, sports facilities, cafes, and other "cultural facilities" took the responsibility of filling up the leisure time of both under-age and adult Soviet citizens, acting as sites for community building and as forms of communist education.[13] Meanwhile, such nonliving spaces as the stairwells of apartment blocks, their yards, and other adjacent territories were planned on exclusively utilitarian principles to ensure the effective passage of people to and from their apartments. To summarize, new microdistricts were meant

FIGURE 4.1. Stairwell of a 1959 khrushchevka in Petrozavodsk. Photo by Aleksei Marakhtanov.

to modernize Soviet society by immersing Soviet citizens into a modern life-style with personal living space and rationally organized public spaces. In many cases, they were symbolically built in place of the ramshackle barracks of Stalin's era as a gesture visualizing the state's adoption of a new, citizen-oriented model of socialism.[14]

Beginning with Oleg Kharkhordin, scholars of the post-Stalinist Soviet Union had argued that the mass housing reform, when Soviet people moved en masse from communal to new individual apartments, did not herald the supremacy of the private sphere over communal values in the USSR. In-stead, new housing became a frontier where the Soviet authorities sought new, more discreet, and decentralized forms of social control.[15] This was all the more true for the social infrastructure of new microdistricts that were designed to "promote ideological and educational work at the local level."[16] At the institutional level, this new regulatory effort found its man-ifestation in the local housing management offices (ZhEK) established by decree No. 322 on March 25, 1959, by the USSR Council of Ministers, "On measures to improve the usage and maintenance of state-owned residential housing."[17] Housing management offices were primarily responsible for the maintenance of apartment blocks and the related infrastructure of their mi-crodistricts. Their functions also included the governance of social order in Soviet urban communities.[18] As organizations that dealt with most aspects of people's out-of-work time, housing management offices were the Soviet state's representatives in the most private corners of Soviet people's lives. The deputy minister of Housing and Utilities of the RSFSR from 1972 to 1981, Vladimir Ladygin, accurately noted in his memoir that "from birth to death, each Soviet person's life was under the careful supervision of the ministry [of housing and utilities] and its structures in every city and settlement."[19]

Unfortunately for the advocates of the Soviet housing-as-enlightenment project, this picture was largely idealized. Understaffed, underfunded, and often inefficiently run, local housing offices could barely cope with the mag-nitude of the task of keeping apartment blocks and public spaces of Soviet microdistricts properly maintained. Soviet authorities consequently solicited the active and voluntary participation of residents to maintain these pub-lic spaces. This participation was institutionalized in the form of residents' committees (domkom) established in 1959.[20] A 1968 joint resolution of the RSFSR Council of Ministers and Central Council of Trade Unions (VTsSPS) prompted apartment blocks residents to form such committees and obliged ZhEKs to seek close cooperation with the latter. The resolution stressed that this alliance had to address "the conditions of apartments, buildings, stairwells, elevators, equipment, and adjacent spaces."[21] Soviet mass media actively advertised the cooperation between ZhEKs and domkoms as a precondition for clean and "cultured" communal living in apartment blocks. In Karelia, this cooperation was among the favorite stories on the local television channel and radio station.[22] In Leningrad, local Komsomol organizations urged their members to contribute to it actively.[23] Finally, the pan-Union mass media circulated stories of the miraculous transformations of urban neighborhoods into green and safe oases through a popular initiative under the caring supervision of the ZhEKs.[24]

Despite these measures, as new microdistricts sprang up all over the USSR, the Soviet authorities and those responsible residents who internalized the official logic of the rationally organized urban environment found themselves in the uneasy position of being a contender for, rather than a hegemon of, Soviet urban space. Although Soviet urban planners assigned stairwells, yards, and streets a purely utilitarian function of transitory spaces between one's private apartment and public facilities for cultured leisure, these spaces soon acquired their own residents who spent most of their free time there rather than in state-funded facilities or at home. As a result, the last decades of the Soviet Union saw a remarkable relationship between stairwells and similar utilitarian public spaces, on the one hand, and certain groups of the urban population, on the other. This symbiosis challenged official moral norms and sincerely scared the more educated and disciplined parts of Soviet society because it threatened to engulf Soviet youth, its future generations.

Sex on Stairs

In a Soviet-era joke, a Parisian woman complains that, when she invited a Soviet man for a romantic outing, he tried to have sex with her on the stairwell leading to her apartment.[25] In another joke, a Russian man explains why the stairwell of an apartment block is the best place to have casual sex: stairs neutralize the height difference between lovers, while an inability to properly finish intercourse can be disguised by pretending to hear an approaching neighbor.[26] In yet another joke from the post-Soviet era, a professor of engineering walks in on his daughter having sex with one of his students in the stairwell of their apartment block. The clumsiness of the situation is overcome when the student presents his professor with a mathematical challenge dealing with male and female anatomical differences.[27]

Archival documents, studies of sexual and everyday life in the USSR, and Soviet and post-Soviet fiction show that these jokes reflected an actual phenomenon: the common use of public places for sexual relationships in conditions where one's personal housing failed to provide privacy (teenagers living with parents in small apartments), when hotel staff demanded an official marriage certificate to rent a room to a couple, and when the harsh climate made outdoor sex problematic during much of the year. In Petrozavodsk during the early 1970s, for example, residents of the Pervomaisky district regularly turned to the police with requests to cleanse their houses of couples having sex in stairwells and nearby garages, because that local children "often become unwilling witnesses of loose behavior of drunken men and women."[28] Stephen Harris mentions at least one similar case in his book on post-Stalinist housing.[29] Scholars of sex in the USSR—such as Adrian Geiges and Tatiana Suvorova, Anna Rotkirch, and Igor Kon—mention stairwells and other similar urban spaces—basements, garages, and city parks—as common sites for premarital sex for youth and extramarital sex for adults.[30] Mark Popovsky, a Soviet immigrant who in 1985 published a book about sex in the USSR, featured Soviet stairwells as the most important dating site for people who were not officially married. To emphasize their importance, he quoted one of his respondents: "We [Soviet people] are born in stairwells, make love in stairwells, and die in stairwells."[31] Even still prudish early perestroika-era Soviet cinematography could not avoid this theme. In Karen Shaknazarov's *The Courier* (1986), based on his 1982 novel, two protagonists trying to start their sexual lives fail to find privacy in a city park and their friends' apartments, and end up in the basement of an apartment block, only to be scared off by a vigilant neighbor before intercourse takes place. Dictionaries of Russian slang recorded at least two special terms for sexual intercourse in the stairwell of an apartment block: "periscope sex," a metaphor implying the necessity to stay alert for possible intrusions, and "biathlon."[32]

It would be wrong to extrapolate from such evidence to the whole of Soviet sexual life or to use it, as Popovsky did, for any simplistic conclusions about the totalitarian suppression of sex in the USSR. What this evidence shows is that the stairwells of Soviet apartment blocks possessed properties that were directly opposite to those assigned to them by Soviet urban planners. In other cultural and historical contexts marginalized groups made similar uses of spaces designed for public transit and leisure. George Chauncey's book about gay life in New York before World War II examines the role of vibrant metropolitan spaces in the making of urban homosexual culture in the United States, whereas James Green suggests that parks, plazas, and beaches were central to the emergence of male same-sex encounters in Brazilian cities.[33] The parallels between different forms of urban modernity are striking: like the streets of New York and the parks of Rio de Janeiro, instead of acting as merely transitory spaces for people circulating between their apartments, jobs, and facilities for leisure and recreation, Soviet stairwells revealed an ability to accumulate people and connect them in various and diverse ways.

In addition to providing shelter for young people exploring their sexuality, stairwells acted as sites for unofficial grassroots sexual education. Igor Kon, in his cultural history of sex in the USSR, describes the repeated failures of Soviet advocates of sexual education to institutionalize it in any mass form.[34] Two educators, Dmitry Isaev and Viktor Kagan, wrote in 1979 that a lack of this education drove teenagers together in stairwells, quoting one of their informants: "It is only in the stairwell that we can discuss important sexual questions."[35] As the gathering places for Soviet youth, stairwells facilitated the circulation of knowledge about sexual life, suggested roles and models of sexual behavior, offered stimulants, such as alcohol and drugs, and provided sexual partners. Isaev and Kagan described what can be called the Soviet stairwell's capacity for the vertical organization of urban juvenile communities, in which the circulation of knowledge—but also of sexual partners—was facilitated by communication between teenagers of different age groups and social backgrounds. For Soviet sexual enlighteners, this facilitation was understandably dangerous since it challenged the dominant model of monogamous sexual behavior in officially registered marriages and the regulated conditions of the spousal bed.[36] But in doing this, stairwells and other similar public places provided Soviet people with the resources to practice sexualities that were alternative to the dominant norm.

In Vladimir Vysotsky's unfinished *Roman o devochkakh* (Novel about Girls; 1977), one episode describes a basement-like gallery that, in the daytime, was used by law enforcement officers to practice prone shooting. Soft pads were placed on the floor for their convenience, and this allowed for the gallery's nocturnal repurposing into a venue where "lewd women" had group sex with "young, tipsy boys trembling from excitement and exhibitionism." The novel's protagonist had his first sexual experience in this place; he later learned that not all girls came to this place voluntarily: "There were other times; there were other, very young girls. They were pulled into the shooting gallery by force; they had sex because of fear and then wept, and Kol'ka [the protagonist] felt pity for them."[37]

Anna Rotkirch's study of sexualities in Soviet and post-Soviet times quoted several similar stories. One section, aptly titled "In the Cellar," deals with the memoir of a man born in 1960 into a suburban workers' family in Leningrad. His description of his first sexual encounter was much like that of Vysotsky's protagonist: "I was about 15 years old . . . I was friends with my classmates, but also with guys who were 3–5 years older than me. My first close meeting with a woman took place in a cellar. My elder brother had brought some girl. Together with his friends we got drunk and then everybody fucked her. Around the tenth turn was mine. I was very nervous, standing in line. The older friends calmed and encouraged me. You won't even have to do anything, they said. Just take off your pants."[38] The same respondent mentions an episode in which he had sex with another girl at an unfinished construction site—another ubiquitous place in the late Soviet urban landscape. Upon realizing that this was his partner's first sexual experience, he protected her from his friends who had already lined up outside of their shelter, anticipating an opportunity for casual sex, which would undoubtedly take the form of group rape. Later, according to his claims, this girl became immersed in this misogynistic culture of Soviet transit spaces.[39] Viktor Pirozhkov, a scholar of late Soviet juvenile delinquency, linked urban public and transit places—such as stairwells, basements, attics, and parks— with "line-up love" (*liubov' v ochered'*), the author's euphemism for sex between one girl and several partners taking turns.[40] Soviet sexologists had to admit the existence of these forms of sexuality. In 1979, the Soviet pediatric journal *Pediatriia* published an article on sexual deviance among children and teenagers based on a study of a group of twenty-three boys and fifty-seven girls between the ages of five and sixteen who had been treated for "clinical forms of sexuality." It discovered that nineteen teenagers ("children of the pubertal age" in the authors' words) from the study group had two or more partners, and eleven had at least once engaged in group sex. As an explanation of this behavior that was contradictory to every norm of socialist sexuality, the authors claimed: "These sexual relations should be considered as part of the teenagers' collective behavior which is regulated by moral norms of the groups [to which the teenagers belonged] that are contradictory to social moral principles . . . Forms of sexual activity practices by the teenagers [under study] are primarily determined by 'group moral norms.' This leads to sexual debauchery with easy consent to casual sexual relations, group sex and even occasional homosexuality."[41]

Soviet sexologists, at least in theory, avoided putting the blame for "sexual debauchery" on a specific girl or boy. Instead, they interpreted alternative sexualities not as individual peculiarities but rather as social phenomena derivative of the particular conditions in which some Soviet teenagers were immersed. Premarital sexual contacts, teenage promiscuity, and group sex— all of these had social roots in the moral norms of the groups that emerged on the margins of Soviet society. As other sources show, these margins had a specific topographic location in Soviet urban space, belonging to its dark public places. Stairwells, basements, and garages stood in a metonymic relationship to those forms of sexual behavior that were disapproved of by Soviet official discourse, partially because of the normalization of sexual violence but, most important, because they also provided resources for non-normative sexualities. These nonnormative forms of sexual behavior were only part of broader social practices that, from the perspective of Soviet officials and intelligentsia, threatened not only the reproductive health but the entire social health of the Soviet nation.

Containing the Stairwell

In 1990, a regional Soviet studio released a short documentary, titled *Pod'ezd* (A Stairwell) and directed by Tatiana Vasilieva. The film started with the director interviewing a group of teenagers who gathered every evening on one of the stair landings in her multistoried apartment block in Sverdlovsk (now Yekaterinburg). The interview was done in 1988 and, for the next two years, the filming crew traced the biographies of these teenagers, as nearly all of them, one after another, ended up in youth detention centers or prisons. The last part of the documentary was filmed on the same stair landing in 1990. The group of teenagers was still there, but its composition had changed dramatically: only one remained from 1988. Yet these two groups had a lot in common: behavior, clothes, body language, ways of speaking, as well as antagonism vis-à-vis their more "civilized" neighbors and the police.[42]

In the documentary, the lives of Soviet teenagers rotate around the stairwell. It is here where they come every night; it is here where they return from youth detention centers. The narrator presses them to reveal why the stairwell is so appealing to them, and their confused and disconnected answers eventually converge into the explanation that it is the only place where they do not feel socially alienated. "We have nowhere else to spend our nights," concludes one of the film's subjects at one point.

The film's stairwell represents both a material and social environment that produced deviance in late Soviet society. The director avoids conventional explanations of juvenile crime, such as failures in educational work or negative peer influence. Vasilieva does not offer any direct causal explanations for why most of the teenagers filmed in the first part of her documentary ended up in the Soviet penitentiary system. The connection between the Soviet stairwell and the Soviet prison in the film is spatial: one's physical presence there is followed by one's imprisonment and then by the return to the stairwell. Teenage bodies represented in this film are derivative of the dark and marginal urban spaces of late socialism.

The most recent and detailed English-language study of social deviance in the post-Stalinist USSR, Brian LaPierre's, *Hooligans in Khrushchev's Russia*, interprets Soviet hooliganism of this period as a product of the new classificatory and regulatory policies introduced by Soviet leaders in an attempt to move from coercive methods of social engineering to more discreet and self-regulatory forms of social control. LaPierre's central argument is that Soviet hooliganism was produced and reproduced daily when "Soviet citizens (both official and ordinary) interacted with, evaluated, and applied interpretive labels to the small-scale social niches around them."[43] LaPierre explains deviance and petty crime as the interplay of social and power relations; his study is primarily an exploration of how Soviet society was policed—in the name of order and progress—in the 1950s and 1960s.

This perspective has proven productive in deepening our understanding of the interaction between society and power in the post-Stalinist USSR. At the same time, I suggest that we complement LaPierre's structural and discursive explanations with those interpretations that Soviet officials and citizens used themselves to make sense of disorderly behavior among their compatriots. Their perspective might account for a more complex picture of how social deviance was produced and negotiated in the USSR. LaPierre mentions references to the "West's intrigues" and "relics of the (bourgeois) past," which were, indeed, a commonplace explanation of hooliganism in Soviet official rhetoric and criminal law.[44] Yet official reports and especially daily talk were dominated by other—materialist—interpretations that linked social deviance to the material conditions of life in Soviet urban areas. Soviet officials and citizens were all too aware that hooliganism did not occur in an abstract social space. City parks, streets, yards, stairwells, and apartments were the places where Soviet citizens experienced and witnessed petty crimes and encountered their traces: broken phone booths, carbonated water machines, and lamps, destroyed vegetation, graffiti on the walls, and spittle on the floor. The Soviet hooligan had multiple faces and flexible definitions, as LaPierre convincingly shows. Yet there was one certainty about his origins, which was reflected in Vasilieva's documentary: he—in the Soviet context, hooliganism was practiced as a deviant yet persistent form of masculinity—spawned from ordinary Soviet people in the dark urban places of socialist cities and towns.

Notably, the launch of the antihooligan campaign in the mid-1950s coincided not with the 1953 amnesty of Gulag prisoners but with the launch of the mass housing program. Its materialist logic that the modern conditions of life in new apartments, houses, and neighborhoods would produce a new, modern, cultured, and disciplined Soviet subject had a reverse side. It made many Soviet people—officials and ordinary citizens alike—strongly believe in a firm link between disorderly space and deviant behavior. Authorities at all levels were overwhelmed with complaints from the residents of new neighborhoods that shared one common message—that the unexpected ability of their spaces of transit to accumulate people, rather than to pass them unhampered, had a dangerous consequence: the potential transformation of local youth into deviant subjects.[45] Residents of a new apartment block in Leningrad's Vyborgsky District explicated this logic at their May 1968 meeting, when they demanded that plans to construct a new parking area instead of a sports club in their yard be canceled: "The parking will occupy the area designated for children's sports facilities . . . We don't want our children and children from the adjacent apartment blocks to idle around in the street and stairwells—they should engage in useful activities."[46]

A 1973 study of juvenile delinquency in the Republic of Karelia prepared for the regional Communist Party committee (obkom) claimed the same "idling around . . . in one's community" (*nichegonedelanie . . . po mestu zhitel'stva*) as its main cause. Its authors suggested that special countryside camps be organized to reduce the juvenile crime level, which would negate the influence of "the street" on teenagers who tended to invest more time there than engaging in "socially useful activities."[47] Responding one year later to this suggestion, party officials from the Pudozhsky District of Karelia reported that they had organized a "military and sports camp" based in a local military garrison, with its daily routine "arranged to resemble the daily routine in the Soviet Army."[48] A 1976 survey of the activities of the Kondopoga Club of Young Technical Designers by the Karelian Komsomol committee praised the work of its kart racing section, because its supervisor was particularly successful in attracting teenagers from "stair landings," as well as "controlling their school progress, communicating with parents" and, finally, pushing them to pursue technology majors in technical schools.[49]

The materialist understanding of the power of "the street and stairwells" to transform Soviet teenagers into delinquents offered Soviet officials and responsible citizens a similarly materialist solution: to extract them from the stairwell and move them to facilities where they would be under the strict supervision of someone endowed with authority. If stairwells were so effective in claiming the bodies and souls of Soviet teenagers, then the latter had to be relocated—by force, if necessary, as party officials from the Pudozhsky District implied—to another material and social environment that would shape their bodies and souls in more appropriate ways. Not surprising, one of the most popular forms of extracurricular educational (*vospitatel'naia*) work among Soviet teenagers both in secondary and professional schools was tourist trips to cultural venues, heritage places, and sites related to Soviet military history—an idea dating back to Soviet pedagogical discourses of the 1920s and 1930s.[50] Trips to the "sites of revolutionary and military glory of the Soviet nation" were regarded as instrumental in the upbringing of Soviet youth since they provided a material environment that stimulated more socially responsible forms of identity performances than those provoked by one's immediate living conditions. If repeated regularly, such trips were supposed—according to the theory and practice of Soviet education—to make Soviet teenagers good socialist subjects.[51]

In these and many other examples, Soviet officials and ordinary citizens did not differentiate between the material and social aspects of deviant behavior among Soviet teenagers. Acting as spontaneous materialists, they recognized the power of stairwells and other public places to grant Soviet teenagers a negative social agency—negative from the perspective of Soviet authorities. Peer influence and the peculiar moral norms of marginal groups were often referred to as the force transforming Soviet teenagers into deviant subjects. Still, the materiality of Soviet stairwells, basements, and streets was just as important. Walls and the darkness of stairwells protected youth from the adult gaze, the central heating offered them shelter from the elements, and landing stairs made for cramped but relatively uncontrolled communication and the creation of spaces for interaction. Stairwells were, in other words, breeding grounds for the social agency of Soviet teenagers.

Gilbert Ryle suggested in *The Concept of Mind* that ways of thinking, emotional response, and behavior stand in a certain relationship to one's position in physical space: "The statement 'the mind is its own place,' as theorists might construe it, is not true, for the mind is not even a metaphorical 'place.' On the contrary, the chessboard, the platform, the scholar's desk, the judge's bench, the lorry-driver's seat, the studio and the football field are among its places. These are where people work and play stupidly or intelligently."[52] Soviet officials and intelligentsia would most likely concur with Ryle's statement in that, in their class logic, they recognized the stairwell, the basement, and the street as places that defined—and not merely reflected—one's social position vis-à-vis the cultural norm. This drove the public effort to purge the transitory spaces of Soviet towns and cities of their unwelcome residents. The latter, devoid of a cultural voice, responded to this effort with the only means available to them—with those literally at hand.

Traces on the Walls

The 1988 criminal drama, *Kriminal'nyi Talant* (A Criminal Talent), directed by Sergei Ashkenazi and produced by the Odessa film studio, starts as an investigation into a series of crimes committed by a young woman who has recently migrated to Leningrad. As the plot progresses, an ordinary criminal investigation gradually transforms into an investigation of the material conditions in which such migrants—young, unqualified laborers in a huge Soviet metropolis—have to spend their lives. In *A Criminal Talent*, the Soviet cinematographic eye rediscovers marginal urban areas with their exploited and voiceless populations. Following its protagonist, a high-ranking officer of the Leningrad public prosecution department, the camera shows us dark and inhospitable spaces that destroy the aspirations, hopes, and dreams of their new residents. The latter are seemingly unable to transform or even challenge these spaces of socialist alienation; the only impact they have on this urban environment is in the form of traces: graffiti in the streets and posters in the rooms of their factory's dormitory (figure 4.2).

Kriminal'nyi Talant reflected the humanist momentum of perestroika cinematography in its attempt to understand how broad swaths of Soviet society became voiceless and marginalized. This is the main way in which it differs from a 1979 namesake novel by Stanislav Rodionov, which avoids any discussion of the antagonist's social roots in late socialist city life.[53] The same humanist momentum—to give voice to marginal urban groups—can be seen in Vasilieva's *Pod'ezd*, in Juris Podnieks's famous 1986 documentary *Vai viegli būt jaunam?* [Is it easy to be young?]) and in *12 etazh* (The twelfth

FIGURE 4.2.   Graffiti in a Leningrad backstreet. A still image from *Kriminal'nyi Talant* (1988).

floor), one of the most remarkable projects of perestroika-era television. *12 etazh* was a talk show broadcast in 1986 and 1987 and built as a dialogue between high-ranking Komsomol and government officials, on the one side, and Soviet teenagers, on the other. The latter were filmed on a stairwell—a reference to the omnipresence of teenage groups in Soviet stairwells. The Soviet TV critic Sergei Muratov referred to *12 etazh* as one of the key landmarks in the history of Soviet television and particularly emphasized that the stairwell became a catalyst of social antagonism revealed by the program: "The 'stairwell,' a group of teenagers who infiltrated the back entrance of one of Moscow's 'houses of culture' (to which they previously had been refused entry), behaved defiantly, sought scandal, and fired aggressive questions at the bureaucrats they invited to the show-bureaucrats whose responses seemed programmed in advance. The 'stairwell' itself quickly assumed the role of an actor in the program."[54]

Perestroika-era cinematography and television exposed the link between urban powerlessness and voicelessness, and in doing so brought into the open public debate about what Soviet people had known for decades as common sense and what Soviet low-level officials and educators reflected in their writings. Petty criminality and the overall despondency of life in Soviet suburbs had a palpable material foundation in broken street lamps, graffiti on building walls, dark stairwells, damp basements, teenage bodies smelling of cigarette smoke and alcohol, their aggressive postures, and physical assaults. This material foundation was, in turn, derivative of the very structure of late socialism. Podnieks voiced this perspective in *Vai viegli būt jaunam?* through one of his characters who says: "Yes, we are dirty, ragged, creepy, but we are your children, and you created us like this with your duplicity and lies . . . Society produced us, and now it's trying to brush us aside."[55] What these perestroika-era films and documentaries also showed is that the Soviet working-class and marginalized urban groups, although devoid of a cultural voice and political power, still retained social agency. They struggled for the appropriation of Soviet public spaces, with that struggle taking very tangible material forms, most characteristically that of vandalism.

Contemporary and historical accounts of modern Soviet neighborhoods describe in detail the impact of these deviant groups on the urban environment, in general, and stairwells, in particular. Residents of a new apartment block in Leningrad complained at a meeting in 1968: "The struggle against drunkards and thieves is carried out poorly. Sometimes they are not punished at all. Nobody is held responsible for the damage to and destruction of the green vegetation—the beauty of our city. Streets are poorly lit; many stairwells are not lit at all; bulbs are missing on many stair landings."[56] The poor illumination of streets and stairwells mentioned above was most likely a product of the intentional destruction of lights by disorderly youth. This is how, for example, a correspondent of the official magazine *Sovety narodnykh deputatov* (Councils of People's Deputies) explained the ramshackle appearance of many Soviet apartment blocks despite the constant efforts of local authorities to maintain them in proper order: "Look into the stairwells of even recently built apartment blocks. Today, one can hardly call them new. It is not the fleeting time that left here sorrowful traces of decay, but human irresponsibility. It is sad to see stairwells with walls scribbled by unknown scribes, with stolen bulbs, with broken lamps."[57]

This quote also refers to another omnipresent feature of Soviet stairwells and other public places: graffiti on walls.[58] The walls of Soviet stairwells were routinely scribbled with carved and painted messages, often with obscene vocabulary. Intermediate landings were commonly used as smoking places, and cigarette butts, together with spittle and litter, were another common spectacle in stairwells. Finally, Soviet teenagers had a particular method of vandalizing ceilings in stairwells that destroyed their whitewash. This method employed matches that were lit and then immediately stuck into the whitewash forming a small black stain with a charcoaled match hanging from its middle; various patterns could be made using a matchbox. Ceilings charcoaled in this manner were a common experience of residents and a headache for the managers of Soviet apartment blocks.

Outside of their apartment blocks, in the public places of the microdistricts, Soviet citizens evidenced similar "traces of decay" left by "human irresponsibility." For a Soviet aviation engineer commissioned in 1966 to Cuba as part of the Soviet technical assistance program to the new revolutionary regime, the lack of urban vandalism was so impressive that he wrote about it in his diary: "Phone booths [in Havana] are located near taxi stands. No surveillance, and yet the phones are in a complete order (I am recalling vandalized Soviet phone booths)."[59] Phone booths were one of the favorite objects of destruction in Soviet cities and towns: in 1983, for example, the newspaper *Sovetskaia Latvia* reported that during the previous year hooligans destroyed or stole 7,200 microphone inlets and 1,700 receivers, and smashed 1,800 square meters of glass in phone booths in the capital city of Riga alone.[60] Street vending machines selling carbonated water were another such object of destruction. In 1979, a resident of the apartment block on 17/1 Friedrich Engels Street in Leningrad sent the following complaint to the city newspaper *Leninskaia Pravda*:

> Under our windows, there are carbonated water machines, which disturb our peace during evenings and nights. As May approaches, shivers

of horror go through our veins. Here is one example that occurred yesterday, overnight into 16.06.1979. At approximately 12.40 am, a group of ten drunken teenagers—and with an additional half-liter bottle of vodka in their hands—came to the machines. And what they were doing is hard to describe. They hit it with flying kicks, broke all glass cups, then there was a sound like a police whistle, and they ran away, but soon returned and started it all over: flying kicks and obscenities. Then they went to the shoe repairman's booth and decided to break glasses in it . . . Can I ask for whom these machines are installed? In mornings, drunkards [*khanygi*] use them to ease a hangover, and in evenings and nights—well, I described you the events of one night, and there are so many similar nights ahead, this is just a nightmare! . . . With such a neighbor as the carbonated water machine, one just wants to go outside and cry out: Help! No peace and no life.[61]

This emotional letter inadvertently provides insight into the parallel affective regimes of interaction with urban space. For a law-abiding citizen with a family and exhausting work schedule, the nightly noise of shattered glass and metal under his windows was connected to feelings of fear and anxiety. Symptomatically, the author of the letter sees the root of his misfortunes in the carbonated water machines themselves, or more precisely in their ability to attract deviant adults and teenagers. It is machines that he calls "neighbors," and it is they that "disturb our peace." His main request was to move these machines "to the vegetable market across the street where they won't disturb people and will work at full capacity."[62] It was affective assemblages of teenage bodies, on the one hand, and stairwells, streets, and other urban spaces of transit with their ability to accumulate these bodies, on the other, that terrified those Soviet citizens who embodied the social norm and thus acquired social voice—for example, by expressing their fears and disgust of their urban environment in letters to newspapers or debates at residents' meetings. As with any modern state, the Soviet Union had its politics of aesthetics, which was built around the dichotomy of cleanliness and dirt, with the former being associated with progress, rationality, and high morality, and the latter with regress, social deviance, and danger.[63] Acting from this aesthetic position, Soviet officials and responsible citizens inevitably evaluated vandalized public property as dirty and acts of vandalism as dangerous, hence the common demands in everyday talk and pedagogical discourse to protect children from "the influence of street and stairwells."

Yet that same affective component was different for those people who were part of these assemblages—for children leaving black stains on the white ceilings of stairwells and elevators, for teenagers smashing glass and tearing off receivers in phone booths, or breaking stairwell lamps for better privacy for casual sex, and for adults smoking and drinking on stair landings and leaving empty bottles, cigarette butts and spittle on their floors. One of my respondents admitted that as a teenager and young adult in Leningrad during the 1970s, he had participated in some of these activities. His explanation was simple: smashing glass in phone booths "was fun," a form of entertainment in an otherwise dull life in the Leningrad suburbs (he was a resident of the Vyborgsky district at a time when it experienced mass housing construction).[64] Soviet writers, who in 1977 assembled at the Plenum of the USSR Union of Writers to define what Soviet adolescent literature should be, ended up discussing the relationship between materiality, emotionality, and social deviance among teenagers. Vladimir Amlinsky suggested that there was a direct connection between the inability—or unwillingness—of teenagers to master the dominant cultural discourse ("withdrawal from the normal language" in his words) and the appeal of "night yards, stairwells . . . stuffy dance floors, aimless walks, cravings for a fight, for a meaningless conflict with anybody under any pretext."[65] Amlinsky recognized that the material environment of urban spaces was affective to the degree that it could define the very selves of Soviet teenagers:

> Mugs are rattling in [open-air] beer stands, domino tiles are clapping, a voiceless guitar is thrumming dully . . . And then sometimes this spiritlessness explodes in aggression . . . I saw teenagers who at one moment were kind and understood normal human language, and at the next—surprising manifestations of unchildish cruelty. Saw their sincere puzzlement after committed misdeeds: "How could I do it? What for?" Where do they come from, these teenagers in dark alleys who just an hour ago were good lads, smiled, made jokes, whistled some tune, and who are now ready to deal you a blow?[66]

Amlinsky identified the autonomy of affect from individual bodies, its material foundation in the environment of "night yards, stairwells [and] stuffy dance floors," its ability to attach itself to people and momentarily change them from "good lads" to dangerous thugs "ready to deal you a blow." In many ways, Amlinsky's and other participants' comments at the 1977 meeting tacitly recognized the fragmented nature of the Soviet teenage self and the social agency of things that made up the Soviet teenager's world. The conclusions they made from this recognition were ambivalent. On the one hand, such recognition opened vast possibilities for the social engineering of Soviet youth through such a powerful material object as the book.

On the other hand, it further underlined the dangers that Soviet spaces of transit brought for the socialist enlightenment project. Sergei Mikhalkov, the union's secretary and the highest profile participant of this discussion, encapsulated these fears and hopes in his call to fellow writers "to understand what kinds of needs bring teenagers together in yards and in stairwells, what problems are solved there, and to respond to these needs with books."[67]

Summarizing these observations, such acts of vandalizing socialist property and, to a certain degree, street violence in the late USSR, were products of a specific historical affective regime of people's interactions with Soviet urban space. In terms of motivation in each case, smashing the glass in phone booths, drinking alcohol on stair landings, or charcoaling the ceiling in a stairwell was "fun," something done to entertain oneself during one's leisure time. Yet by leaving traces of their social existence in the public spaces of Soviet microdistricts, disorderly Soviet urban groups entered into affective assemblages with these spaces, appropriated them, made them scary for the Soviet educated public. In this respect, they engaged in a conflict with the values and principles of the dominant socialist discourse on the orderly, progressive. and purist transformation of social reality.[68] The social agency of urban groups devoid of political power and cultural voice emerged from their assemblages with stairwells, basements, garages, and city parks. At stake in this social conflict was the very livability of late socialist urban space.

Ditmar Rozental was a Soviet Samuel Johnson; his name is associated with some of the most popular vocabularies and guidebooks of the Russian language. One of these, published in 1981, is *Government in the Russian Language*, a reference book of noun inflections in combination with the most common verbs. Each entry consists of a verb, a preposition used with it (if any), the case inflection of dependent nouns, and one or several examples of its usage. One of its entries, the verb *berech'* ("protect"), provides an example that is curiously relevant for this chapter: "to protect children from the influence of the street."[69]

"The street" of this example was one of those late socialist spaces of transit which, when not countered by persistent effort on the part of authorities and society, was perceived as corrupting the young Soviet generation. The inclusion of this example in a dictionary, a cultural product that supposedly operates with the most common and neutral meanings, betrays a social concern so profoundly rooted in the dominant culture that it is no longer interpreted as something to be questioned. By the time of the publication of Rozental's guidebook, it was part of the Soviet common sense that Soviet streets (or stairwells, or basements) were socially dangerous.

This chapter shows how the drive "to protect children from the influence of the street" became a cornerstone of Soviet educational discourse, in general, and extracurricular activities, in particular. In chapter 2, I discussed the constructive agenda of extracurricular activities in the USSR: Soviet educational theorists regarded them as pedagogical tools that would teach Soviet children and teenagers values, attitudes, and skills for responsible Soviet citizenship. But the network of hobby clubs, houses of Young Pioneers, and sports complexes that the Soviet authorities were incessantly developing also had another preventive agenda to distract children from spending their out-of-school time "idling around in the street and stairwells."[70] This didactic drive became translated into the life biographies of many children from educated families whose leisure time was occupied with music and dancing lessons, arts and crafts, sports and amateur engineering and, of course, reading at home.[71] A responsible Soviet subject was one who, as a teenager, invested their free time in books, models, and other socially responsible things and activities. Their antipode was someone who spent their free time in a stairwell. This logic found the perfect expression in the novels and pedagogical practice of Vladislav Krapivin, a popular Soviet juvenile literature author and strong advocate of extracurricular education. In 1961, Krapivin, an educator, established and for many years supervised the Young Pioneers' experimental club Karavella (Caravel), which organized the free time of its members through fencing classes, filmmaking workshops, outdoor trips and, most important, the building and operation of sailing ships, hence the name.[72] As for his books, his main protagonist is a suburban teenager who challenges his material environment and its associated vices. The spatial structure of his novels is based on a contrast between the simultaneously dull and dangerous Soviet city, on the one hand, and imaginary romantic spaces, such as the sea or parallel worlds, on the other hand; most plots are organized as the protagonist's escape into the latter. It is not surprising then that one of Krapivin's most fervent Soviet-era critics accused his writing of nurturing social antagonism.[73]

The significant absence of urban public places in the life biographies of Soviet intelligentsia is too often translated into silence about their vibrant social lives. Many Western scholars, who tend to evince solidarity with Soviet and post-Soviet intelligentsia due to a shared class position, reproduce this silence. For example, Caroline Humphrey in *The Unmaking of Soviet Life*, referring to Svetlana Boym's studies of late socialist spaces, wrote: "There was no mediating space in Soviet Russia between the public and the private, no space of conventional socialization; you were either in the space of official decorum or in the nooks of domesticity. Any other space, like the stairwells or backyards of apartment blocks, was a space of alienation, belonging to everyone and no one, and often a hangout for drunks and strewn with rubbish and graffiti."[74]

Humphrey writes from an aesthetic position ("strewn with rubbish and graffiti"), which can be found in abundance in Soviet official and dissident discourses alike and which disguises the social antagonism that was generated by the specific material environment of Soviet urban space. This antagonism, in turn, generates statements that dehumanize their populations in cultural and academic representations. Humphrey refers to the stairwells and backyards of apartment blocks as "spaces of alienation"—which they were, but only for the Soviet educated public; having occupied this specific social position, she then dismissively characterizes these public spaces (and their residents) as "hangouts for drunks." Another interesting example can be found in *Prisoners of Power* by Arkady and Boris Strugatsky, who seem to consciously play with this stereotype. Early in the novel, their protagonist, a highly educated and intelligent adventurer from a communist society of the future, is confronted by a street gang in a dark alley archway reminiscent of similar places in Soviet microdistricts. His imagination immediately transforms the gang members into apes, which allows him to massacre the entire group: "Something clicked in his brain and the people vanished . . . [Instead of people], dangerous animals stamped clumsily through the mud."[75] *Prisoners of Power* and its sequels have distinct elements of a Bildungsroman, and the Strugatsky brothers' character gradually learns to deal with the antagonism caused by his move from a socially homogenous environment of the Communist future into a world riven by class conflicts.

Post-Soviet culture has actively exploited the imagery of the stairwell and similar urban common places in the blossoming genres of the crime novel and telenovela. The stairwell's place as the absent signifier of Soviet and post-Soviet subjectivity allows authors writing or making films in these genres to represent it as an endless source of criminality to populate it with social outcasts and to induce excitement and anxiety among their audience, which easily recognizes this imagery. It is hardly surprising that some of the most productive authors in this genre are highly educated and come from a very different social background than their characters.[76] Their writing reproduces and perpetuates social knowledge that—to return to Michel Foucault's argument in his debate with Noam Chomsky—acts as a form and measure in social struggle.[77]

As for the stairwell itself, it has undergone a significant transformation since the collapse of the USSR. In 1977, Sergei Mikhalkov expressed his belief that good books were capable of reforming disorderly Soviet youth; he argued that "we should not put a lock on an entranceway door."[78] Ironically, it was the mass spread of tumbler security locks and especially house intercoms in Soviet stairwells that transformed them over the last two decades.[79] The contemporary Russian stairwell is, on average, cleaner and lighter than its late Soviet counterpart. It also lives a different social life, reflecting—as well as objectifying and influencing—new post-Soviet social structures.

CHAPTER 5

The Men of Steel

Repairing and Empowering Soviet Bodies with Iron

> I receive lots of letters in which young men complain
> that they shy away from dating girls because of
> physical weakness. To the authors of these letters
> I always successfully prescribe "iron pills."
>
> —Georgi Tenno, "Not a Cult, but Culture"

> We also have basements. Yet we are not "getting high"
> in them, but rather exercising! Boxing, weightlifting—
> in other words, "pumping iron," and this gives a lot to
> us—strength, health, self-assurance.
>
> —A Soviet teenage bodybuilder's letter to
> *Komsomolskaya Pravda* (1987)

Among the many waves of moral panic that overwhelmed the Soviet Union in its final years, one can be connected to two articles that appeared simultaneously in *Ogoniok* and *Sobesednik*, two of the most popular Soviet weeklies, in February 1987.[1] The articles were the result of a joint investigation of youth behavior in one of Moscow's satellite towns, Liubertsy. These youths were reported to be enrolling in large numbers in basement gyms and then traveling in organized groups to Moscow to "beat-up" punks, hippies, and metalheads, as well as teenagers who dressed and behaved in conspicuously Western, non-Soviet fashions. In interviews, the *liubery* (they named themselves after their hometown) insisted that they were acting as exemplary Soviet citizens: "Hippies, punks and metalheads are a disgrace to the Soviet way of life. We want to cleanse the capital of them."[2] As another *liuber* wrote in a letter to a Soviet youth magazine: "I am 18. I can say without any misgivings that I love my Motherland. And I contribute to it more than many Komsomol members. Lots of maggots have multiplied like rabbits these days: fascists, punks, metalheads, rockers . . . That is why I fully support the *liubery* and never miss a single raid of these lads in their hunt for the shadow of the rotten West."[3]

The articles in *Ogoniok* and *Sobesednik* had a huge resonance.[4] They were one of the earliest examples of the Soviet press tackling social conflict, a notable change from a mass media that for years had described Soviet society as conflict-free. Among Western-oriented liberal intellectuals who hailed Mikhail Gorbachev's reforms, the practice of bodybuilding for the sake of street fights against conspicuously Western subcultures presented the grim prospect of a conservative revolution from below.[5] The authors of the articles, which represented the *liubery* and other similar groups of teenage bodybuilders as a social threat, accentuated that the latter belonged to the suburban youth with a "low" educational and cultural background and even developed a conspiracy theory that cast them as a street school of some mafialike organization, an allegation that has never been confirmed by scholars of late Soviet youth subcultures.[6] Their threat to the social order was additionally underlined on the rhetorical and visual levels: for example, the illustration accompanying Vladimir Iakovlev's article "The Shady Business of the '*liubery*'" (one of the two which triggered the panic about the *liubery*) obscured the heads of its protagonists with the headline, thereby focusing the readers' gaze on their bodies, represented in ostensibly aggressive postures.

Yet contemporary assessment of this practice was far from uniform. Other influential Soviet magazines, such as *Nedelia* (Week) and *Tekhnika— Molodezhi*, published laudatory articles about the bodybuilding gyms in Liubertsy and those regularly visiting them. These articles emphasized a different aspect of this practice, namely that local youth enrolled in these gyms in order to prepare their bodies and minds for military service in the Soviet Army, in particular, and for proper Soviet adulthood and citizenship, in general. From this perspective, basement bodybuilding emerged as a socially useful, even desirable activity. One of these articles quoted a Soviet Army captain who had just returned from Afghanistan, claiming that, "They [athletes from Liubertsy] were my right hand in raids against jihadists."[7] Another journalist went so far as to suggest that Soviet authorities should promote bodybuilding as a standard physical activity for teenagers in order to prepare them for proper Soviet manhood and citizenship, thus referring to Liubertsy as an exemplar for the entire Soviet Union.[8] Yuri Sorokin, one of the pioneers of bodybuilding in the USSR, responded to this call by publishing, in an impressive run of 365,000 copies, *Athletic Training of a Pre-Conscription Teenager* (1990). The book's cover featured a muscular teenager with a kettlebell and a Soviet airborne force commando—the teenager's presumed alter ego—in the background, with both figures radiating strength and self-confidence. The text instructed its teenage readers on how to develop physical and mental preparedness to properly perform national duty in the Soviet Army.[9]

For this chapter, the most important aspect in the story of young bodybuilders from Liubertsy is that all of the participants—the athletes; the critical and the laudatory press; local municipal, party, and police bodies; and Soviet Army officers—recognized the key role of material objects (the weightlifting equipment, or "iron," as it was known among weightlifters) and the material environment (basement gyms) in the production of Soviet bodies and Soviet selves. The critics of bodybuilding feared that "iron" (here meaning objects and equipment used to transform one's body into a muscular form) and "basements" empowered working-class suburban teenagers to the degree that they could generate negative social change. A possible resurgence of normative Sovietness driven from below by an army of underground bodybuilders and weightlifters encapsulated the worst fears of Western-oriented intellectuals in the USSR. By contrast, practitioners and advocates of bodybuilding linked the muscular body with proper citizenship ("I love my Motherland," in the words of a *liuber*). For them, basement gyms were a key to obtaining "strength, health, self-assurance," the qualities that physically, by way of muscle growth, imprinted one's devotion to national duty on the individual body. The difference between critics and advocates of Soviet bodybuilding was not in substance but in modality; both recognized that the assemblage of iron, basements, and bodies generated social agency, but differed on whether iron and basement gyms produced normative or deviant bodies and behaviors.

This chapter traces the history of assemblages of iron, basements, disabled and muscular bodies, and associated social meanings in late Soviet cultural context. Iron as well as steel, its derivative, have provided powerful and long-lasting ways of imagining the new socialist man in Soviet culture from the first years of the Soviet state. Aleksei Gastev, a vocal proponent of scientific management and a prominent avant-garde poet, wrote extensively during the late 1910s and 1920s on how the individual and collective socialist body would eventually become one with machines. "We Grow Out of Iron" (1923) was the title of one of his poems, in which he described a body melting into and merging with the metal of factories. Rolf Hellebust's *Flesh to Metal*, a comprehensive study of "the alchemy of revolution," explored in depth how the "metallization of the revolutionary body" became one of the key themes in early Soviet culture. Metal acted as a powerful symbol to describe the envisioned transition from an organic and decadent bourgeois society to the communist utopia of steel and machines.[10] This symbolism carried ostensible gender implications, since in modern cultures iron and steel, when used as metaphors, signified the transformation from organicity, with its implications of femininity, irrationality, softness, passivity, and decay to metallicity and machineness, associated with masculinity, rationality, rigidness, durability, strength, and hygiene.[11] Yet in the Stalinist era, the union between iron and Soviet people dreamed of by Gastev and other Soviet avant-gardists remained mainly nominative, finding expression in the naming conventions for ships, aircraft, and other vehicles. The Soviet propaganda plane ANT-20, the largest aircraft of the 1930s, was named *Maxim Gorky*; the two series of Soviet heavy tanks were named after Klim Voroshilov and Joseph Stalin; and Soviet merchant and warships were en masse named after various prominent figures from the Russian and international revolutionary pantheon.

In the second half of the twentieth century, this rhetoric and imagery became increasingly contested. Mikhail Heller's antimachinist criticism of Soviet society, as well as the rise of the architectural preservation movement grew from broader skepticism among Soviet intellectuals in regard to the modernist discourse and visions of the Soviet leadership. At the same time, iron in Soviet culture acquired an even stronger connection with health and strength through popular medical and fitness knowledge. The union of iron and human bodies, a formerly metaphoric figure, found bodily manifestations in the patients of Gavriil Ilizarov, a famed Soviet physician, and Valentin Dikul, a circus artist and self-taught rehabilitation specialist, as well as in Soviet bodybuilding. These phenomena shared one common ground: a belief in the unlimited possibilities of the human body in terms of its physical recovery or development.

Iron as Medicine

In 1944, Gavriil Ilizarov (1921–92), a fresh graduate of the Simferopol Medical School, received a job placement as the only physician in a Siberian village of Dolgovka. He worked there for the following six years, during the time when World War II veterans were returning home, many of them with war wounds that due to mistreatment or negligence were progressing into disabilities. Despite being overburdened with his regular work, Ilizarov began to practice reconstructive surgery but soon became disappointed with the conventional orthopedic methods that were ineffective in treating complicated and neglected wounds. Since his hospital had only the most basic medical tools, Ilizarov experimented with makeshift equipment, including the use of steel rods as bone implants. The main problem that he faced in his experiments was how to fixate the fractured bones; at that time, plaster cast was used for external fixation, which could not provide adequate rigidness in complicated cases, while at the same time severely restricting the patient's mobility. His hospital had no motor transport, and Ilizarov was forced to visit his outpatients in a horse cart or sleigh, depending on the season. He later recollected that it was the design of the Russian harness with its shaft bow that suggested to him the idea to use metal rings as external fixators for steels rods (figure 5.1).[12]

In 1950, Ilizarov successfully treated first patients with this new technique; according to semi-apocryphal accounts, the first version of his apparatus was made from spare bicycle parts.[13] The same year he moved to the Siberian city of Kurgan, where he could finally specialize in orthopedic surgery and further develop his method. Next year he patented his apparatus to reduce fractures and correct bone deformities that otherwise doomed people to a life of immobility. The frame of metal rings, rods, and spikes revolutionized orthopedic surgery; it and its derivatives remain a preferred method of treatment for severe fractures and deformities.[14] Yet the initial response of the Soviet medical establishment to this invention was lukewarm or even straightforwardly hostile because the new method undermined the hierarchies and reputations built on the conventional orthopedic approaches. It

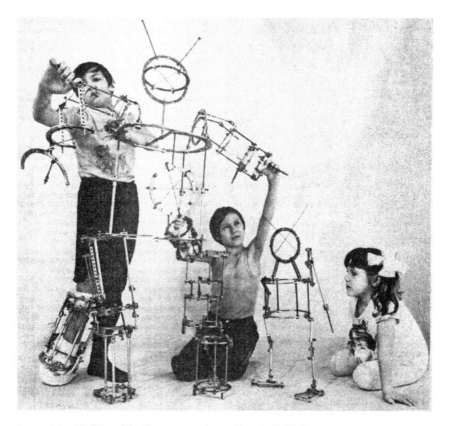

FIGURE 5.1.   Vitalities of the Ilizarov apparatuses. Photo by Ye.M. Rogov, 1982.

took Ilizarov almost two decades to achieve the professional and public recognition of his technique. Only in 1968 Ilizarov and his apparatus became nationally renowned after he successfully treated a Soviet celebrity athlete, the 1964 Olympic men's high jump champion, Valery Brumel.

Brumel, who dominated high jump in the first half of the 1960s and became the American Broadcasting Company's Wide World of Sports Athlete of the Year in 1963, broke his right leg in a motorcycle accident in October 1965. Subsequent conventional treatment in the best Moscow hospitals lasted for two and a half years but failed to heal him. With chronic osteomyelitis and the looming threat of leg amputation, Brumel traveled to Ilizarov, who at that time was still struggling for recognition of his technique. Brumel later described the treatment in his memoir: "The surgery took place a week later [after arrival]. My tibia was cut at the location of the fracture and just beneath the knee . . . Then it was pegged with metal spikes, which were connected with some rings and rods, and everything was fastened with screw-nuts."[15]

Less than five months after this operation Brumel walked out of the clinic without crutches and soon even returned to his sport's career, although no longer as the leading athlete in his discipline.[16] Brumel's case publicized the Ilizarov technique in the USSR, and his national fame was further spurred by the international acclaim that Ilizarov gradually acquired throughout the 1970s and 1980s, after having successfully treated two other celebrities: Soviet composer Dmitri Shostakovich and Italian explorer Carlo Mauri. Soviet mass media widely reproduced images of Ilizarov's patients with shiny metal constructions around their limbs, cyborgs of a sort, whose biological shortcomings were corrected by the power of iron to heal human bodies.[17] This futuristic association with cyborgs did not escape Ilizarov's contemporaries. Critics of his method from the Soviet orthopedic establishment pejoratively dubbed his method a "machinist [*slesarnyi*] approach to surgery,"[18] while Valery Brumel, in his second memoir, described Ilizarov's clinic in Kurgan as "a strange planet populated by people with iron legs and arms."[19] A photo placed by *Nauka i zhizn'*, the leading Soviet popular science journal, as an illustration to an article about Ilizarov (figure 5.1), featured three child patients from his clinic wearing the Illizarov apparatuses and assembling anthropomorphic figures from other Ilizarov frames.[20] The involvement of iron frames in the children's play emphasized the vitality of metal and its transformative nature. This assemblage of iron and children's bodies was affective in the sense that it enticed those reading the article and viewing the image with the promise of health. This and other innumerable domestic and international publications would call Ilizarov the "magician from Kurgan," a title perhaps inspired by his hobby of conjuring tricks, but his medical magic was apparently instrumental, stemming from his apparatuses.

Another phenomenon that connected iron with health and strength in popular medical knowledge in the late Soviet Union was the history of Valentin Dikul (b. 1938). In 1962, Dikul, then a beginner circus athlete, broke his spine during a show. His subsequent treatment lasted for eight months but left him paralyzed below the waist. Facing the near certainty of a lifetime disability, Dikul developed a system of load exercises, at the core of which was weightlifting. He later claimed that it was this system that gradually restored his physical abilities through exhausting daily exercises. Dikul started walking again five years after the injury; moreover, regular weightlifting exercises built his physique to the degree that in 1970 he returned to work in the circus not as an aerialist, but as a strength athlete. At the peak of his circus career Dikul was capable of lifting a midsize Volga sedan.[21] "I fell in love with metal, because it saved me," a Soviet sports journalist quoted Dikul later, adding in his own words, "For it was, indeed, iron that saved, healed, and literally put Dikul back on his feet."[22] This experience left Dikul with the conviction that iron—that is, weightlifting equipment—could cure the most severe traumas and even congenital diseases.

During the 1980s, Dikul's assertion that his system, which was based on the use of specially designed weightlifting equipment, might rehabilitate people with disabilities made him a Soviet celebrity of the same prominence as Ilizarov. Soviet magazines publicized his methods to their multimillion-strong audiences, causing a flurry of letters to Dikul from all over the USSR and a pilgrimage on behalf of those who had failed to overcome their disabilities by way of conventional medicine.[23] In 1985, this popular obsession with his methods was featured in a full-length documentary, *Piramida* (Pyramid).[24] It intertwined two plotlines: Dikul's preparation and premiere of his new circus act (the lifting of the Volga), and the visits and letters of numerous people seeking to overcome their physical disabilities. The film focused on a five-year-old boy, Dima, born with a congenital defect causing severe locomotor impairment that left him incapable of walking or even standing. Throughout the film, Dikul is repeatedly shown using his makeshift weightlifting equipment to restore Dima's physical abilities. These and other episodes in which iron helps Dikul and his patients struggle against bodily debilitation are interwoven with reminiscences of Dikul's own story of overcoming his spinal cord trauma and with his workout routines and circus tricks using huge kettlebells, barbells, and Volga. The spectacle of Dikul's exceptional strength acquired through his interaction with iron builds a promise of healing for his patients, and at the end of the film Dima is shown standing on his feet for the first time in his life and then watching, gratefully and passionately, Dikul's performance.

Ilizarov and Dikul developed the early Soviet mythology of the power of metal to a new level by providing the Soviet cultural imagination with numerous images of and texts about people regaining and acquiring health, strength, and power through their bodily contact with iron. In both cases, the magic of iron became institutionalized. The Kurgan Research Institute of Experimental and Clinical Orthopedics and Traumatology was established in 1971 with Gavriil Ilizarov as its director, and in 1988 the first rehabilitation center of Valentin Dikul was founded in Moscow. The power of iron that they tamed also granted them political power: in 1989, Ilizarov and Dikul became People's Deputies of the USSR Supreme Soviet.[25]

Both Ilizarov and Dikul emphasized on numerous occasions that iron was important only because it helped to release the unlimited hidden potential of the human body for healing and regeneration. One of Ilizarov's colleagues described his first trip to the Kurgan Research Institute of Experimental and Clinical Orthopedics and Traumatology: "I was lucky—genuinely lucky!—to experience the method of transosseous osteosynthesis and Ilizarov's system that returned his patients to an active, full-blooded life, to experience its humanism based on the belief in the unlimitedness of capabilities and possibilities of the human body."[26] Another doctor described in very similar terms Dikul's "belief in man's unlimited capabilities, in his ability to be stronger than any circumstances."[27] Underlying this belief was a holistic and individualistic understanding of the self as possessing nearly infinite "inner reserves," to which a patient had to resort to reacquire health. This was particularly true for Dikul, whose claims that he had overcome his disability through an individual effort, without any support from the official medical establishment, resonated deeply with many Soviet people suffering from untreatable (at that time) spinal injuries. The original design of Dikul's equipment allowed it to be installed in small Soviet apartments and used on one's own, without external help.[28] The message to his patients was clear: any change for the better had to start within themselves, which was additionally reinforced by Dikul's assertions that it was self-discipline, self-control, and self-responsibility that helped him overcome his trauma.[29]

In the anthropology of post-Soviet societies, it has become commonplace to argue that a boom of self-help and self-improvement advice in Russian popular culture after 1991 has been a product of neoliberal economy and the dismantlement of Soviet-era social welfare programs and structures. Tomas Matza in his book on psychotherapeutic networks and institutions in post-Soviet St. Petersburg argued that the technologies of the self they popularize are inseparable from a neoliberal governmentality adopted by the Russian state in the aftermath of the Soviet collapse, a vision that implies "autonomization of society" (subjects as "self-governing machines") as an ultimate goal.[30] Michele Rivkin-Fish and Suvi Salmenniemi developed similar arguments in their research on post-Soviet medical care and self-help literature, respectively, when they argued that it was the post-Soviet neoliberal order that produced social alienation which, in turn, fueled the demand for self-help advice.[31] Yet Dikul's insistence that severe physical disabilities could (and often had to) be overcome entirely on one's own, through vigorous daily self-improvement, is an evidence that a certain "autonomization of society" was a feature of the Soviet social life as well.[32] In this form of cultural imagination, the Soviet body was autonomous; it derived its health and strength from its "inner reserves," rather than from a collective, with "iron" acting as a key to these reserves. To a certain degree, this understanding of the body reflected the treatment of illness and disability in the Soviet Union, which was often an experience of social isolation and alienation.[33] Dikul's equipment, which was originally designed for a pointedly autonomous usage at home, outside of any kind of medical facility, materialized precisely this experience that Dikul lived through personally. But even Ilizarov, who had remained a part of the official medical system, insisted that the overall urge for recovery should originate from within the patient. In interviews for his biography by Boris Nuvakhov he recollected cases when he was rejecting treatment to depressed or apathetic patients until they recovered faith in the ability of their body to heal. He argued that, rather than a whim or an act of cruelty, this rejection was a necessity, because "a surgical operation . . . would not produce a result" unless a patient would "actively struggle for a normal healthy life."[34]

This individualistic understanding of the human body as possessing an infinite potential for physical recovery and development—a potential that "iron" could unleash—was not reduced to two prominent individuals of the post-Stalinist era. We can find it in other historical phenomena, including the Soviet version of bodybuilding, known during most of the Soviet era as athletic gymnastics.

In a Gray Zone of Soviet Sport

Historians of Soviet bodybuilding—most of whom were members of the bodybuilding community—date its origins to the turn of the 1960s.[35] It was then, in the heyday of Khrushchev's Thaw and the declared return to Leninist humanism, that Soviet cultural production reaestheticized the human body and re-emphasized its individualizing, intimate aspects.[36] This

Thaw-era decentralization of social life was the historical background in which Soviet sports enthusiasts discovered bodybuilding. Ben Weider, a co-founder of the International Federation of Bodybuilding and Fitness and a key figure in the history of bodybuilding, visited the Soviet Union in 1955 trying to promote bodybuilding, only to face a seeming lack of any official interest.[37] Despite his failure, the claims of Western advocates of bodybuilding that "iron" was capable of producing aesthetically perfect human bodies did not go unnoticed by some of the people responsible for the development of Soviet sport. Beginning in 1962, several sports officials employed at the Central Research Institute of Physical Culture in Moscow published articles and exercises on how to develop one's musculature in order to pursue an aesthetic ideal of the perfect human body.[38] By the end of the 1960s, the first books on "athleticism" and "athletic gymnastic," as bodybuilding was dubbed in Soviet sport terminology, appeared. One of them—Georgi Tenno and Yuri Sorokin's *Atletizm*—became a de facto standard guide used in Soviet bodybuilding gyms.[39] The sports magazine *Sportivnaia zhizn' Rossii* (Russia's sport life) became the mouthpiece of Soviet bodybuilding when, beginning in 1962, Tenno started to contribute regularly to the "athleticism" section. Despite the waves of official criticism, it kept on publishing advice and exercises on how to use the iron to build one's perfect body throughout the last three decades of the Soviet Union.[40]

To a certain degree, Soviet bodybuilding was a transnational product of the Cold War era when, beginning in the mid-1950s, the Iron Curtain increasingly turned from a dividing line into an active contact zone. Tenno, the most prominent advocate of bodybuilding in the USSR in the 1960s, had served during World War II as an English-language military interpreter in the Allied convoys to North Russia. In 1948, his international connections led to his arrest and trial in which he was charged with espionage activities and sentenced to imprisonment (he was an inmate with Aleksandr Solzhenitsyn, who wrote two chapters about him in *The Gulag Archipelago*).[41] After Tenno's release and rehabilitation in 1956, he was employed at the Central Research Institute of Physical Culture in Moscow. This position gave him access to Western bodybuilding magazines, to which the institute had a special subscription, as they were otherwise unavailable for a private subscription. Tenno's job responsibilities included the translation of foreign materials into Russian either for internal use in the institute or for their reproduction in Soviet periodicals.[42] The influence of Western muscle magazines on Tenno and his colleagues later became one of the central criticisms of Soviet bodybuilding by the conservative Soviet sports press.[43] Bodybuilding also made its way to the USSR through Czechoslovakian, Polish and East German sports magazines.[44] Both Western and Eastern European magazines were usually obtained through acquaintances who traveled abroad or on the black market, and clippings from them with workout routines and photos of professional bodybuilders decorated most Soviet bodybuilding gyms. Many Soviet-era photographs of bodybuilding and weightlifting facilities show these clippings in the background (see figure 5.3).

Some Soviet citizens may have been enthusiastic about bodybuilding (Tenno claimed to have received thousands of letters after his first publications in the Soviet press), and it was supported by the Central Research Institute of Physical Culture and several influential sport, popular and political magazines with large circulations, most prominently *Tekhnika—Molodezhi* (Technology to youth), an analog of *Popular Mechanic*.[45] At the same time, it received a more ambiguous reception in the official Soviet sports milieu, especially among its top officials.[46] Early assaults on bodybuilding began with its appearance in the USSR, and the first major wave of criticism of the Soviet young people's obsession with iron came in 1966. This was after a series of articles appeared in the main Soviet sports newspaper *Sovetskii sport* (Soviet sport) and pedagogical magazine *Teoriia i praktika fizkul'tury* (Theory and practice of physical culture), which denounced bodybuilding for its ideologically bourgeois, non-Soviet nature.[47]

To soften the criticism, proponents of bodybuilding stopped using the borrowed terms "culturisme" (from French) and "bodybuilding" and disguised their clubs as groups and studios of "athleticism" and "athletic gymnastics." They thus pushed to the forefront bodybuilding's genealogical relationship with prerevolutionary Russian and early Soviet traditions of physical culture.[48] This tactic proved fruitless: even though Tenno and Sorokin's 1968 bodybuilding guide was published under the title *Athleticism*, it received negative reviews in *Sovetskii sport*.[49] The campaign against bodybuilding intensified in the 1970s. On January 24, 1973, the USSR Sports Committee passed a resolution that instructed sports organizations to disband groups of women's soccer, karate, and yoga, and to reorganize the work of the bodybuilding groups to remove "ideologically alien" elements borrowed from Western bodybuilding and make it a worthy representative of Soviet sports:

> Recently, many physical activities that have nothing in common with the Soviet system of physical education have infiltrated from the West . . . [These activities] can potentially spread sport tendencies that are alien to Soviet society, and are socially harmful . . . Most so-called athletic gymnastics groups popularize and spread [Western] bodybuilding. The only exercises are weight training aimed at the unrestricted growth of

muscle mass and artistic posing . . . Narcissism, extreme egoism, showing off of the so-called body culture—all this contradicts the humanism and applicable orientation of the Soviet system of physical culture
and sport, which educate people in terms of collectivism, labor and
political activism, [and] promote harmonious physical development.[50]

In 1977, following an article written by the 1954 world weightlifting
champion Dmitry Ivanov (one of the most vocal critics of bodybuilding),
the USSR Committee of Physical Culture and Sport launched another major
attack on bodybuilding when it issued a resolution, "On serious drawbacks
in the work of groups of athletic gymnastics."[51] The resolution condemned
the "perverted ideas of power-building [*razvitie sily*], the cult of 'the beauty
of the body,' [and] all kinds of illegally functioning groups that reduce their
activities to illiterate, mindless muscle weight gain."[52]

Dimitrios Liokaftos, a historian of Western bodybuilding, argues that
from the 1940s to the 1970s, the Western spectacle of a perfect masculine
body transformed from a "holistic model," in which muscular development was seen as a derivative of more essential masculine qualities, primarily health and strength, to a new perception of normative masculinity with
an emphasis on appearance. In doing this, bodybuilding facilitated a shift
from an essentialist understanding of manhood to manhood understood as
a set of acquired characteristics, of which visible muscularity was one of the
most important.[53] This new vision of the masculine body had its Western
critics. Liokaftos quotes an article from a 1955 issue of *Strength and Health*,
which renounced bodybuilding in strikingly similar language to that of its
Soviet critics: "Athletic fitness and muscular coordination and superb health
are completely meaningless to [bodybuilders]."[54] Yet by the 1960s—the time
when bodybuilding appeared in the USSR—the spectacle of hypermuscular
bodies in the Western popular culture led to a situation in which male selfhood became strongly associated with muscularity for the sake of aesthetic
impression, rather than utilitarian purposes.[55] Western bodybuilding magazines, which were instrumental in the development of Soviet bodybuilding
at its formative stage, helped to transfer the understanding of the masculine
body as an individual aesthetic object to the Soviet cultural milieu.

Soviet critics accused bodybuilding of a fixation on muscle mass at the
expense of "health and harmonious bodily development."[56] For them, an uncontrolled affection for bodybuilding was dangerous, because it threatened
to produce distorted and unhealthy, rather than beautiful bodies. Dmitry
Ivanov described bodybuilding competitions as "panopticons of monstros-
ity" (*panoptikumy urodstva*).[57] Others emphasized that bodybuilding's focus

on muscles at the expense of other body parts (lungs, heart) and functions (stamina, coordination, blood flow) brought more harm than good and was aesthetically dubious.[58] The underlying criticism appears to be that bodybuilding advanced a fragmented image and understanding of the human body, in which the body consisted of muscles to be "pumped" and body shapes to be achieved.[59] This preoccupation with the shaping of the body challenged an older holistic way of thinking about athletes' bodies as aspects of the socialist whole, of the collective of Soviet people, that initially emerged as a theory of "mass action" in the early Soviet period and became the foundations of the official Soviet sport.[60] This holistic corporeal imagination decried the individualistic thinking of one's body provoked by bodybuilding with its fetishization of biceps, triceps, and other muscles. That is why the counterargument from bodybuilding advocates that officially recognized sports produced "less harmonious" bodies than bodybuilding fell on deaf ears.[61] Other officially supported sports in the USSR, such as cycling or fencing, could be less effective in shaping overall muscular bodies. However, their emphasis on the subjugation of the body to the mind and collective interests made them much more appropriate for sports managers than bodybuilding, which turned sporting bodies into aesthetic objects. When Soviet sports journalists and bureaucrats condemned bodybuilding as an "ideologically alien" sport, it was the exhibitory and narcissistic nature of bodybuilding exercises and competitions and bodybuilding's alleged aversion to anything collective that sparked their most fervent reaction: "Bodybuilding is one of the typical products of bourgeois culture. Its ideological nature aims, primarily, to separate the youth from social and political activism. The man is urged to retreat into oneself, to stay inside the four walls of one's own self."[62]

The anti-bodybuilding campaign of the 1970s spearheaded by *Sovetskii sport* and supported by the USSR Committee of Physical Culture and Sport did not translate into a legal prohibition of this sport, yet discouraged local officials from allocating resources (infrastructure and equipment) to bodybuilding enthusiasts. Moreover, since the Communist Party and Komsomol were responsible for maintaining proper moral standards among their members, they would publicly criticize those who resorted to weightlifting equipment in order to shape their bodies in accordance with transnational—rather than Soviet—understanding of masculinity. A Soviet-era bodybuilder from Petrozavodsk mentioned that in the early 1980s he and his friends frequented the gym of the local university (he also complained that the gym was designed for Olympic weightlifting and had only barbells), yet had to be discreet about the true purpose of their exercises: "I can imagine what would have happened if we put [Arnold] Schwarzenegger's photos on walls there.

If anyone knew, we would have been thrown away from the gym immediately . . . If I would have told at the university that I pumped iron in their gym, I would have been at once summoned to the [university] committee of the Komsomol."[63]

Engaging in bodybuilding in the USSR could thus potentially endanger one's social status and standing. This attitude had never been a universal phenomenon: for example, one of the earliest bodybuilding clubs in the USSR opened in Tyumen in the mid-1960s after Evgeny Koltun, a local enthusiast of bodybuilding, successfully lobbied support for it at the city committee of the Komsomol.[64] Yet local bureaucrats tended to act overcautiously and to discourage, whenever possible, the Soviet youth from this sport through public criticism and nonprovision of funding.

As a result, throughout the last three decades of the Soviet Union bodybuilding existed in a gray zone of Soviet sport. Its supporters among sports functionaries and experts produced a large and loyal audience through publications in mass journals, yet the opposition from some other sports officials and decision-making bureaucrats prevented the large-scale, centralized development of bodybuilding classes and clubs. This situation had a notable impact on the spatial distribution of bodybuilding in Soviet society. Throughout the 1970s and 1980s, it gained the most popularity in factory neighborhoods where local youth had little or none social capital to lose, and where the large-scale program of urban development created ubiquitous facilities that they could repurpose for bodybuilding gyms, such as local clubs, garages, and most important basements of apartment blocks.

Basements, Filthy and Clean

In chapter 4, I described how the revival of modernist architecture in the post-Stalinist era, combined with a new trend in urban planning to build entire residential areas as relatively self-sufficient neighborhoods, translated into an effort to ensure effective circulation of people between their apartments, workplaces, and places of leisure. The transitory places of new Soviet neighborhoods such as stairwells, doorways, and streets were, consequently, planned in an ostensibly utilitarian manner. The same utilitarian approach was applied to another important locale in late socialist housing: the basements of new apartment blocks. Before the mass housing campaign launched by Nikita Khrushchev in the mid-1950s, the acute shortage of urban housing led to the commonplace use of apartment block basements for residential dwelling units.[65] The designers of industrially produced new homes since the mid-1950s had discouraged the possibility of such use of their basements. They had low ceilings, no windows other than for ventilation, and had been assigned a purely utilitarian function to accommodate heating, electric, sewage, and water supply infrastructure systems. The usage of the free basement space was delegated to local housing management offices (ZhEK). Sometimes they allocated it for private storage units but in most cases basements remained unoccupied and unused. It was then that marginalized Soviet youth reclaimed them as their "own space," usually after getting the permission of housing managers, sometimes by squatting.

Soviet bodybuilders who were devoid of access to the public sports infrastructure were active in claiming these basements for their gyms. Their memoirs and interviews describe this process as spontaneous and noncoordinated, yet it happened simultaneously all over the Soviet Union. Sergey B., a resident of Petrozavodsk who got into bodybuilding in 1982, at the age of fifteen, described the following trajectory of himself and his friends in the city space in search of a place for their bodybuilding gym. Initially, they learned about bodybuilding at school from their physical education teacher, who had just graduated from college and apparently was a bodybuilding enthusiast himself. He encouraged them to use the school gym for weightlifting exercises after classes and introduced this small group of schoolchildren to basic bodybuilding complexes. Yet, at the end of the school year, somebody "informed" the school principal of their group, and it was immediately disbanded. Since there were no facilities or clubs in Petrozavodsk that could host teenagers devoted to bodybuilding, they had to resort to their own resources. At first, they worked out in somebody's garage, where they cleared a corner and put a workout bench. This solution was good only for the summer; since the garage had no heating, in the fall the teenagers had to start looking for another place:

> At first we tried to work out at home, but it was a bad idea: there were always other family members around, and it was too loud and cramped. But then we were very lucky. It turned out that there was a semi-official youth club in the basement of one of the apartment blocks in our neighborhood. The mother of one of these teens worked in the ZhEK, and they kind of turned a blind eye on it. Those guys gathered there together, played the guitar, sang some songs. We had already finished school, and they were younger, but we were neighbors, and they gave us shelter. It was in this basement that we organized our first gym.[66]

Although Sergey framed the finding of an appropriate basement for their gym in terms of luck, in reality it was a commonplace phenomenon, and most other bodybuilders of the Soviet era worked out in similar conditions. In 1986, a bodybuilding enthusiast in the city of Kirov used the atmosphere of the perestroika to squeeze out permission from the local committee of the Komsomol to establish a regional federation of bodybuilding and fitness. At that time, as he mentioned in a 2016 interview, approximately 10,000 young people in Kirov more or less regularly attended basement gyms, which could be found in abundance in the city with a population of ca. 450,000; he personally knew at least 150 of these gyms but also claimed that their total number was bigger.[67] In 1988, one journalist writing on teenage bodybuilders from Liubertsy mentioned that there were over one hundred basement gyms in this town with a population of 165,000.[68] Liubertsy was notable for its higher-than-usual density of such gyms, but Soviet-era bodybuilding enthusiasts claimed retrospectively that semilegal basement gyms were ubiquitous all over the USSR (figure 5.2).[69]

To make exercising in their basement more comfortable, Sergey B. and his friends spread sand on the floor for protection and soundproofing. This was a quite common practice since otherwise the noise of dropped barbells could lead to a conflict with neighbors. Its side effect was clouds of dust that were raised when someone would incautiously drop equipment on the floor. Low ceiling meant that some exercises such as the overhead press were

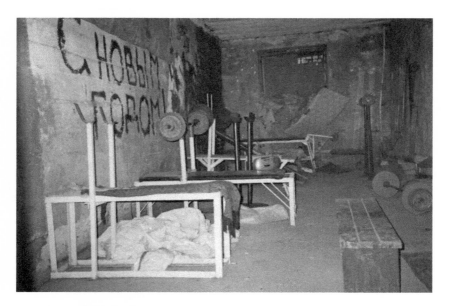

FIGURE 5.2.   A basement gym in a Khrushchev-era apartment block that has survived mostly unchanged since the 1980s. Liubertsy, 2006. Photo by Dmitry Gromov.

impossible to perform. As a solution, bodybuilders sometimes dug holes in the floor and did these exercises standing in them.[70] The popularity of bodybuilding among urban youth also led to many cases when, once the word about a new gym spread in the local community, it immediately became overcrowded. Cherepanov described a particular gym in which he worked out in the 1970s: "When someone brought mirrors and hung them on the walls, it wasn't just condensation—water was literally running down them. Because the number of people who were exercising simultaneously—I am speaking about my first gym that was located in a 60 square meter [ca. 646 square feet] room—could be as high as fifty."[71] Nikolai Yasinovsky, who in the 1990s became the first Russian bodybuilder to compete professionally in the United States, mentioned in his memoir that in his first bodybuilding gym he sometimes had to work out in underwear, which was "neither a whim, nor narcissism, but rather a necessity, because in the summertime the basement was as hot as a sauna."[72]

Finding an appropriate basement was only one of the many problems to which Soviet enthusiasts of bodybuilding had to apply their social networks and ingenuity. Getting the equipment for it was another. During the entire late Soviet era, they faced a shortage of kettlebells, barbells, and dumbbells in the Soviet retail trade. More advanced weightlifting machines such as squat stands and cable trainers were simply unheard of. Some of them sent letters to the Soviet press with requests to help solve this supply crisis.[73] Yet most used the vast opportunities provided by the Soviet informal economy or produced basic equipment with their own hands. Sergey B. told that they acquired equipment for their first gym when their neighbors, a worker at the local machine shop, approached them and asked if his teenage son could enroll in the gym: "He was taking orders for fences, railings and other stuff, making them at the shop. After all, the year was 1984, and the labor discipline was low. So, the father wanted his son to train with us, and—imagine—he made a barbell for free: a shaft and plates."[74] Here, he describes a typical situation for the Soviet shadow economy, when workers used the resources of their workplace as a source of extra income or to exchange favors.[75] Bodybuilders actively used these informal economic relations. Those of them who were students at vocational colleges could produce barbells and dumbbells at their schools' equipment. Others asked for help from relatives and friends employed in factories. Yet others pooled their money and "entered the commodity-money relations" with the workers of local factories.[76] As a result, late Soviet gyms had no lack of custom-made barbells and dumbbells.

Sports nutrition and specialized literature were two other problematic issues for Soviet bodybuilders. The Soviet journals that popularized bodybuilding, such as *Sportivnaia zhizn' Rossii* and *Tekhnika—Molodezhi*, played the role of a catalyst that sparked the interest of Soviet citizens in the use of "iron" for muscle gain. But having created a broad audience of bodybuilding enthusiasts, they failed to satisfy its demand for weightlifting complexes, nutritional tips, and stage techniques. Tenno and Sorokin's *Atletizm* provided some of this information, but its publication year (1968), a relatively small number of copies in the first print run (100,000), and the fact that it was not reprinted meant that it immediately became a rarity. Soviet-era enthusiasts warmly remember this book that provided advice to several generations of bodybuilders: "It passed from hands to hands, people read it voraciously, and all copies that I saw were in extremely used condition."[77] Yet Soviet bodybuilders also craved for the cutting-edge information on their sport, which could only be found in foreign magazines. Here, once again, their social networks came to help. Soviet bodybuilders used their friends and acquaintances among diplomats, sailors, or just tourists to get a hold of U.S., Eastern and Western European bodybuilding guides and magazines. The black market was another opportunity: Nikolai Yasinovsky mentioned in his memoir that he once paid seventy-five rubles (an equivalent of one-half of the average monthly salary in the USSR at that time) for two issues of *Muscle and Fitness*.[78] Just like with Tenno and Sorokin's book, the purchased journals often became a collective property shared among members of one or several gyms: "We got our first bodybuilding magazines from Finland. We kept in them in the gym, and they were soiled and worn out like porn magazines."[79]

The same informant mentioned that first specialized sports nutrition appeared in Petrozavodsk in the 1980s through the same channel—Soviet tourism to Finland, but its deliveries were only occasional, and bodybuilders had to rely on whatever they could find in the Soviet retail trade to create improvised diets. Finding necessary information on the theory of sports nutrition was never a problem: for example, Tenno and Sorokin's *Atletizm* had an entire section, titled "Fuel for the Living Motor," that further developed the metaphor of iron.[80] Most bodybuilders were satisfied with generic advice to eat larger quantities of protein-rich products such as meat, fish, eggs, milk, or cheese. For others, however, an appeal of professional Western bodybuilding translated into attempts to imitate professional protein supplements. Dmitry Gromov mentions that it was quite common for bodybuilding enthusiasts in Liubertsy to consume infant formulas and—in some more extreme cases— whey protein powder for pigs.[81] It was among the latter group of more devoted enthusiasts that steroids and drugs gradually acquired popularity in the latter half of the 1980s.[82]

The specific material conditions in which Soviet bodybuilders exercised contributed to negative assessments and stereotypes about this sport among sports officials and journalists. When Soviet bodybuilders moved en masse to basements, organizing semilegal gyms with makeshift equipment and decorating the walls with clippings of workout routines and posters of famous U.S. bodybuilders, they aggravated the fears of their opponents in Soviet officialdom. For them, not only was bodybuilding genealogically rooted in capitalist ideology, but it also dragged athletes from specially allocated premises, such as stadiums and "palaces of sport" (the Soviet term for sports complexes), where they exercised under the supervision of professional trainers, into dark, stuffy, and dirty basements where they trained without properly educated supervisors. In other words, Soviet bodybuilders moved from the purity and hygiene of a materiality which was ordered in a centralized manner and which was transparent to the gaze of power embodied by state-appointed trainers, into the domain of an allegedly filthy and unsanitary material environment where the norm of an ideal body was set by images of hypermuscular athletes from U.S. posters, and where the power to plan, control, and judge an individual's approximation to this ideal belonged to a bodybuilder's own gaze in a mirror.

Dmitry Ivanov's 1977 article in *Sovetskii sport*—"Deviation" ("Izlom")—is remembered by Soviet-era bodybuilding pioneers as one of the most severe attacks on their sport.[83] It encapsulated the fears that bodybuilding, when practiced away from the controlled material environment of official sports infrastructure, produced deviant bodies and minds. This article opened as a journalist investigation into a criminal case in which a bodybuilder killed one man and critically injured another. To understand what pushed the athlete to commit these crimes, Ivanov toured Moscow basement gyms. What he found was "an extremely unhealthy bodybuilding environment," where the focus on increasing one's muscle weight produced "a negative impact on character building [vospitanie] and, consequently, on this person's entire life." Throughout the lengthy article—published over three issues—Ivanov emphasized that it was the lack of any official guidance in these studios that was the main reason why people emerged from these basements with numerous deviancies. According to Ivanov, these ranged from damaged health to bachelorhood and an unwillingness to have children, to a tolerance of homosexual relationships, to criminality. In the absence of proper state control in the form of a trainer's gaze, iron dangerously empowered people's bodies and produced social deviations. "How much dirt I have seen in these gyms!," exclaimed Ivanov in the last part of his article, before concluding with a recommendation to disband bodybuilding gyms and clubs and replace them with official weightlifting groups in order to save young athletes from "from the filthy, cramped basement."[84]

Mary Douglas has famously suggested that "where there is dirt there is [a] system. Dirt is the by-product of a systematic ordering and classification of matter."[85] With the use of this concept, Ivanov invoked a system of social classification which displaced bodybuilders into the domain of social deviation. When some of my informants mentioned that they disguised their workouts as Olympic weightlifting or general fitness, they intentionally avoided this classification scheme. The same scheme produced derogatory myths about bodybuilding in late Soviet society, such as that bodybuilders are sexually impotent, and that their muscles are "hollow," having only volume, but no strength. Yet the case of the *liubery* is illustrative in the sense that bodybuilders refused to regard themselves as deviations from the Soviet social norm. Instead, they and their supporters appealed to the same vocabulary of purity and dirt as had been applied to them, but inverted it to use against visually distinct youth groups, of which they aspired to "cleanse" Soviet society. One apologetic article about the *liubery* relentlessly emphasized how clean and orderly their basement gyms were. As additional evidence, it printed a photo of one of them that hid its low ceiling and featured a mirror in the background, thereby transforming the basement gym into a spacious and immaculate environment, with people passionately engaged in the empowerment of their bodies.[86] Some informal youth groups even called themselves "cleaners" or "janitors" to emphasize their self-imposed social function as guardians of social hygiene.[87] Although the name *liubery* did not carry this association, in both contemporary and retrospective interviews, these young (or formerly young) Soviet bodybuilders also emphasized this aspect of their activities. Vladimir Yakovlev, in his 1987 article, wrote that bodybuilders repeatedly described themselves as using their raids to "cleanse the capital."[88] One of Dmitry Gromov's respondents claimed that, when encountering instances of unorderly behavior by soccer fans, *liubery* fought them in order "to restore the [public] order";[89] and in a recent interview, a former *liuber* explained the motivation of he and his friends' raids in Moscow in a similar way: "For us, the teens from the working suburbs, these [new subcultures] looked wild. All our brothers and fathers had served in the [Soviet] Army, worked in factories . . . And suddenly, all these dirty, hairy ones emerged. For example, metalheads were walking through the park, shouting and smashing bottles. There was nothing about them to like . . . We looked normally, behaved normally. Without any whims."[90]

Late Soviet cultural production—with a varying degree of irony—also noted this tendency of the *liubery* to borrow the language of social hygiene.

The musician Yuri Shevchuk, leader of the popular rock band DDT, ironically sang about a *liuber* who "supports the iron order . . . and is rescuing Moscow from foreign contagion"; and Pavel Lungin's 1992 film *Luna-park*, inspired by the *liubery*, featured a violent anti-Semitic bodybuilding group that called themselves "The Cleaners." The 1988 film *Menia zovut Arlekino* (My Name Is Harlequin) is another cinematic reflection on this working-class vigilante phenomenon. In one scene, young bodybuilders from a suburb round up a hippie and give him an impromptu haircut so that he will look "like a normal person." The victim recognizes this as an act of power, rather than of deviance, when he compares their actions with those of the Soviet police (*militsiia*) who had previously done the same to him.[91] In a historical perspective, the discourse of cleansing utilized by Soviet teenage bodybuilders comprised reused and repurposed Soviet discourses dating back to the cultural revolution of the late 1920s and early 1930s and the Great Purge of the late 1930s.[92] The *liubery* raids, in which they cut the hair of metalheads, punks and hippies, destroyed their clothes and took their accessories, also resembles those of state-encouraged groups of Komsomol activists in the 1950s and 1960s, who confronted a different, but also Western-inspired subculture of *stiliagi* (a Soviet analog of the 1940s subculture of hipsters in the United States), often using violent means to impose proper social norms, including forced haircuts and the slashing of clothes.[93]

There were other, less violent ways in which Soviet bodybuilders performed their loyal Soviet identities and affirmed their citizenship as normative. One of them was organizing bodybuilding contests on Soviet holidays, such as Victory Day on May 9, which symbolically attached bodybuilding to the calendar of Soviet rituals. Another was the advocacy mentioned above for the inclusion of bodybuilding and weightlifting in the training program of preconscription age teenagers to prepare them for compulsory military service in the Red Army.[94] Finally, from 1989 to 1991, after having joined the International Bodybuilding Federation, professional Soviet bodybuilders competed with their U.S. counterparts as the "Team USSR" in four USA-USSR bodybuilding contests.[95]

To summarize, the official criticism of bodybuilding marginalized its enthusiasts spatially, forcing them to move to the basements of Soviet apartment blocks and, to a certain degree culturally, creating routinely reproduced patterns of representation that depicted them as balancing on the brink of criminality and deviance. However, it failed to marginalize them socially despite very dedicated attempts on behalf of some Soviet officials from the USSR Sports Committee and journalists like Dmitry Ivanov. Moreover, Soviet bodybuilders appropriated certain discourses of power and joined the performance of Soviet rituals. When the *liubery* transformed their bodies into weapons to restore the social order, or when teenagers in Liubertsy and elsewhere in the USSR enrolled in basement gyms to qualify for the Soviet airborne forces, even though it meant a higher chance of being sent to Afghanistan, or when professional Soviet bodybuilders rallied under the flag of the USSR in order to perform on the international arena, the biopolitical agenda in these cases relied on and pushed forward normative masculinity and citizenship. Their claims to represent and perform the proper socialist manhood came from a strong realization that iron made their bodies cultured.

Cultural Bodies, Hybrid Selves

Bodybuilding advocates called their sport "athletic gymnastics" to tone down its Western roots, yet they also interchangeably used the French term *culturisme* throughout the late Soviet era. They deployed this term strategically as it allowed them to invoke a different genealogy. "*Culturisme* is indeed a Western influence [veianie Zapada]. But I am intentionally not saying "a new influence." Because its origins can be found in many centuries before the common era, or, more precisely, in Ancient Greece."[96] The author of this 1971 article in the youth magazine *Smena* built his argument in support of bodybuilding by developing a contrast between the "harmoniously" muscled body of antiquity, which was an expression of classical culture, and the "hypertrophied" body of Western bodybuilding. He called on Soviet teenagers to strive to build the former, while avoiding any temptation to imitate the latter:

> Any good idea, if reduced to absurdity, becomes absurd. Such distortions can be found in bodybuilding, too, because it came to us from across the Atlantic in such an obscene form. We should rebuild it in our own fashion . . . Let's be fair and treat it like we would treat it like a painting by an old master, whose canvas was later used by a third-rater who slapdashed something worthless on it. Let's be art restorers. Let's approach carefully the work of the genius, remove the accretions of later ages, this irrelevant dribble-drabble, and restore what has been lost.[97]

Here, the author's rhetoric bears a surprising similarity to the arguments of Soviet architectural preservation experts in the sense that they also sought in history aesthetic ideals that had been contaminated by later capitalist influences. The tasks of socialist sport—just like the tasks of socialist architectural preservation—was thus a rediscovery and popularization of the past ideals among the Soviet population. In the context of bodybuilding, this argumentation provided Soviet audiences with narratives and imagery of the muscled body as a cultural body. Commonplace references to the classical imagery of the male body in Soviet bodybuilding literature served to reinforce this idea: for example, Tenno and Sorokin's *Atletizm* was illustrated with collages that superimposed posing bodybuilders on ancient Greek sculptures. Many athletes who practiced this sport reproduced this argument in their later interviews and memoirs, as for example a certain Dmitry Kononov who, writing in 2004 in the professional bodybuilding magazine *Iron World* nostalgically wrote: "[In the Soviet era] our sport was called *culturisme* . . . and it was indeed a culture of body and mind . . . a system that guaranteed, to a certain degree, a balanced development of an athlete."[98] It is hardly surprising that teenage bodybuilders framed their confrontations with punks, metalheads, and similar nonconformist youth groups as a struggle between the dominant culture and countercultures. Moreover, they often reduced the latter to "unculturedness," as did unnamed bodybuilder quoted above who referred to conspicuously vandalistic behavior of his opponents in order to explain why he and his friends sought to beat them up: "Metalheads were walking through the park, shouting and smashing bottles. There was nothing about them to like."[99] Another unnamed bodybuilder whose letter to *Komsomolskaya pravda* was quoted in the epigraph to this chapter capitalized on a similar opposition between the "uncultured" urban places, in which young Soviet people satisfied their base natural instincts by getting drunk, drinking alcohol, or having extramarital sex, and basement gyms where a cult of the cultured body reigned supreme: "We also have basements. Yet we are not 'getting high' in them, but rather exercising! Boxing, weightlifting—in other words, 'pumping iron,' and this gives a lot to us—strength, health, self-assurance."[100]

Few bodybuilders disputed that cultured bodies could also be produced through the centralized system of sport, but it was the power of iron to transform human bodies that promised a shortcut to health and strength, and that was appealing for them. This understanding of the power of iron was close to those of Gavriil Ilizarov and Valentin Dikul, as Soviet bodybuilding enthusiasts, especially Tenno, equated iron with bodily and mental health. This equation became encapsulated in the term "iron pills" that Tenno coined for weightlifting equipment to show its remedial potential.[101] In his writings, Tenno extensively quoted letters from his readers, which described miraculous transformations from disease and weakness to health and strength, including cases of full restoration from wartime wounds, heart defects, hepatitis, and rheumatism—all this was attributed to the nearly limitless potential of iron.[102] The transformations that their authors attributed to the power of iron were as miraculous as the stories of Ilizarov's and Dikul's patients:

> I spent seven years in a plaster cast all over my body due to bone tuberculosis. I recovered, and although I didn't have a humped back, I was very thin, frail, and constrained. It was at this time that I learned about [your] weight training system. The desire to overcome my physical disability was so strong that I became fanatically devoted to bodybuilding. After fourteen months of exercise I changed so much that my friends do not recognize me. My weight gained from fifty-nine to seventy-one kilograms. I even joined an [Olympic] weightlifting club. I would have never even dreamed of that, if it hadn't been for bodybuilding.[103]

Ivanov and other Soviet critics of bodybuilding recognized this power of iron—after all, Ivanov was a world weightlifting champion himself. What they attacked and official sports resolutions sought to administer was not bodybuilding exercises per se, but rather the perceived attempt to remove bodybuilding from the surveillance system of centralized Soviet sports management. If iron were a medicine, then its abuse in the basement could make it a dangerous drug. From the perspective of Soviet sports officials, it was because of the power of iron that its use for building one's body could not be left unattended and had to be regulated. The perception of weightlifting equipment in medical terms, as having the power to heal and transform the body, explains why critics of bodybuilding tried to discredit its leading proponents as charlatans and its enthusiasts as sick people whose unhealthy, nonsupervised addiction to iron led to mental disorders.[104]

Alan Klein, the author of an influential ethnography of a bodybuilding community in California, argued that the desire to make the body hypermuscular and hypermasculine stemmed from internal feelings of personal inadequacy (hence the "little" in the title of his book, *Little Big Men*).[105] Soviet excitement about bodybuilding, by contrast, revealed the elemental materialism of Soviet culture, which implied a reverse relationship between the body, on the one hand, and the material environment of the bodybuilding gym, on the other. For Klein, an obsession with iron was an indication of "a shaky psyche," and bodybuilding gyms acted as compensatory mechanisms for people "working out a range of personal issues."[106] Soviet critics of bodybuilding shared this opinion on the personal inadequacy of bodybuilders, but their materialism pushed them to offer a different explanation: it was not a cause, but rather an effect of iron's abuse outside of the panoptic supervision of the state-controlled sport system. For them, basement gyms took normal

Soviet citizens and transformed them into self-centered, egoistic, "pompous peacocks," to use Ivanov's term.

It is important to emphasize that critics of bodybuilding did not advocate for its total ban, unlike, for instance, with karate groups, which were made illegal by the 1973 resolution of the USSR Sports Committee. They attacked not bodybuilding exercises per se, but rather their system: the "pumping of iron" in front of mirrors in basement gyms which allegedly created a self-obsession with one's own body, provoked a disregard for collective interests and provided no opportunity for direct intervention on behalf on the authorities. It was the belief that iron could shape human bodies and selves, shared by both advocates and critics of bodybuilding, which made their conflict so dramatic. And it was the same materialist recognition of the power of iron that, from the perspective of Soviet enthusiasts of bodybuilding, was vitally important for embodying their understanding of proper masculinity and citizenship. From a historical perspective, the fears of Soviet journalists and officials proved false: instead of egoists absorbed in the creation of their bodies as spectacle, basement gyms produced loyal and socially active Soviet citizens who had a strong sense of belonging to Soviet society and were eager to enforce the social norm as they understood it. Moreover, as a place where young people worked on their body culture, it often stood in opposition to "disorganized" urban spaces discussed in chapter 4, such as hallways and streets. Many Soviet-era bodybuilders refer to this; as one Belorussian bodybuilder recalled later in an article for a professional bodybuilding journal: "I was growing up, as they say, 'in the street,' and it was gradually engulfing me, I could feel it myself. Bodybuilding saved me. My friends and I found and equipped a basement of some forty square meters, called it 'Club 73.' We had our own charter: no booze, no smoking, no girls or even friends."[107]

Soviet bodybuilding emerged in the writings of its enthusiasts as a Soviet athletic system of building a perfect body and thus was a product of Khrushchev's Thaw with its tendency to decentralize and diffuse the articulation of power. In the context of Soviet biopolitics, one's individual involvement in the production of power was not only discursive or ritualistic (participation in Soviet mass festivals) but also bodily. The concept of "good" citizenship had been firmly connected to one's physical fitness since 1931, when the Soviet government introduced the GTO system (GTO is an acronym for "Ready for Labor and Defense") as a propaganda tool to encourage mass participation in physical culture, but also to evaluate one's approximation to the ideal level of fitness understood as one's ability to contribute to the public good.[108] Therefore, when Soviet enthusiasts of bodybuilding argued that its value was exactly in its ability to empower people's bodies to become good citizens, their position was deeply rooted in the Soviet discursive field. "Muscles are given to man not for narcissism, but for work," wrote Tenno and Sorokin at the end of their 1968 bodybuilding guide, appealing to the understanding of men's muscles as instruments; they concluded: "Iron works miracles, but will and persistence will do even more."[109]

Oleg Kharkhordin argued that the de-Stalinization of Soviet society did not lead to any lesser degree of social surveillance. In fact, the opposite happened, which Kharkhordin qualified as a gradual transformation from top-down surveillance of Stalin's years to "increasingly pervasive mutual surveillance in everyday life" during and after Khrushchev's period in power.[110] Bodybuilding, with its tendency to bring the male body into the domain of the visual, seems to be part of this transformation. Apart from bodybuilding contests which the critical Soviet press derogatorily, but also insightfully dubbed "pageants," the presentation and performance of one's muscular body as an aesthetic object took the form of spending time at local beaches and wearing sleeveless shirts in summer.[111] These forms of performing one's masculinity reflected the complex voyeuristic space of Soviet bodybuilding gyms. A photo of a basement gym in Liubertsy (figure 5.3) gives an idea of this complexity. Clippings of bodybuilders on the wall in the left side of the image acted as posters, with Western professional bodybuilders providing their bodies as models and muscles as fetishes, but also acting as sources of the authoritative gaze like that of Lord Kitchener from the famous 1914 British propaganda poster and its later imitations. This authoritative gaze played a similar mobilizing function, provoking the fetishization of muscles and urging those who viewed these posters to engage in the pursuit of muscle gain. When a former athlete at one of the Liubertsy gyms recalled his attempts at increasing the size of his biceps, he explicitly referred to this voyeuristic logic:

> At that time, my nickname was the Thin One [Khudoi]. Thin—because my biceps did not grow. I kept on pumping them with dumbbells, with barbells. Because what are the main muscles for a teen? Biceps. So that you could put on a sleeveless shirt, and everyone would see huge arms, like those of [Arnold] Schwarzenegger. [In response to a question of whether or not he envied more muscular men] When you go to the gym with someone, measure your biceps together every week and see that his grow, while yours do not . . . Of course, I couldn't help but envy him.[112]

Apart from a reference to Schwarzenegger's biceps, this quote invokes another dimension of the Soviet bodybuilders' voyeuristic space: their drive to

FIGURE 5.3.   A basement gym in Liubertsy, 1980s, http://www.furfur.me.

train their bodies as a spectacle for the public gaze. In the image in figure 5.3, the public gaze is reified in the poster of a young woman in the background wall (similar posters were featured in the basement gym recreated in the film *Menia zovut Arlekino*), and, in a similar fashion, the quotation above referred to its author's fantasy in which "everyone would see [his] huge arms, like those of Schwarzenegger" as a major motivating force behind his workout efforts. Images of professional bodybuilders nurtured an inferiority feeling for those possessing "insufficient" muscles, but this inferiority only made sense in a more immediate surveillance system—that of the public gaze, which promised an immediate affective punishment of one's lack of formidable muscularity.

The image in figure 5.3 provides an insight into one more aspect of the voyeuristic space of Soviet basement gyms. While it is not quite clear what the bodybuilder in its center is looking at, it is likely the most common object, after weightlifting equipment, found in bodybuilding gyms: the mirror. The evaluative nature of his gaze suggests that the culture of surveillance that basement bodybuilding helped to create in Soviet symbolic space was deeper than just the mutual surveillance of which Kharkhordin speaks. In the absence of a state-appointed trainer to supervise physical activities, every Soviet bodybuilder had to become a trainer for himself. To practice bodybuilding, one was required to engage in voluntary and willing self-surveillance.

Tenno and Sorokin's bodybuilding guide was exemplary in this respect, since a large part of the book focused not on exercises per se, but on practices of self-surveillance, with its final section eloquently titled "You are your own mentor and trainer." The authors insisted that all major muscles and body proportions had to be regularly measured and recorded in a personal diary, so that the athlete could keep track of the changes in his body. "Before getting to exercises, chart the frontier from which you will start your offensive on weakness, ill-health, physical imperfection," they wrote, using the mobilizing language of war.[113] The critical history of anthropology has shown how the anthropometric efforts of nineteenth-century Western scholarship were deployed as a form of state power over domestic populations and colonial people alike.[114] When Soviet bodybuilders were advised to engage in self-anthropometry, it represented a step from abstract centralized state power toward an intimate form of power of self-control and self-regulation. Moreover, the authors of the first Soviet bodybuilding guide suggested that athletes should "supplement anthropometry with photography," taking regular and repeated sets of photos of themselves facing forward, in profile, and from the back. A succession of such photos would "eloquently narrate the story of your achievements," Tenno and Sorokin strove to convince their readers.[115] Just like with anthropometry, this advice is strikingly similar to the modern use of photography (especially in the form of the photographic archive) for the policing and classification of populations.[116] Creating a home archive of one's own mug shots ("face forward and in profile") represented the internalization of this practice: a form of self-policing of one's own progress from physical weakness to a perfect physical form, which guaranteed that its owner was a worthy member of both his local community and the Soviet nation.

The quintessence of this regulatory effort was the advice to keep a personal diary. In addition to one's anthropometric record, it had to include "objective and subjective data about one's health and labor productivity [*rabotosposobnost'*]," such as sleep, appetite, weight, training load, and any unusual feelings.[117] In their studies of Soviet diary-keeping, Jochen Hellbeck and Anatoly Pinsky showed how the diary became an important medium in the internalization of Soviet values and meanings, thus acting as the forge of one's Soviet self.[118] The nature of a bodybuilder's diary, with its intimate observations about physical development, appears to be different from the private diaries that Hellbeck and Pinsky analyzed, but it worked to the same end: as a performative medium, capable of bringing into being the very things being written about, the diary assisted in making oneself into a Soviet subject whose physical beauty and strength were important socially, just as they were individually. As Tenno and Sorokin wrote: "Muscles are given to man not for narcissism, but for work . . . Iron works miracles, but will and persistence will do even more."[119]

What Soviet bodybuilding skeptics misrecognized as institutionalized egoism was thus a new, subtler, discreet, and modern form of self-governance of people's bodies and loyalties. It was another, more individualist form of Soviet selfhood that challenged the collectivist culture of the body inherited from the 1920s and 1930s, but was nonetheless Soviet. Unlike the mass forms of physical culture like jogging or cross-country skiing, which were popularized in a centralized manner, bodybuilding was more effective, due to the power of iron, in transforming one's body to comply with new transnational standards of fitness. It also did not require developed sports infrastructure, something the USSR could not boast, especially in factory neighborhoods and small towns. Bodybuilding provided a unique opportunity to overcome this difficulty and to build one's Soviet body in a decentralized fashion. This had already been revealed in the basic advice of Soviet bodybuilding enthusiasts: a perfect body could be produced at home. Tenno and Sorokin emphasized that weightlifting exercises did not necessarily require specialized infrastructure since iron transformed any quarters into a gym.[120] Basements turned out to be a convenient solution to a situation in which the public sports infrastructure was unavailable for objective or administrative reasons, but virtually any space could be turned into a bodybuilding gym with the use of makeshift equipment.[121]

It is important to emphasize that when Soviet people repaired and empowered their bodies with iron, this was a particular form of the care of the self. Soviet bodybuilding did absorb the dominant understandings of masculinity and citizenship, but the bodies it produced were a result of lengthy, costly, and tedious efforts focused on one's personal fitness. Self-improvement and self-reliance were important for Ilizarov's treatment and an absolute prerequisite for Dikul's techniques. During the late Soviet era, these experiences of vigorous self-building became part of the Soviet culture of the body through the narratives and imagery of Ilizarov's cyborgs, Dikul's patients, and hypermuscular bodies of teenage bodybuilders. Ilizarov and Dikul emphasized that their methods returned formerly disabled people to society as its full members and, in a similar way, Soviet bodybuilders claimed that they represented and embodied the social norm. But in all these cases, the human bodies performed a new kind of normalcy—the one where one's social empowerment was derived from the agency of things, rather than from socialist collectivity. Soviet people's affection for iron produced hybrid selves whose ideological structure was incommensurable with bodily experience.

CHAPTER 6

Ordinary and Paranormal

The Soviet Television Set

> We are deceived by the mundanity of the television's intrusion in our life. We are willing to accept it, as we had previously accepted the introduction of matches, electric shavers, and pencil sharpeners. We solemnly install the beaming box ten centimeters away from the sewing machine and cozily cover it with a tablecloth. Now television is like a house cat. It is ordinary. It is domesticated. It pretends to be happening as if in the past tense. And it doesn't even come to us that we are standing on the threshold of a revolution in the means of human communication which has just barely started.
>
> —Sergei Muratov, *Cinema as a Form of Television*

The last three decades of the Soviet Union were unusually rich in paranormal phenomena. It all started with unidentified flying objects (UFOs). In the late 1950s, Soviet citizens who attended the public lectures of Moscow professor Yuri Fomin were shocked to learn that Earth was being visited on a regular basis by UFOs. The official topic of Fomin's lectures was about how the universe works, but Fomin used his forums to present numerous facts and detailed descriptions about alien explorations of Earth. Typewritten copies of the lectures soon circulated broadly among the Soviet educated public, leading *Pravda* and *Komsomolskaya pravda* to provide an official refutation in 1961.[1] Despite the refutations, news of UFO sightings continued to emerge in the Soviet press with an ever-lowering degree of skepticism, culminating in October 1989, when TASS, the main Soviet information agency, officially released a report that "an unidentified flying object" with a crew of several tall humanoid creatures and "a small robot" landed in the city of Voronezh.[2] But UFOs were just one of the many paranormal phenomena that haunted the late socialist society. In the late 1950s, sightings of abominable snowmen (yeti) in the Pamir Mountains intensified to the degree that in 1958 the Soviet Academy of Sciences organized a special expedition there.[3] While its failure to find any evidence of the living Bigfoot precluded any other official effort to find the yeti, groups of unofficial searchers kept on exploring Pamir, as well as the Caucasus, Arctic taiga, and other Soviet regions in search of the mysterious *homo trogloditus*.[4] Beginning in the early 1980s, the Soviet Union experienced a steady growth of news about poltergeists arriving from many regions, which skyrocketed in late 1988 when the Soviet television broadcast the story of a poltergeist named Barabashka allegedly living in a construction workers' dormitory in Moscow.[5] In addition, the Soviet public in the post-Stalinist period was well aware of paranormal activities outside of the Soviet borders. Stories about the Bermuda Triangle, the Loch Ness Monster, and other mysterious creatures were reported—usually as criticism, but sometimes as hypotheses or op-ed pieces—in *Tekhnika—Molodezhi* (which had a special rubric "Anthology of mysterious cases"), *Nauka i zhizn'*, *Khimiia i zhizn'*, *Znanie-sila*, and the TV show *Ochevidnoe-neveroiatnoe* (Obvious yet unbelievable).

The same post-Stalinist period saw a dramatic rise in the number of extrasensory perception experts in the USSR. Wolf Messing and Ninel' Kulagina were the two key figures that publicized telekinesis, telepathy, and other forms of special psychic abilities in the 1960s more than anyone else.[6] In the late 1960s, the Soviet press widely discussed allegedly successful experiments in telepathic communication.[7] Official sources, including the third edition of *The Great Soviet Encyclopedia*, cautiously admitted the possibility that the human body could possess hidden abilities of which official scholarship was as yet unaware.[8] The concept of body energy (*biopole*) acquired a particularly strong following among Soviet scholars to the degree that a special laboratory for the study of human energy was established in 1981 at the Institute of Radio-engineering and Electronics of the USSR Academy of Sciences.[9] The head of the laboratory, Eduard Godik, published a memoir about this late Soviet project to scientifically study extrasensory human abilities, in which he wrote that their research was initiated and supported at the top level of the Soviet leadership.[10]

In this remarkable list of mysterious phenomena that Soviet society encountered in its last three decades, it is easy to overlook the fact that the most paranormal object of late socialism was neither the UFO nor the poltergeist but the ordinary Soviet television set. After all, only a handful of people claimed firsthand experience with the paranormal phenomena; most learned of them indirectly, from rumors or the mass media. Yet nearly every Soviet person had a personal experience with the healing séances of Anatoly Kashpirovsky and Allan Chumak that were broadcast on Soviet television in 1989. Kashpirovsky and Chumak initially appeared on the main Soviet channel, Channel 1, with claims that they were capable of using their psychic powers to heal audiences sitting in front of their television sets. Both proved extremely popular. Kashpirovsky's séances were broadcast on prime time every second Sunday from October to December 1989; each show lasted for over an hour. Chumak's séances were shorter, lasting between eight and ten minutes, but during the summer and autumn of 1989 they were broadcast daily, with the exception of Sunday, early in the morning as part of the entertainment show *90 minut* (90 minutes) (later renamed *120 minut* [120 minutes]). In 1990, both healers disappeared from central television but made occasional appearances on regional TV channels until 1993, when a new law was passed in Russia on public health that explicitly banned healing séances through mass media.[11]

Kashpirovsky and Chumak addressed Soviet television audiences from TV screens that showed close-up views of their faces, creating the illusion of eye-to-eye contact between the healers and viewers. Kashpirovsky spoke in a hypnotizing voice giving commands and suggestions that supposedly mobilized the "inner reserves" of people's bodies to heal themselves. By contrast, Chumak remained silent for most of his TV shows: after a brief introduction, in which he explained that he was going to transmit his healing energy via the TV signal, he performed mesmeric passes that represented the aforementioned transmission of energy to the audience. He additionally claimed that he was capable of charging liquids with his healing energy and encouraged TV viewers to put jars of water and cosmetic creams in front of their screens. After the séance was over, the water and creams were allegedly charged with his energy and could be applied for internal and external use.[12] As a result, accounts of how Soviet TV audiences watched Chumak's séances routinely mention innumerable jars and other vessels with various liquids that viewers put in front of their TV screens and then used to treat various diseases.

In 1990, the All-Union Center for the Study of Public Opinion (VTsIOM) conducted a nationwide poll that included the question, "Do you watch the psychotherapy sessions of Anatoly Kashpirovsky on TV? If yes, how closely?" The option "I put everything aside and sit in front of the TV" gathered an impressive 57 percent of the answers, and an additional 30 percent responded that they watched them occasionally.[13] A recent documentary claimed that at the peak of their fame in the latter half of 1989, Kashpirovsky and Chumak reached a television audience of roughly 150,000,000 people, which more or less correlates with the statistical data above (according to the 1989 census, the population of the USSR at that time was 287,000,000 people).[14] In other words, the overwhelming majority of Soviet citizens took seriously—even if only for a brief moment of time—the alleged healing powers of

Kashpirovsky and Chumak, to the degree that they "put everything aside" to watch the healing TV séances of the two paranormalists.

Most explanations of this historical phenomenon have been centered on the personalities of Kashpirovsky and Chumak as two charlatans who found themselves in the right place at the right time. In his Pulitzer Prize-winning book *Lenin's Tomb*, David Remnick, the *Washington Post*'s Moscow correspondent between 1988 and 1992, compared Kashpirovsky to Rasputin as a figure coming at the end of an epoch to captivate the popular imagination by personifying everything irrational and mystical that had been previously suppressed.[15] Soviet academics who in late 1989 gathered for a special conference on "telepsychotherapy," a term that Soviet mass media coined to refer to both Kashpirovsky's and Chumak's healing TV séances, also focused on the personalities of these mass healers. Some of the conference participants attributed to them actual hypnotic abilities; others argued that this duo duped their television audiences into believing obvious nonsense.[16] A variation of this explanation emphasizes the gullibility of Soviet TV audiences, interpreting the Kashpirovsky-Chumak phenomenon as exploitation of popular beliefs in bodily energy and extrasensory experts capable of controlling it. This is, for example, the interpretation of Yuri Bogomolov, a prominent Russian TV critic.[17] Finally, the term obscurantism (*mrakobesie*) often comes up as a sociocultural explanation of the popularity of late Soviet extrasensory perception experts. Interpreted as an innate feature of Soviet culture that had survived decades of centralized enlightenment and rationality, obscurantism is credited with producing both Soviet paranormalists and their audiences by the writer and extreme left-wing politician Eduard Limonov, popular TV host Vladimir Solovyev, and some of my informants.[18] Being highly emotional and judgmental, this term encapsulated the affective response of the Soviet educated class to what they perceived as a grand failure of Soviet rationality.

These explanations leave largely unnoticed, despite its conspicuous visibility, another important actor in this story: the television set. Its role might seem purely technical since Soviet apartments had television sets before and after Kashpirovsky's and Chumak's TV séances, and so any direct cause-and-effect relationship would be far-fetched. There are, however, reasons to suggest that the role of the television set in this historical phenomenon was more than merely a medium for delivering certain content. Let us imagine an ethnographic description of the practice of watching Kashpirovsky's and Chumak's tele-séances in Soviet households. Such a description would assign this practice to the domain of healing magic, as its explicit purpose was to obtain health outside of the framework of the system of medical care.

The practice itself would then be described as a ritual involving people and material objects, in which the latter allegedly possess medical powers to cure people's bodies. The most important of these objects was the television set, and in the case of Chumak's TV shows also jars and bottles with liquids that allegedly acquired healing properties after the ritual. Of course, certain conditions had to be followed for this ritual to become magical, namely the television set had to be turned on at the right time to show a certain set of images. But the presumable transfer of healing energy within the immediate domestic space occurred between the television set and people's bodies. The actual failure of Soviet rationality was taking place not in the television studios where Kashpirovsky and Chumak demonstrated their alleged paranormal abilities, but in the apartments of Soviet people, who were sitting down in front of their television sets to get rid of their illnesses. Kashpirovsky admitted in late 1989, while still at the full zenith of his fame, that his "own power is very weak. It is, primarily, the television effect that is at work here." Any impostor (he explicitly referred to his competitor Chumak) could act as an extrasensory perception practitioner because all medical effects were due to "the affective power of the television screen."[19]

The TV shows of Soviet paranormalists are important as a symptom that gives a fresh perspective on how the television set as a material object changed Soviet domestic space and Soviet selfhood. I focus on both the content and material form of television in order to argue that its inclusion in Soviet domestic space instigated new forms of identity performances that cannot be reduced to the content of television programs, but can rather be traced to "the affective power of the television screen." The materiality of television that I describe in this chapter is revealed on several levels. First, its presence at home is material. A television set is an object of the apartment interiors, the main property of which is the permeability of its frontal surface to light. As a number of scholars argued, this dramatically changed the materiality and temporality of the modern home, as this permeability allows the television screen to attract the attention of apartment residents by projecting images "from the outside" to the domestic space.[20] Unlike TV images that are volatile, the presence of the set itself at home is monumental. Taken in the Soviet historical context, this presence produced a physical transformation, namely, changes in the late socialist hierarchy of domestic objects, the reorganization of the Soviet home and its accelerated transformation into voyeuristic space built along the principles of visual pleasure.

The second level is the materiality of the bodies of people watching television. Thanks to the programs that it broadcasts, the television set punctuates the day and attracts people to the living room. In doing so, it arranges people's bodies spatially and temporally. Moreover, its influence has a physical dimension on them, affecting vision, weight, muscles, heart, and breath—an influence that became increasingly worrying for Soviet officials and scholars, especially pediatricians.[21] But just as it could take health away, the television set could assist in regaining it: this logic is visible not only in Kashpirovsky's and Chumak's TV séances but also in the popularity of instructional television series, such as *Esli khochesh' byt' zdorov* (If you want to be healthy), *Utrenniaia razminka* (Morning exercises) and especially *Ritmicheskaia gimnastika* (Rhythmic gymnastics, a Russian term for aerobics), which was broadcast beginning in 1984. These TV shows appealed to Soviet television audiences to join their hosts in doing fitness exercises in front of their TV screens—a performance aimed at energizing and repairing bodies.[22]

Finally, an analysis of the material aspects of Soviet television shows an intricate connection between the television set and Soviet selfhood. From the very beginning, Soviet scholars of television, when describing its psychic effects, extensively used the vocabulary of family relations, prosthetic devices, and mental disorders. Its everyday presence at home and its vital and vibrant materiality (the "presence effect") often rendered it as a "family member" or "family friend."[23] Its ability to momentarily transmit images and sounds from everywhere in the world prompted Sergei Muratov, a prominent Soviet theorist of television, to call it "the planetary vision and worldwide hearing of humanity."[24] Meanwhile, Soviet doctors coined a special term "telemania" for the tendency to spend vast amounts of time in front of TV screens.[25] The use of this vocabulary betrays the cultural recognition that the television set objectified the complex, decentralized and diffuse selfhood, made manifest this diffusion and thus problematized—in historical perspective—Soviet cultural fantasies of total control over the material world. Muratov described this destabilizing quality of the television set as the "quicksand surface of the display," a metaphor hinting at the uncertainty of the border between the screen and the self, and implying a danger of the latter to be absorbed by the former.[26]

Although studies of Soviet television are numbered in the hundreds, if not the thousands, the majority of them, including key works in this field, are focused on its content.[27] When it comes to the television set, an insightful observation by Mihaly Csikszentmihalyi and Eugene Rochberg-Halton—made in another historical and geographic context—remains true: "researchers are not interested in how *the television* affects people but only in the effects of *programs* . . . The thing itself, the set that transmits the communication, is supposed to be neutral."[28] However, it is not. As media theorists and critics show in arguments that can differ in modality, yet are similar in the main idea, the television set, through its presence—that is, independent of transmitted content—irrevocably changes the cultures in which it has been introduced.

Theorists of early Soviet television, such as Vladimir Sappak and Iraklii Andronikov, emphasized the ability of the television to reestablish the connection between individuals and larger social entities, its potential to overcome social alienation, and its capacity to build and reinforce communities.[29] Sappak, as well as Muratov, also saw how it changed the spatial coordinates of the Soviet household, destroying its "petty apartment world" (*kvartirnyi mirok*) by bringing in images of a larger world behind its four walls.[30] Their perspective on the television's potential in reorganizing the domestic space and lifestyle resonates with Marshal McLuhan's views, who wrote that the television acts as a prosthesis extending human selves into space and time, securing domination over them, but also transforming the nature of human selfhood.[31] Friedrich Kittler's approach was even more radical; he removed ideology from his explanatory framework and accentuated the transformative agency of the media per se, in their very materiality, without the need for any external force.[32] The historical change that television brought with it was not determined by any particular political system, official ideology, or social conditions in which this medium was introduced. Rather, the historical change was produced by television as a network of material objects, which produced its effects through humans' contact with the screen ("surface effect," in Kittler's gloss). In one of his latest interviews, Kittler claimed that the technological process led to human beings becoming "a reflection of their technologies," and then added: "After all, it is we who adapt to the machine. The machine does not adapt to us."[33]

The common denominator for these media theorists is their interest in the complex relationship between the materiality of television (independently of its content) and selfhood. This chapter does not reconcile or hybridize their views, but it is informed by this general understanding that the television set is not neutral, nor is it an innocent object belonging to apartment interiors. It explores the various ways in which Soviet television audiences discovered that the television set and networks had a power over their bodies and selves, and how this discovery was translated into the paranormal séances of Kashpirovsky and Chumak on Soviet television.

The Voyeuristic Revolution of Soviet Apartment Interiors

The early 1960s to the mid-1980s saw the mass introduction of television sets in the USSR. According to the 1989 statistical book on Soviet domestic trade, the private ownership of television sets grew from 24 per 100 families in 1965 to 103 per 100 families in 1988.[34] Urban areas initially dominated in the ratio of television sets per capita, but by the 1980s rural communities caught up with the city: a study of leisure time in rural areas of Tatarstan, for example, discovered that, whereas in 1967 only 15 percent of rural dwellers had television sets, by 1983 this figure had grown to 96 percent[35]

The advent of television was, in many respects, revolutionary for the domestic space. Lynn Spiegel, in her study of "television in the family circle" in post–World War II United States, noted that the mass introduction of television sets in U.S. culture had a profound influence on domestic interiors. The U.S. living room became rearranged around the television set, which became the focal point organizing the U.S. home and the leisure time of the U.S. family.[36] A similar transformation occurred in the USSR, as the mass appearance of television sets in Soviet apartments reorganized their interior design. Being a high-status object of possession and a new focal point of home residents, it changed the hierarchy of domestic objects by installing itself on top. Sofas and armchairs lined up in a semicircle around the TV set, accommodating apartment residents in their new capacity as television audiences and confirming the TV set's dominant position in the Soviet apartment.[37] In addition, in most households the television set exiled the radio to the kitchen, where it could be listened to during cooking or meals and led to the increased use of books as home design objects.

The mass introduction of TV sets in Soviet apartments was accompanied by another peculiar phenomenon that affected Soviet domestic space in the 1970s: the advent of the *stenka*, a massive floor-to-ceiling wall cabinet occupying the longer walls of the rectangular living rooms of Soviet standardized apartments that replaced the more rag-tag living room furniture of the Khrushchev's era.[38] Susan Reid, who described this dynamic, emphasized the enlightening and disciplinary state effort behind this change and interpreted it as a modernist campaign to impose a new, socialist, hygienic and orderly lifestyle among the population where the majority were first—or second-generation migrants from rural areas. With its modern, laconic design, the *stenka* had to help apartment residents perform their modern, socialist identities.[39] Serguei Oushakine emphasized the functional character of the *stenka* and its genealogy in the pragmatic turn among Soviet interior designers in the post-Stalinist period.[40] At the same time, the *stenka* and the television set launched together a voyeuristic revolution in Soviet domestic space.

As a furniture style, the *stenka* combined cabinets with solid wood and glass doors. The latter transformed it into a spectacle: proud owners of *stenkas* did their best to put into them such high-status commodities as china sets, crystalware, and valuable souvenirs. In the Soviet retail trade all these items were hard to obtain; the purchase of a wall cabinet and such high-status commodities as East German china sets or Czechoslovak crystalware required ingenuity, useful connections (*blat*), luck, and patience. Accounts of former Soviet tourists are full of stories of how these precious items were obtained and transported back to the USSR.[41] These precious china sets and crystalware were used only on the most solemn occasions several times a year; all the rest of the time they stood behind the glass doors as home exhibits: visual but not haptic objects.

Together, the *stenka* and the television set facilitated the reorganization of late socialist living rooms in terms of visual pleasure. The construction of the voyeuristic gaze into Soviet apartments was not something new for Soviet homes. The post–World War II emphasis on domesticity among the Soviet "middle class" that Vera Dunham described in her *In Stalin's Time* was, to a considerable degree, about creating domestic interiors in which assemblages of Soviet things and bodies would create "a small, gay, and bright paradise." Since such a paradise was practically impossible to reach in the conditions of the postwar shortage of all but the most necessary consumer commodities and it was late Stalinist fiction that took the task of creating representations of domestic life in terms of visual fantasies of beautiful home interiors.[42] In a similar way, Reid and Steven Harris showed how in the post-Stalinist period, being a modern socialist person acquired the meaning of possessing a modern-looking home.[43] It was household objects that performed modern socialist identities together with (and sometimes instead of) their owners by looking modern. The performativity of Soviet interiors already implied the presence of the voyeuristic gaze, which did not belong to the apartment owners but emerged through advice literature and fiction. Irina Kriukova in her overview of the history of post-Stalinist interior designs described this process in spatial terms, as a transition of Soviet apartments from places where domestic objects obstructed both the gaze and people's movement to a transparent and visually enjoyable space:

> [Stalin-era furniture] occupied disproportionately much space and, in addition, created the visual feeling of darkness, [and] transformed rooms into dismal corridors, into narrow crevices . . . The incredibly difficult work of architects, artists, designers, entire factory collectives carried out in the short span of the late 1950s and early 1960s transformed the [Soviet] domestic designs . . . It seemed that every piece of furniture now wanted to become less visible, to shrink its size . . . Horizontals and, to a lesser degree, verticals became the dominant lines; everything tended to transform into flat surfaces.[44]

This change in Soviet apartments cleared the way for the transformation of their residents into television audiences. The open and glass-door cabinets added to the creation of visually enjoyable space by creating domestic displays of china sets and crystalware: miniature Hermitages of a kind. The mass production and import of television sets and *stenka*-type furniture translated this cultural message from discourse into the matter. Indoor scenes in advice literature, typical photographs of Soviet-era living room interiors, and their cinematographic representations embodied the unobstructed voyeuristic gaze in their composition, providing a standardized perspective on television sets and on the "flat surfaces" of new furniture.

This tacit domestic revolution had another important aspect: the changed position of books as domestic objects. Soviet sociologists noted that the private possession of a TV set dramatically decreased the amount of leisure time spent reading books and magazines. A sociological study of urban Soviet families carried out between 1965 and 1968 mentioned that, in families with a TV set, "television . . . displaces books and magazines."[45] At the same time, books retained their superior position in the official hierarchy of Soviet culture, and "communication with the book [obshchenie s knigoi] as the supreme and critical form of man's intellectual development," as Aleksandr Tvardovsky put it at the Twenty-First Congress of the CPSU, was vigorously promoted through all channels of official propaganda.[46] Having a good home library was a social convention, and books were proudly featured in Soviet *stenkas* together with china sets and crystalware. Yet the transformation of Soviet domestic space into a site of visual pleasure and the decreasing amount of time spent with books brought about a social tendency in which books were purchased to fill in domestic space, to stand as interior objects, rather than to be read. Late Soviet intellectuals often dismissively and begrudgingly described this tendency as the purchase of books "to fit the color of the wallpaper," that is, as a sign of vanity.[47] Such dismissive statements misrecognized the fact that the possession and display of books at home was a necessary prerequisite for performing one's modern socialist identity. The underlying concerns of their statements were that many Soviet citizens increasingly denied the power of books to transform their selves and instead spent an increasing among of time in front of their TV screens. And as the Soviet television set became ordinary and domesticated, it entered into symbiotic relations not only with objects but also with people populating the homes where it was installed.

New Rhythms of Life

In its triumphant conquest of the Soviet home in the course of the 1960s and 1970s, the television set virtually chained its viewers in front of itself. Writing in 1962, the Soviet television critic Vladimir Sappak described this process: "The TV set was purchased, and immediately started behaving very aggressively. It occupied a notable place in our rather small apartment (it was allocated the best corner in the dining room), and very soon became the foundation of all aspects of our daily routine. We watched TV shows every night. All of them. Even boring ones . . . The fear to miss something 'really interesting,' or maybe even sensational, overwhelmed us. The magic of the 'free spectacle' had a full reign over us."[48]

This magnetism of the television set—its ability to keep people immovable in front of their TV screen—worked independently of its content, as Sappak somewhat bitterly noted. Its physical effects were also visible: the TV set became an active contributor to a new curse of late socialism: the sedentary lifestyle, which was dubbed hypodynamia by Soviet physicians. Since the late 1970s, in particular, they were increasingly worried that leisure time spent by people in front of the TV set led directly to cardiovascular disorders and extra body weight.[49] But the curse could also become a cure, and in the mid-1980s the Soviet television set became a witness to how some of its audiences, after having watched it rather immovably during the previous decades, stood up and started doing physical exercises in front of their TV screens. What enabled the Soviet TV set to animate its viewers was the introduction of exercise television shows.

In an article for a 1985 issue of the Soviet magazine *Televidenie i radioveshchanie* (Television and Radio Broadcast), Aleksandr Ivanitskii, the chief editor of the Sports Programs Bureau of the Soviet Central Television and Radio between 1973 and 1991, wrote that, beginning in 1981, his bureau had been working on new TV shows "aimed directly at improving the health of the audience." Initially, the focus was on propaganda for a healthy lifestyle through such programs as *Esli khochesh byt' zdorov* and *Stadion dlia vsekh* (A stadium for all).[50] In 1984, with the introduction of the new TV show *Ritmicheskaia gimnastika*, the Soviet television engaged its viewers in a more immediate and intimate way. The show was inspired by home videotapes of *Jane Fonda Workout*, a 1982 exercise video that popularized aerobics worldwide. The Sports Programs Bureau asked the Research Institute of the Physical Culture of the Russian Academy of Science to modify aerobics for Soviet television audiences; the name "aerobics" was also dropped as too Anglophone and instead a Russian neologism, "rhythmic gymnastics," was coined.[51] Between 1984 and 1991, thirteen episodes were filmed. Each of them was broadcast several times a week and stayed in rotation for at least several months, and sometimes for over a year.[52]

Both contemporary and later accounts claimed that the social effects of the new show were immense: it triggered an aerobics craze in the USSR among many Soviet women and transformed the TV set into a site of sexual desire for many Soviet men. This popular fascination with aerobics was addressed in Leonid Parfyonov's *Namedni* and a recent short documentary on Channel One Russia devoted to the thirty-year anniversary of *Ritmicheskaia gimnastika*. Both mentioned how a popular demand on everything related to this TV show catapulted unitards and legwarmers into women's sports fashion, led to the production of workout routines in newspapers and of vinyl records with its soundtracks, and kept the program among the most popular shows of Soviet television until the collapse of the USSR. At the same time, its hosts, clad in tight-fitting dresses and performing in a very uninhibited way under disco rhythms, looked dramatically different from the otherwise still purist Soviet television programming. It was only natural that the TV show was perceived in terms of visual pleasure: "Those who did not exercise gazed," and its most devoted male audiences were soldiers of the Soviet Army and prison inmates who watched it in an ostensibly voyeuristic manner.[53] There was also negative response: Ivanitskii mentioned that an early version of *Ritmicheskaia gimnastika*, which was tested at some point in the early 1980s, led to an avalanche of "letters, telegrams, and calls from furious pensioners";[54] and one of the hosts of *Ritmicheskaia gimnastika* quoted in an interview with me a letter that she received after her appearance in the TV show from a vigilant Soviet woman: "What can Natasha Efremova's bedroom positions and looks teach Soviet youth?"[55]

Both negative and positive reactions demonstrate that Soviet exercise TV shows became a manifestation of new female corporeality and sexuality. The omnipresent television set brought this corporeality into every Soviet apartment and made it a social phenomenon. Triggered by Western imagery of the exercising female body and introduced by Soviet enthusiasts of aerobics, the television set inscribed this imagery into many Soviet women's bodies by prompting them to stand up and exercise in front of their TV screens. The privileged position of the TV set in the Soviet home helped translate imagery into bodily practice. With television infrastructure networks permeating Soviet society, one no longer needed a gym to acquire a better body: fitness was delivered to the home, transforming Soviet apartments into fitness clubs. In the Soviet popular imagination of the late 1980s, the television set substituted for a fitness trainer and, for a short period in 1989, it also replaced the physician.

Paranormalists on TV

Anatoly Kashpirovsky's rise to national fame began in April 1988, when the popular TV show *Vzgliad* broadcast a teleconference between its studio in Moscow and a hospital in Kiev. The actual medical background is hardly possible to recover, but the storyline dealt with a patient allergic to anesthetics who had a breast tumor that had to be surgically removed.[56] Kashpirovsky managed to convince the patient, the medical staff, and the management of *Vzgliad* that he would successfully use his hypnotic abilities to provide remote psychic anesthetic through the TV screen. The operation took place on March 31, 1988, and several days later the multimillion-strong audience of the Soviet Channel I saw a middle-aged man with a commanding voice who put the woman into a trance from a distance of 800 kilometers by way of a small television set installed in the operation room. The surgery was reported as a success, done without medical anesthesia, and became a topic of discussion in major Soviet newspapers.[57] Following his newly acquired popularity, Kashpirovsky started organizing mass healing sessions in Kiev and Moscow. Later in 1988, he also appeared on Ukrainian TV in a series of five TV broadcasts which, he claimed, were designed to help children suffering from bedwetting.[58] In March 1989, Kashpirovsky was once again shown on Channel 1 delivering remote anesthesia from Kiev to two patients undergoing abdominal surgery in Tbilisi, a distance of over 2,000 kilometers. As with the previous case a year before, the TV coverage of this teleconference was shown nationwide and generated a huge interest in his alleged hypnotic and psychic abilities among the Soviet public.[59]

Kashpirovsky became a Soviet celebrity of the first order after his live session in the Ostankino Concert Hall, the heart of Soviet television, broadcast on July 27, 1989, and six subsequent healing séances broadcast biweekly on Sunday prime time from October 8 to December 16, 1989, all of them on Channel 1. Many other séances were broadcast by regional TV channels. His first healing séance, broadcast by Channel 1 on October 8, 1989, started with Kashpirovsky appearing in front of a huge auditorium in Ostankino and claiming that his "curing influence" starts its work on the bodies and minds of TV viewers from the first seconds of the program. He then read aloud excerpts from several letters from the viewers of his previous TV show that allegedly "evidenced the effectiveness of my TV healing":

> After your séance, the postdelivery umbilical hernia from which I suffered for twelve years has disappeared. I can now sleep without pills . . .
>
> I am undergoing treatment in front of the TV set. The twenty-eight-year-old scars on my chest have dissolved. Blood pressure is back to normal . . .
>
> I was holding my two-year son suffering from hemophilia in front of the TV set. Since then he hasn't had any bleeding, and it has already been two months. Is it possible that it is over? . . .

After your séance, a tumor the size of a three-kopeck coin in the breast of my fourteen-year-old daughter has dissolved. . .[60]

After reading the letters, Kashpirovsky asked the audience members to share their experiences of how his healing powers helped them. Several oncology patients claimed that they successfully substituted radiation and chemotherapy treatments with Kashpirovsky's séances, and some other audience members narrated stories of how his TV broadcasts successfully treated scars, tumors, obesity, cerebral palsy, hepatitis, postinfarction complications, amyotrophic sclerosis, and many other diseases. Letters and personal accounts emphasized that the distance from Moscow did not play any role in the effectiveness of TV treatment: success stories were coming from all over the USSR.

In the second part of the TV show, Kashpirovsky moved on to address the television audience. With the camera showing close-ups of his face and soothing music playing in the background, he commanded in a deep, assured voice:

I've been giving you a suggestion for healing from the very first second that we've been communicating . . . The effects will be only positive . . . Many of you feel that your arms are moving, are lifting [by themselves] . . . Some of you feel pleasant flows of heat in your body. It is blood circulating. Your blood pressure is becoming normal . . . Your body itself will find what needs to be destroyed, what it needs to get rid of.[61]

The show ended with Kashpirovsky counting to ten, suggesting that the TV audience "is feeling itself great" and then announcing the séance over, with his close-up view gradually dissolving into a nature scene of a mountain lake.

Kashpirovsky's appearance on the central Soviet TV channel, with its audience of over 200,000,000 people, was a social phenomenon on a national scale. Remnick spoke of Kashpirovsky's "cult of personality" and described packed concert halls and soccer stadiums with people desperately wishing to see their idol.[62] The Soviet press exploded with feature articles, op-ed pieces, and letters from readers addressing Kashpirovsky's spiritual powers.[63] In November 1989, the Institute of Philosophy of the Russian Academy of Sciences organized a public debate, titled "Telepsychotherapy: The Stretches of the Real," with prominent doctors, psychiatrists, philosophers, journalists, and Kashpirovsky, which served as a public forum to discuss the pros and cons of the popular ways of healing oneself in front of the TV screen. Most participants took the effects of Kashpirovsky's séances on Soviet TV audiences seriously but disagreed on whether they had more positive or negative influences.

Simultaneously with Kashpirovsky, another paranormalist appeared on Soviet television. In the spring of 1989, a popular TV show devoted to amateur engineering *Eto vy mozhete!* (You can do it!) broadcast a short healing séance held by Allan Chumak, a former journalist who claimed possession of a gift to manipulate alleged human bioenergy. Then, during the summer of 1989, his short séances were broadcast during the morning entertainment show *90 Minutes* from Monday to Saturday. Unlike Kashpirovsky, Chumak communicated with his television audiences only at the beginning of each episode, when he announced that he was going to transmit his healing energy through the television network to TV viewers and that this day's séance would focus on certain disease groups: different weekdays allegedly addressed cardiovascular deceases, locomotor impairments, gastric deceases, and some others. He then added that those viewers who wanted to benefit from his healing energy during the entire day could put jars and bottles with water or any other drink, as well as cosmetic creams, in front of their TV screens to charge them with curing properties. After this brief announcement, Chumak stayed silent for several minutes (a typical show lasted between eight and ten minutes), making mesmeric gestures that symbolized the transmission of his energy through the TV network. At the end of the séance, he reiterated that the fluids placed in front of the TV screen had become a universal remedy and could be applied externally or internally throughout the day.

The public reaction to Kashpirovsky's and Chumak's TV séances tended to gravitate either to acceptance, often on the brink of reverence, or to rejection that routinely took equally radical forms, such as the labeling of these TV shows and the popular practice of watching them as obscurantist. This divide had an explicitly social nature: my analysis of the followers and critics of the Soviet paranormalists shows that the two key factors that influenced (although did not determine rigidly) one's standpoint on TV healing were education and gender. Women dominated in their audiences, and a higher educational level made people more likely to dismiss the claims that Kashpirovsky or Chumak actually possessed paranormal power.[64] A typical critic of healing TV séances was an urban male intellectual; a typical adept was a middle-aged or senior woman without a university degree. As one—male and educated—Soviet journalist patronizingly described the opposing camp, "the audience of [Kashpirovsky's] séances is dominated by a certain type of woman: with agitated looks, rusty, fatty, of a hairdresser type [parikmakherskogo vida]."[65] The latter took for granted the claims of Soviet paranormalists that their TV shows were beneficial for bodily health; the former rang the alarm that these shows facilitated the physical and moral degeneration of Soviet society. What united them was the firm belief that TV séances influenced people's bodies and minds. At the Institute of Philosophy's conference in November 1989, Kashpirovsky mentioned that his home archive held 60,000 letters from those TV viewers who reported positive effects of his séances.[66] His opponents, in response, cited the statistics of emergency room visits, as did one Moscow doctor at the same conference:

> What happened after Kashpirovsky's séance? By nightfall, there was a sharp increase in the number of emergency room visitors. Most of the cases were difficult: pulmonary edemas, cardiac dysrhythmias, and hypertensive crises. The death rate triples during the days of his séances! In the following three days, the doctors of the [Moscow] Polyclinic No. 23 noted a sharp recrudescence of cardiovascular diseases. The psychoneurological dispensary had huge lines of patients with neuropsychic disturbances . . . Somebody has earlier said that it's everyone's own business whether to watch TV or not . . . It turned out that among adults, women with secondary-level education are most susceptible to teletherapy, . . . and I want to draw your attention to the fact that the most vulnerable group to this faith cure were children . . . [These TV séances] are damaging not only people's health, but also the ecology of our society's psychic life.[67]

The use of medical knowledge in this speech is openly politicized, as its author refers to "women with secondary-level education" and children as victims incapable of resisting Kashpirovsky's influence as transmitted through the TV signal. This vocabulary allows him to claim the authority to dismiss the question of whether "it's everyone's own business whether to watch TV or not," as rhetorical. Of course, it is not, since the television's power is dangerous for the national body. If left unchecked, it would damage the physical and mental health of the nation, represented by a conventional reference to women and children as powerless subjects needing protection.

From this perspective, the use of the concept "obscurantism" to refer to both Kashpirovsky and his audiences was highly politicized, since it aimed to discredit in the public discourse another form of power that threatened the monopoly of the Soviet educated class—or, more precisely, its male part—on defining the Soviet national body. After all, the use of this term was genealogically rooted in the feeling of shame for one's compatriots—an emotion that some authors expressed explicitly in the context of the popularity of these paranormal TV shows.[68] In this historical context, shame produced an identification effect similar to the one that Eve Sedgwick described in *Touching Feeling*: it disrupted one's conventional identity as a Soviet intellectual,

but immediately imposed another form of identification, that of a responsible member of the Soviet public body; in Sedgwick's own words shame
makes "the double movement . . . toward painful individuation, toward uncontrollable relationality."[69] For the predominantly male Soviet intelligentsia, the appearance of Kashpirovsky and Chumak on the Soviet television
screen brought into their homes an undesired unity with Soviet society. This
was not an ideal imagined and rational society regulated by productivist language or any other official discourse, but a society that performed other,
presumably irrational, individual and collective identities. This feeling fright-
ened them since this society refused to perform rational Soviet identities according to the values that Soviet intellectuals wanted to see as social norms.
Referring to their popularity as obscurantism was an emotional reaction to
regain distance from "the rest of society" that the presence of the TV set in
their homes threatened to violate. Muratov called television "a revolution in
the means of human communication" and "a shortcut between a man and
humanity."[70] The use of the term "obscurantism" was meant to block this
shortcut, to restore the autonomy of one's private space, and to hide the
"uncontrollable relationality" that the TV set provoked by virtue of its very
material presence in every Soviet home.

Let's look more closely at the opposite camp—those who sincerely believed in the curing effects of Soviet paranormalists' TV shows. Neither Soviet nor foreign medical scientists have confirmed any actual bodily effects
of these séances, although during debates with Kashpirovsky his opponents
referred to the medical statistics that allegedly demonstrated a higher rate
of emergency room visits after his séances, thus inadvertently and paradoxi-
cally crediting him with medical power—the one that damaged rather than
healed.[71] Yet Kashpirovsky and Chumak received thousands of enthusiastic
and grateful letters from their followers, some of which had been reproduced in print editions or read aloud during their broadcasts. In addition,
people gave their personal testimonies during live TV shows of Kashpirovsky
and later of TV shows of both healers. If we put aside conspiracy explanations that all this feedback was fabricated either by paranormalists themselves, or even by Soviet security services, the most reasonable explanation is
that claims of actual healing were a result of translation into medical terms
of some other forms of personal experience. These claims were not accurate
descriptions of one's medical conditions, but were themselves symptoms sig-
naling recognition of "the affective power of the television screen." While
each separate testimony can probably be explained by certain psychological
factors, their sheer mass, numbering in the tens of thousands, made them a
social phenomenon and an interesting historical source.

If these testimonies were a symptom, then what did they signal? The historical background of the Soviet paranormal TV shows suggests an answer. Perestroika provoked public debates about the nature of Soviet society and the socialist system, and television played a key role in transmitting these debates to Soviet homes through such TV programs as *600 sekund* (600 Seconds) and televised proceedings of the First USSR Congress of People's Deputies in the spring and summer of 1989. In doing so, Soviet mass media broadcast not only political pluralism and dissent opinions but also a growing sense of insecurity.[72] The promise of personal healing in the confinement of one's private space at the time when the Soviet national body was falling apart found resonance among Soviet audiences, as their letters to Chumak and Kashpirovsky show.

Iraklii Andronikov, a literature historian and public intellectual who was among the first Soviet scholars to give lectures on TV beginning in 1954, described the main difference between cinematography and television in terms of audience's performance: "What makes the TV set different from the movie screen? One wonderful feature . . . A spectator in a cinema is an observer of the film events. A TV viewer is a co-participant, or—to be more precise—a silent participant in the events. [The TV set] addresses him, converses with him, the television events happen in his house."[73]

Andronikov emphasizes the ability of the TV set to instigate performance among its audiences, to act as a force that brings its viewers into motion. In their positive or negative reaction alike, Soviet viewers recognized the power of the television to demand co-participation on behalf of the public. Writing thankful letters to Soviet paranormalists—as well as exposing one's body to the TV screen to receive their perceived healing power—were some of the forms of this performance. By engaging in them, Soviet viewers reflected their experience of living in a rapidly atomizing society, as well as inadvertently coparticipated in the discrediting of Soviet rationality as a historical product of techno-utopian visions of Soviet intellectuals.

The gloss of Kashpirovsky and Chumak was full of terms such as "psyche," "(bio)energy," "(psychic) influence," and "gift" referring to beliefs in the supernatural and the paranormal. In reality, the Kashpirovsky-Chumak phenomenon revealed a different, much more materialist power that was part of social change in the late Soviet Union: the power of the television set. It transformed Soviet domestic space and undermined its privacy by co-opting its viewers into various forms of performance that, despite its intimate character (watching TV at home), united them into a larger social entity.[74] In doing so, it problematized—in the historical perspective—Soviet cultural fantasies of total control over the material world, as it demonstrated the power of a material object to animate people in ways contrary to those that official discourses desired.

In Soviet culture, books and magazines have traditionally been the medium that sought to promote Promethean fantasies of the Soviet man transforming the material world around himself and becoming a better—enlightened and rational—Soviet subject in the process. Soviet discourse on reading always emphasized this self-transformational aspect of one's engagement with books. The written word endowed the Soviet educated class with the power to define Soviet norms and values. The television, by contrast, revealed an ability to organize its audience along different social structures and beliefs. In doing so, the television challenged the established cultural hierarchy in Soviet society and granted agency to people without a cultural voice—as a Soviet journalist dismissively characterized them to that "certain type of women: with agitated looks, rusty, fatty, of a hairdresser type." The cultural conflict around the Soviet television set, in general, and TV shows of Soviet psychics, in particular, followed the logic of class struggle over social power, with social distinctions imprinted in the people's bodies ("fatty, of a hairdresser type") as well as their material possessions.

It is hardly surprising, therefore, that the television set remains one of the most antagonistic objects in contemporary Russian society. The consolidation of control over TV channels by the current political establishment associated with President Vladimir Putin resulted in the widespread use of television propaganda to popularize official politics and discredit political opposition. As a result, in the critical public discourse of the 2000s and 2010s, regular viewing of television strongly associates with a lack of critical thinking. This logic was exemplified in a satiric cartoon produced by a Russian graphic designed, Andrei Barkov, in 2004 that became immediately popular in the Russian-language segment of the Internet. The cartoon (figure 6.1) shows three fatted pigs eating swill in front of a television set equipped with a surveillance camera. Meanwhile, a skinny piglet in a pilot helmet stands in the corner of the sty, looking at a poster of a Soviet streamlined fighter jet with eyes full of tears. The caption reads, "We used to know how to fly. We just forgot it . . . But we will remember . . . We will definitely remember."

Apart from obvious intertextual references to George Orwell's *Nineteen Eighty-Four* and *Animal Farm*, this cartoon illustrates many of the topics that I discussed in this book in regard to Soviet materiality. Objects of this image perform different, socially conflicting temporalities. A poster with a fighter jet acts as a mnemonic object conserving a memory of the national progress through technological innovation. In turn, a television set stands

FIGURE 6.1.   Andrei Barkov, "We used to know how to fly," 2004. Courtesy of Andrei Barkov.

for hedonistic depravity and promises no future for its audience. Body is another important category here: the little piglet looks ascetic, having left the base pleasures of life in front of a TV set to rise up to the challenge of Soviet technological grandeur; the three bigger pigs, overfed and with tiny thoughtless eyes, embody the corporeal and moral degradation that Soviet and post-Soviet intelligentsia often associated with watching too much TV. The MTV icon on the screen adds another—conspiratorial—twist to this image pointing at the alleged American influence lurking behind the moral and physical degradation of Russian society. By contrast, the Soviet technological heritage acts as a path to a social and cultural salvation. Overall, this image reflects the logic of social antagonism in the late Soviet and post-Soviet Russia. On one side of this conflict was a community of people united by the understanding of national history as technological progress and conquest of national space. In chapter 1, I discussed how Soviet techno-utopian discourse envisioned an ideal society organized around machines; it is a form of cultural imagination that the author of this image takes as normative, disregarding its specific social origins in cultural fantasies of Soviet technical intelligentsia. On another side is a community of people who are not interested in this grand techno-utopian historicity. Instead, they are fascinated with a television set that structures their social time cyclically, rather than linearly, with a focus on a bodily and visual pleasure rather than on asceticism that in Soviet and post-Soviet culture is associated with a pursuit of the communal good.[75] The logic of social conflict and struggle is materialized in and through bodies and objects.

The historical role of the television set in the Soviet and post-Soviet contexts thus included the undermining of the social power of large narratives by reorganizing personal time into cyclical, repetitive patterns structured by TV shows. At the same time, at least in some families, as my field observations in Russia showed, watching TV at home has become a performative act that creates an imaginary connection to the larger national body, especially during the periods of international crises such as the Russo-Georgian War of 2008 or the 2014 Ukrainian revolution. The form here is just as important as the content; to recall Muratov's quote, "A TV viewer is a co-participant, or—to be more precise—a silent participant in the events." One of the basic political distinctions in Russia these days is drawn over the question of whether to connect one's domestic space to the national television network, or to the World Wide Web with its numerous other imagined communities.

Conclusions

Soviet Objects and Socialist Modernity

The academic interest in materiality studies of the last three decades has been driven by two major factors. One is the epistemological potential offered by materiality-focused research on societies and cultures. In the introduction to this book, I discussed some of the approaches to the study of material objects and their social lives from the epistemological perspective. Many authors who offered new interpretations of materiality's role in social change also repeatedly emphasized that their research and writing have an explicit political agenda. In many cases, this political agenda is the leading force of the new materiality studies. Positioning themselves vis-à-vis the scholarship that accentuates the primary character of language and linguistic symbolism in humanities and social sciences, authors such as Michel de Certeau, Bill Brown, Daniel Miller, and Jane Bennet do not challenge the main arguments of this scholarship, namely, that language is helplessly "colonized" by power relations and meanings or that any writing has its own politics and organizes itself—often independently of its author's will—through ritualized and hence uncritically reproduced writings practices. By contrast, these arguments serve as their launch pad when they claim materiality is resistant to hegemonic power and has emancipatory political potential.[1] Materiality studies of the twenty-first century argue that politically and analytically dominant conceptualizations of matter and things as passive objects of human will are political acts structuring our understanding of the world as anthropocentric and encapsulating all those power practices that also serve as the basis of racism, chauvinism, and orientalism.[2] Only defamiliarization of the material world, the political effort to "make the stone *stony* . . . to make objects 'unfamiliar,' to make forms difficult" (in this respect, Russian Formalists sound astonishingly contemporary to the agenda of new materiality studies) can help lead to a more egalitarian and just society.[3]

My study of how Soviet objects and spaces substantiated individual and collective selves shows that the ability of things to materialize emotions, to objectify social understandings of the past and future, and to shape human bodies—in other words, their ability to act in a potentially subversive manner—was contested by the Soviet authorities and intellectual elite who sought to regulate, manipulate, and subordinate the vibrant lives of Soviet things. Yet the "elementalness" of matter, its unpredictability, and resistance provided innumerable obstacles in the pathway of the rational social transformation of the Soviet people. The materiality of Soviet objects such as stairwells, weightlifting equipment, or television sets created hybrid social creatures whose practices were influenced not only by ideology and language but also by things around them. As a result, Soviet artifacts had their politics. Since the late 1960s, official texts claimed that Soviet society had entered into developed socialism characterized by the absence of fundamental social contradictions, yet natural and man-made objects generated active public debates, provoked conflicts, mobilized communities, and helped produce a social and cultural diversity that challenged the social engineering efforts of Soviet authorities and intelligentsia.[4]

Symptomatically, this effort was based on the recognition of the power of things to structure and change Soviet society. Elemental materialism, as a part of the cultural logic of late socialism, supplied officials and intellectuals with persistent and routinely reproduced metaphors that assessed people through their mastery of professional equipment, consumption practices, and hobbies. It also influenced the social topography of late socialism, as it helped induce moral panics over the Soviet national body that could allegedly become corrupted by too intimate a contact with the materiality of such spaces as semilegal basement gyms or the virtual reality of the television set, but could also be healed through interaction with others at such locales as open-air museums of heritage architecture, Palaces of Young Pioneers, or public gyms and stadiums. Elemental materialism contributed to an important transformation of late Soviet society into a more inclusive social and political order through claims that such material objects and spaces as wooden churches and archaic northern landscapes were socialist by nature.

Elemental materialism reconciled within the discursive field of late socialism the Prometheanism of Genrikh Altshuller with the architectural preservationism of Aleksandr Opolovnikov, and the petrified plastic historicity of scale modeling with the voyeuristic space of basement bodybuilding gyms. The historical agency of socialist objects originated from the elementalness and spontaneity of materiality, its affectivity that appealed to Soviet people and forced them to change their bodies and selves, its innate ability to produce social effects that were not anticipated by the hegemonic discourse and forced it to react and adapt. Soviet materiality was instrumental in creating communities, performing new meanings, producing and objectifying certain regimes of knowledge.

It would be wrong to categorize these effects only in terms of hegemony and subversion. Studies of Soviet history have long been fascinated with these questions, especially when it comes to understanding and interpreting how Soviet people were produced as a distinct historical category. It has become a commonplace to argue that Soviet civilization shaped Soviet people, first of all by teaching them how to "speak Bolshevik." Yet as my analysis of various historical forms of interaction between Soviet people and materiality shows, this process was more complicated. Soviet objects and spaces interfered in the processes of subjectivation by suggesting forms of selfhood that fell out of the civilizing frameworks of the Soviet enlightenment project. When Soviet underground bodybuilders turned to weightlifting equipment to gain muscle weight, or when the members of the club Polar Odysseus searched White Sea villages for remnants of traditional boat designs, new hybrid bodies and identities were suggested by affective objects that called these people into social being as "men of iron" and the "last Pomors," respectively. In contrast to some of the claims made within the field of new materialism that attribute social agency directly to objects, my empirical sources suggest a different model of the relationship between the material and the social. Soviet materiality acquired its historical agency through the bodies of people who were fascinated with various material objects of late socialism and for whom these objects were instrumental in suggesting and objectifying their individual and collective selves.

A social history of Soviet objects and spaces is also important for our understanding of the Soviet Union in the global context, including one of the most interesting questions in Soviet history: What was the place of the USSR in the landscape of modernity? Was the Soviet Union a specifically, yet quintessentially modern state? Or did it represent a separate, socialist variant of modernity? Or has it ever been modern at all?[5] My study of Soviet materiality shows that many phenomena in late socialism were inspired, triggered, or caused by the transnational circulation of objects, ideas, and people. In the 1960s, when Georgi Tenno transplanted U.S. bodybuilding to Soviet soil, he sought to exploit the potential of weightlifting equipment to produce the modern Soviet body. In the 1970s and 1980s, Soviet suburban youth found this Western cultural product to be a useful technique to transform their bodies into weapons not only to survive with dignity compulsory service in the Soviet Army with its institutionalized abuse and harassment, but also to assert their class visions of what the proper Soviet collective body should look like. In doing so, they clashed with other, on average more educated social groups among Soviet youth whose lifestyles were inspired by other Western subcultures, such as hippies or punks.

Meanwhile, many Soviet women of the 1980s embraced the Soviet version of aerobics inspired by Jane Fonda's fitness videos and popularized by Soviet television. Soviet modelers mastered their hobby using plastic model sets designed in England. They also built collections that—in terms of ideology and politics—were barely distinguishable in their glorification of the national past from similar model collections constructed elsewhere in the Global North. Soviet architectural preservation enthusiasts looked at the Skansen Museum in Stockholm as an exemplary open-air museum and even called their discipline "skansenology." These and other phenomena of the late Soviet era—the popularity of yoga and karate or the search for the abominable snowman and UFOs—demonstrate that transnational communication between the Eastern and Western blocs was not homogeneous. Rather, it was rather structured along social categories, such as class, gender, and ethnicity. The concept of entangled modernities popularized by Göran Therborn is helpful for the understanding of late Soviet society. Yet we should add an important aspect to it: the divisions between modernities followed not only ideological, national and cultural but also social borders.[6] Age, gender, and class mattered in Soviet society as they did in Western Europe or North America, and transnational entanglements across the Iron Curtain demonstrate that different social groups had their own understandings and practices of what it meant to be modern. Objects encapsulated and communicated across national borders these different, class-based visions and practices. To speak of a separate Soviet modernity would mean to discard an immense diversity of social and cultural life in the USSR, and to imply that the essence of Russian history lies in its strong centralized system of government—something that often translates into the writing and teaching of Russian history as a history of its rulers.

From this perspective, a focus on objects and spaces in the Soviet context can help us make another significant conceptual move. A history of Soviet materiality provides an important intervention into the ways of writing and teaching Russian history that allows us to see otherwise invisible or obscure historical trends, social structures, and cultural meanings. Material objects of late socialism encapsulated different and often conflicting visions of the past, present, and future, structured the social landscape, and suggested various forms of navigating through it. Examining the ways they did so makes it possible to better understand Soviet society as a complex historical phenomenon that proved resistant to the persistent efforts of the Soviet political and cultural elites to transform it into a rationally organized, disciplined, and easily controllable community.

NOTES

Introduction. Elemental Materialism in Soviet Culture and Society

1. National Archive of Republic of Karelia (NARK), f. R-2359, op. 1, d. 2/14, l. 12.

2. Katerina Clark, *Moscow, the Fourth Rome: Stalinism, Cosmopolitanism, and the Evolution of Soviet Culture, 1931–1941* (Cambridge, MA: Harvard University Press, 2011), esp. 136–68.

3. NARK, f. R-690, op. 11, d. 514/2393, ll. 43–44.

4. NARK, f. P-3, op. 26, d. 140, l. 4.

5. Bill Brown, "Thing Theory," *Critical Inquiry* 28, no. 1 (October 1, 2001): 3.

6. Friedrich Engels, *Herr Eugen Dührings Umwälzung der Wissenschaft* (Zürich: Berlags-Magazin, 1886), 129.

7. Friedrich Engels, "Anti-Dühring. Dialectics of Nature," in Karl Marx and Friedrich Engels, *Collected Works* (New York: International Publishers, 1987), 25: 128.

8. Engels, "Anti-Dühring. Dialectics of Nature," 467.

9. M. I. Ananieva et al., *Dialekticheskii materializm* (Moscow: Mysl', 1989), 47.

10. Brown, "Thing Theory," 3.

11. Ernst Gombrich, *Art and Illusion: A Study in the Psychology of Pictorial Representation* (London: Phaidon Press, 1977), 96.

12. Judith Butler. *Excitable Speech: A Politics of the Performative* (New York: Routledge, 1997); Slavoj Žižek, *The Sublime Object of Ideology* (London: Verso, 2008); Oleg Kharkhordin, *The Collective and the Individual in Russia: A Study of Practices* (Berkeley: University of California Press, 1999); Igal Halfin, *Terror in My Soul: Communist Autobiographies on Trial* (Cambridge, MA: Harvard University Press, 2003); Jochen Hellbeck, *Revolution on My Mind: Writing a Diary under Stalin* (Cambridge, MA: Harvard University Press, 2006).

13. Bernward Joerges, "Technology in Everyday Life: Conceptual Queries," *Journal for the Theory of Social Behaviour* 18, no. 2 (1988): 220.

14. Bronislaw Malinowski, *Argonauts of the Western Pacific: An Account of Native Enterprise and Adventure in the Archipelagoes of Melanesian New Guinea* (LaVergne, TN: Malinowski Press, [1922] 2008); Igor Kopytoff, "The Cultural Biography of Things: Commoditization as Process," in *The Social Life of Things*, ed. Arjun Appadurai (Cambridge: Cambridge University Press, 1986), 64–91; Pierre Bourdieu, *Distinction: A Social Critique of the Judgement of Taste* (Cambridge, MA: Harvard University Press, 1984); Daniel Miller, *Material Culture and Mass Consumption, Social Archaeology* (Oxford: Blackwell, 1987); Bennett, *Vibrant Matter*; Diana H. Coole, and Samantha Frost, eds., *New Materialisms: Ontology, Agency, and Politics* (Durham: Duke University Press, 2010).

15. Tretiakov, "The Biography of the Object," 60.

16. Roland Barthes, "Death of the Author," in *Image, Music, Text*, trans. Stephen Heath (New York: Hill and Wang, 1977), 142–48.

17. Tretiakov, "The Biography of the Object," 61.

18. Tretiakov, "The Biography of the Object," 62.

19. This form of the cultural negotiation of gender is discussed in Serguei Oushakine, "'Chelovek roda on': Znaki otsutstviia," in *O muzhe(n)stvennosti*, ed. Serguei Oushakine (Moscow: NLO, 2002), 21–23.

20. Donald Raleigh, *Russia's Sputnik Generation: Soviet Baby Boomers Talk about Their Lives* (Bloomington: Indiana University Press, 2006); Alexei Yurchak, *Everything Was Forever, until It Was No More: The Last Soviet Generation* (Princeton, NJ: Princeton University Press, 2006); Vladislav Zubok, *Zhivago's Children: The Last Russian Intelligentsia* (Cambridge, MA: Harvard University Press, 2009).

21. Carlo Ginzburg, "Morelli, Freud and Sherlock Holmes: Clues and Scientific Method," trans. Anna Davin, *History Workshop*, no. 9 (April 1, 1980): 11.

22. On the Soviet avant-gardist debates about the relationship between things and representational techniques, see Serguei Oushakine, "'Ne vzletevshie samolety mechty': O pokolenii formal'nogo metoda," in *Formal'nyi metod: Antologiia russkogo modernizma*, ed. Serguei Oushakine (Moscow: Kabinetnyi uchenyi, 2016), 1:9–20.

23. Viktor Shklovsky, "Kuda shagaet Dziga Vertov?" in Oushakine, *Formal'nyi metod*, 247.

24. Marshall McLuhan, *Understanding Media: The Extensions of Man* (New York: McGraw-Hill, 1964). Oushakine makes this comparison in "'Ne vzletevshie samolety,'" 38.

25. Viktor Shklovsky, "Art as Technique," in *Russian Formalist Criticism: Four Essays*, ed. Lee T. Lemon and Marion J. Reis (Lincoln: University of Nebraska Press, 1965), 12.

26. Tretiakov, "The Biography of the Object," 62.

27. Bruno Latour and Stève Woolgar, *Laboratory Life: The Social Construction of Scientific Facts* (Princeton University Press, 1986); M. Norton Wise, "Mediating Machines," *Science in Context* 2 (1988), 77–113; Leora Auslander et al., "AHR Conversation: Historians and the Study of Material Culture," *American Historical Review* 114, no. 5 (December 1, 2009): 1355–404.

28. Victor Buchli, *An Archaeology of Socialism* (Oxford: Berg, 2000); Christina Kiaer, *Imagine No Possessions: The Socialist Objects of Russian Constructivism* (Cambridge: MIT Press, 2008); Emma Widdis, "Faktura: Depth and Surface in Early Soviet Set Design," *Studies in Russian and Soviet Cinema* 3, no. 1 (2009): 5–32; Brandon Schechter, *The Stuff of Soldiers: A History of the Red Army in World War II through Objects* (Ithaca, NY: Cornell University Press, 2019).

29. On consumption, see Susan E. Reid, "Cold War in the Kitchen: Gender and the De-Stalinization of Consumer Taste in the Soviet Union under Khrushchev," *Slavic Review* 61, no. 2 (2002): 211–52; Susan E. Reid, "Khrushchev Modern: Agency and Modernization in the Soviet Home," *Cahiers du monde russe* 47, no. 1/2 (2006): 227–68; Susan E. Reid, "Who Will Beat Whom? Soviet Popular Reception of the American National Exhibition in Moscow, 1959," *Kritika: Explorations in Russian and Eurasian History* 9, no. 4 (Fall 2008): 855–904; Lewis H Siegelbaum, *Cars for Comrades: The Life of the Soviet Automobile* (Ithaca, NY: Cornell University Press, 2008); Natalya Chernyshova, *Soviet Consumer Culture in the Brezhnev Era* (London: Routledge, 2013). On housing, see Lynne Attwood, *Gender and Housing in Soviet Russia:*

Private Life in a Public Space (Manchester: Manchester University Press, 2010); Mark B. Smith, *Property of Communists: The Urban Housing Program from Stalin to Khrushchev* (DeKalb: Northern Illinois University Press, 2010); Steven E. Harris, *Communism on Tomorrow Street: Mass Housing and Everyday Life after Stalin* (Washington, DC: Johns Hopkins University Press, 2013); Christine Varga-Harris, *Stories of House and Home: Soviet Apartment Life during the Khrushchev Years* (Ithaca, NY: Cornell University Press, 2015).

30. See, in particular, Natalya's Chernyshova exemplary work on late Soviet consumption: Chernyshova, *Soviet Consumer Culture*.

31. This understanding is based on Jacques Lacan, *The Four Fundamental Concepts of Psycho-Analysis*, ed. Jacques-Alain Miller, trans. Alan Sheridan (London: Hogarth Press, 1977); Louis Althusser, "Ideology and Ideological State Apparatuses (Notes towards an Investigation)," in *Lenin and Philosophy, and Other Essays* (New York: Monthly Review Press, 1971), 127–93; Michel Foucault, *Discipline and Punish: The Birth of the Prison* (New York: Pantheon Books, 1977).

32. Stephen Kotkin, *Magnetic Mountain: Stalinism as a Civilization* (Berkeley: University of California Press, 1995); Kharkhordin, *The Collective and the Individual in Russia*; Hellbeck, *Revolution on My Mind*; Halfin, *Terror in My Soul*; Igal Halfin, *Red Autobiographies: Initiating the Bolshevik Self* (Seattle: University of Washington Press, 2011); Yurchak, *Everything Was Forever*; Lilya Kaganovsky, *How the Soviet Man Was Unmade: Cultural Fantasy and Male Subjectivity Under Stalin* (Pittsburgh: University of Pittsburgh Press, 2008); Anatoly Pinsky, "The Diaristic Form and Subjectivity under Khrushchev," *Slavic Review* 73, no. 4 (December 1, 2014): 805–27; Emma Widdis, *Socialist Senses: Film, Feeling, and the Soviet Subject, 1917–1940* (Bloomington: Indiana University Press, 2017).

33. The works of Emma Widdis and Lilya Kaganovsky are two important exceptions, but both address the Stalinist period.

34. Yurchak, *Everything Was Forever*, 21–24, 295.

35. Viktor Shklovsky, "Zoo, ili Pis'ma ne o liubvi," in *Zhili-byli* (Moscow: Sovetskii pisatel', 1964), 130–31.

36. Karl Marx, *The Eighteenth Brumaire of Louis Bonaparte* (New York: International Publishers 1981).

Chapter 1. Techno-Utopian Visions of Soviet Intellectuals after Stalin

1. Mikhail Geller, *Mashina i vintiki: Istoriia formirovaniia sovetskogo cheloveka* (London: Overseas Publication Interchange, 1985); English translation: Mikhail Heller, *Cogs in the Wheel: The Formation of Soviet Man* (New York: Knopf, 1988).

2. Heller, *Cogs in the Wheel*, 259–61.

3. Heller, *Cogs in the Wheel*, 89. Heller's section on the Soviet language is introduced with the opening line from the Gospel of John (John 1:1): "In the beginning was the Word," which, coupled with his argument that Soviet leaders, in particular Vladimir Lenin, were the authors of the new Soviet language, adds to these demiurgic implications.

4. Jacques Derrida, "'To Do Justice to Freud': The History of Madness in the Age of Psychoanalysis," trans. Pascale-Anne Brault and Michael Naas, *Critical Inquiry* 20, no. 2 (January 1, 1994): 245. See also Eva Horn, *The Secret War: Treason, Espionage,*

and Modern Fiction, trans. Geoffrey Winthrop-Young (Evanston, IL: Northwestern University Press, 2013), 82–100.

5. Heller, *Cogs in the Wheel*, 6.

6. Leonid Brezhnev, "Otchetnyi doklad TsK KPSS XXIV s'ezdu KPSS," in *XXIV s'ezd Kommunisticheskoi partii Sovetskogo Soiuza. 30 marta–9 apr. 1971 g. Stenogr. otchet. V 2-kh t.* (Moscow: Politizdat, 1971), 1:114.

7. Lev Vygotsky's influence was notable throughout the entire Soviet period, both through his writings and the work of his former students such as Aleksei Leontiev, Alexander Luria, or Lidiia Bozhovich, who became prominent psychologists and theorists of education in the USSR. See Alex Kozulin, "The Concept of Activity in Soviet Psychology: Vygotsky, His Disciples and Critics," in *American Psychologist* 41, no. 3 (1986): 264–74.

8. Klara Shvartsman, *Etika . . . bez morali (kritika sovremennykh burzhuaznykh eticheskikh teorii)* (Moscow: Mysl', 1964); Vasilii Gromeka, *Nauchno-tekhnicheskaia revoliutsiia i sovremennyi kapitalizm* (Moscow: Politizdat, 1976).

9. On the language of socialist dissidents as the inverted official language, see Anna Wierzbicka, "Antitotalitarian Language in Poland: Some Mechanisms of Linguistic Self-Defense," *Language in Society* 19, no. 1 (March 1, 1990): 1–59; Oushakine, "The Terrifying Mimicry of Samizdat."

10. Heller, *Cogs in the Wheel*, 217.

11. Aleksei K. Gastev, *Kak nado rabotat'* (Moscow: Ekonomika, 1972), originally published in 1921; Alexander A. Bogdanov, *Vseobshchaia organizatsionnaia nauka (tektologiia)*, 2 vols. (Moscow: Ekonomika, 1989), originally published in 1922; Boris Arvatov, "Everyday Life and the Culture of the Thing (Toward the Formulation of the Question)," trans. Christina Kiaer, *October*, no. 81 (Summer 1997): 119–28. On Arvatov and other Soviet Productivist theorists and practitioners, see Christina Kiaer, *Imagine No Possessions: The Socialist Objects of Russian Constructivism* (Cambridge: MIT Press, 2008).

12. Dziga Vertov, "We: Variant of a Manifesto," in *Kino-Eye: The Writings of Dziga Vertov*, ed. Annette Michelson, trans. Kevin O'Brien (Berkeley: University of California Press, 1984), 8.

13. Louis Althusser, "Ideological State Apparatuses," in *Lenin and Philosophy, and Other Essays* (New York: Monthly Review Press, 1972), 163ff.

14. For an argument that the authoritative Soviet language became increasingly ritualized during the late socialist era, see Yurchak, *Everything Was Forever*, 21–28.

15. Alexei Kojevnikov, "Science as Co-Producer of Soviet Polity," *Historia Scientiarum* 22, no. 3 (2010): 167–68.

16. Nikita Khrushchev, "Otchetnyi doklad TsK KPSS XX s'ezdu partii," *XX s'ezd KPSS. 14–25 fevralia 1956 g. Stenograficheskii otchet* (Moscow: Politizdat, 1956), 34–36; Vladislav Zubok, *A Failed Empire: The Soviet Union in the Cold War from Stalin to Gorbachev* (Chapel Hill: University of North Carolina Press, 2007), 125–29.

17. This belief found a reflection in an impressive body of writing on the role of Soviet youth in the "scientific-technical revolution." For an annotated bibliography, see V. G. Bylov and I. G. Minervin, eds., *Molodezh i nauchno-tekhnicheskii progress* (Moscow: INION RAN, 1985). For a scholarly discussion of these beliefs, see Julian Cooper, "The Scientific and Technical Revolution in Soviet Theory," in *Technology and Communist Culture: The Socio-Cultural Impact of Technology under Socialism*, ed.

Frederic Fleron (New York: Praeger, 1977): 146–79; Harley Balzer, "Education, Science and Technology," in *The Soviet Union Today: An Interpretive Guide*, ed. James Cracraft (Chicago: University of Chicago Press, 1988), 233–43; Mark Lipovetsky, "Traektorii ITR-diskursa," *Neprikosnovennyi zapas*, no. 6 (2010): 213–30. Of course, this was not a uniquely Soviet feature. For the link between technical education and the visions of national development in other national contexts, see Gabrielle Hecht, *The Radiance of France: Nuclear Power and National Identity after World War II* (Cambridge: MIT Press, 1998), 23–26; Andrew Hartman, *Education and the Cold War: The Battle for the American School* (New York: Palgrave Macmillan, 2008).

18. For a cultural impact of the Soviet space program, see Eva Mauer et al., eds., *Soviet Space Culture: Cosmic Enthusiasm in Socialist Societies* (Basingstoke: Palgrave Macmillan), 2011; James T. Andrews and Asif A. Siddiqi, eds., *Into the Cosmos: Space Exploration and Soviet Culture* (Pittsburgh: University of Pittsburgh Press, 2011).

19. Alexey Golubev, "Affective Machines or the Inner Self? Drawing the Boundaries of the Female Body in the Socialist Romantic Imagination," *Canadian Slavonic Papers/Revue canadienne des slavistes* 58, no. 2: 141–59; Galina Orlova, "Fizikiadershchiki v bor'be za kosmos. Apokrif," *Vestnik PNIPU*, no. 2 (2018): 108–26.

20. Jessica Werneke, "The Boundaries of Art: Soviet Photography from 1956 to 1970" (PhD diss., University of Texas at Austin, 2015), 103–14.

21. Lev Sherstennikov, *Ostalis' za kadrom* (Moscow: Muzei organicheskoi kul'tury, 2013), 219–22.

22. "Moshchnyi otriad fotografov" (editorial), *Sovetskoe foto*, no. 1 (1957): 2. The discussion of photojournalism in *Sovetskoe foto* lasted throughout the entire launch year.

23. Dziga Vertov, "The Birth of Kino-Eye," in Vertov, *Kino-eye*, 41.

24. Yakov Gik, "Fotoreporter—eto zhurnalist," *Sovetskoe foto*, no. 1 (1957): 14.

25. L. Podvoiskii, "Chego ne videl fotoglaz na zavode," *Sovetskoe foto*, no. 2 (1957): 29.

26. "Sibir' v shestoi piatiletki," *Ogoniok*, no. 29 (1956): 2.

27. See, for example, V. Chilizubov, "Pust' s mashinoi podruzhit kazhdyi," *Agitator*, no. 6 (1963): 134–35; N. Aleksentseva, "Distsiplina—litso kollektiva," *Agitator*, no. 5 (1980): 6–8.

28. B. Soskin, "Doroga v zhizn'," *Smena*, no. 13 (1956): 15.

29. Yurii Stoliarov, "Kosmos v rebiachih glazakh," *Modelist-Konstruktor* 7 (1978): 2.

30. Ilya Kukulin, "Prodistsiplinarnye i antidistsiplinarnye seti v pozdnesovetskom obshchestve," *Sotsiologicheskoe obozrenie* 16, no. 3 (2017): 152–57.

31. V. I. Lenin, *Polnoe sobranie sochinenii* (Moscow: Politizdat, 1962), 35:57. See examples of such writing in the 1970s and early 1980s: D. M. Aptekman, *Formirovaniie ateisticheskoi ubezhdennosti rabochego klassa v razvitom sotsialiticheskom obshchestve* (Leningrad: Izd-vo LGU, 1979), esp. 27; T. I. Snegiriova, *Dukhovnaia kul'tura razvitogo sotsialisticheskogo obshchestva* (Moscow: Nauka, 1981), esp. 125–27.

32. Anna Paretskaya, "A Middle Class without Capitalism? Socialist Ideology and Post-Collectivist Discourse in the Late-Soviet Era," in *Soviet Society in the Era of Late Socialism, 1964–1985*, ed. Neringa Klumbyté and Gulnaz Sharafutdinova (New York: Lexington Books, 2013), 46–50.

33. "Uchit' tvorchestvu!," *Modelist-Konstruktor*, no. 1 (1978): 1–3, 25; Iu. Gerbov, "Pokoleniie tvortsov i iskatelei," *Modelist-Konstruktor*, no. 10 (1982): 3–4, 32; D. Filippov, "V edinom stroiu," *Tekhnika—Molodezhi*, no. 11 (1977): 2.

34. Prometheus was an important symbol of the official Soviet culture and ideology. For example, a youth-oriented Soviet publisher Molodaia Gvardiia published under this title, starting since 1966, an almanac with biographies of famous (at least in the Soviet system of coordinates) people.

35. Genrikh Altshuller and Igor Vertkin, *Kak stat' geniem: Zhiznennaia strategiia tvorcheskoi lichnosti* (Minsk: Belarus, 1994), 10–18; Genrikh Altshuller, *TRIZ Keys to Technical Innovation*, trans. and ed. Lev Shulyak and Steven Rodman (Worcester, MA: Technical Innovation Center, 2002), 11–13.

36. Inna Lisnianskaia, "Khvastun'ia," *Znamia*, no. 1 (2006): 18–19.

37. Zinaida Vasilyeva, "Soobshchestvo TRIZ: Logika i etika sovetskogo izobretatelia," *Etnograficheskoe obozrenie*, no. 3 (2012): 29–46.

38. Genrikh S. Altshuller, *Algoritm izobreteniia* (Moscow: Moskovskii rabochii, 1973); Genrikh S. Altshuller and Aleksandr B. Seliutskii, *Kryl'ia dlia Ikara: Kak reshat' izobretatel'skie zadachi* (Petrozavodsk: Kareliia, 1980); Genrikh S. Altshuller, *Naiti ideiu* (Novosibirsk: Nauka, 1986).

39. Altshuller, *Naiti ideiiu*, 185.

40. "Pismo G. Altova ANu, 21 aprelia 1964," in., *Neizvestnyie Strugatskie. Pis'ma. Rabochiie dnevniki. 1963–1966 gg.*, ed. Svetlana Bondarenko and Viktor Kurilskii (Moscow: AST, 2009), 170–71.

41. Aleksandr Seliutskii, *Derzkiie formuly tvorchestva* (Petrozavodsk: Karelia, 1987), 175.

42. Genrikh Altshuller, "Food for thought," a memo to TRIZ schools, July 25, 1981, in Chelyabinsk Regional Universal Scientific Library, collection "Fond materialov po TRIZ," file A58 R2059, 1–4; Interview with Alexander Seliutskii and Alla Nesterenko. Interviewer: Aleksandr Osipov. Petrozavodsk, July 15, 2016.

43. "How to teach TRIZ (1985 edition)," in Chelyabinsk Regional Universal Scientific Library, collection "Fond materialov po TRIZ," file 3, 5; B. Zlotin and A. Zusman, *Mesiats pod zvezdami fantazii* (Kishinev: Lumina, 1988), 48.

44. NARK, f. R-3665, op. 1, d. 9/154, ll. 4–6. See also Vasilyeva, "Soobshchestvo TRIZ," 34.

45. On the Constructivist notion of the "friendly things," see Kiaer, *Imagine No Possessions*.

46. Altshuller, *Naiti ideiiu*, 173–85; Altshuller and Viortkin, *Kak stat' geniem*.

47. Altshuller and Seliutskii, *Kryl'ia dlia Ikara*, 3.

48. NARK, f. R-3665, op. 1, d. 9/154, l. 5.

49. Genrikh Altshuller, "Recommendations of how to teach TRIZ classes in the 1976–77 academic year" (a typewritten manuscript), Chelyabinsk Regional Universal Scientific Library, collection "Fond materialov po TRIZ," file 5, 2.

50. NARK, f. R-3665, op. 1, d. 9/154, l. 1.

51. Aleksandr B. Seliutskii, ed., *Pravila igry bez pravil* (Petrozavodsk: Karelia, 1989), 3–6; Yuri Dral', "Rezul'taty obiazatel'no budut," *Narodnoe obrazovanie*, no. 3 (1990): 45–49; Leonid Shub, "Fantaziia v upriazhke ili dialektika dlia vzroslykh (O razvitii tvorcheskogo voobrazheniia doshkol'nikov)," *Detskaia literatura*, no. 4 (1991): 48–50.

52. See, for example, the website of the Russian TRIZ Association: http://ratriz. ru. One of its sections targets a teenage audience with the following slogan: "Do you want to be lucky in life? Do you want to learn how to solve any problem? Do you

want to be an interesting person for your friends? Do you want to study easily and pleasantly? Then learn TRIZ!"

53. *Modelist-Konstruktor*, no. 1 (1966), back side of the front cover.

54. Z. Fomina (dir.), *Novosti dnia / Khronika nashikh dnei*, no. 45 (Studiia documental'nykh fil'mov, 1966); "Molodost plius umenia," *Za rulem*, no. 12 (1967): 17–18; V. Demchenko, "Marsh-parad v 3000 kilometrov," *Za rulem*, no. 2 (1972): 18; O. Iaremenko, "Serioznyie samodelki," *Za rulem*, no. 12 (1982): 12–13.

55. K. N. Kurdenkov, *Suda: Stroim sami* (Moscow: Sudostroieniie, 1964); B. S. Ivanov, *Elektronika svoimi rukami* (Moscow: Molodaia gvardiia, 1964); V. M. Gesler, *Avtomobil svoimi rukami* (Moscow: DOSAAF, 1970); G. M. Novak, *Katera, lodki i motory v voprosakh i otvetakh: Spravochnik* (Moscow: Sudostroienie, 1977).

56. "Valga-Kombi: Avtomobil iz fanery," *Modelist-Konstruktor*, no. 8 (1980): 4–8 and a color inlet between 8 and 9; "Pokhodnaia elektrostantsiia," *IuT dlia umelykh ruk*, no. 3 (1980): 1.

57. The Soviet comedy film *Ivan Vasil'evich meniaet professiiu* (Ivan Vasilyevich Changes Profession [1973]) involves a time machine made by an amateur engineer in his apartment from basic radio components.

58. "K chitateliam," *Katera i yakhty*, no. 1 (1963): 3.

59. Timo Vihavainen, *The Inner Adversary: The Struggle against Philistinism as the Moral Mission of the Russian Intelligentsia* (Washington, DC: New Academia, 2006).

60. R. Nudelman, "Voobrazheniie po pravilam," *Iunyi tekhnik*, no. 1 (1968): 58–59; D. Bilenkin, "Voobrazheniie—sila," *Iunyi tekhnik*, no. 6 (1977): 78–80.

61. Iu. S. Stoliarov, B. P. Iusov, and V. I. Leibson, "Child Creativity," in *The Great Soviet Encyclopedia* (New York: Macmillan, 1975), 8: 19–22.

62. Iu. S. Stoliarov, *Iunye konstruktory i tekhnicheskoe tvorchestvo* (Moscow: Izd-vo DOSAAF, 1966), 36.

63. Stoliarov, *Iunye konstruktory*, 37–61.

64. Boris Groys, *The Total Art of Stalinism* (London: Verso, 2011), 21–22; Evgeny Steiner, *Stories for Little Comrades: Revolutionary Artists and the Making of Early Soviet Children's Books* (Seattle: University of Washington Press, 1999), 97.

65. Although Soviet women's magazines focused on domestic space and the female body, their discourse with its infinitely repeating advice on how to reuse or remake old things brought the same connotations: the idealized Soviet subject through do-it-yourself practices had to perform mastery over the material world. In other words, their relationship to materiality was framed in similar fantasies of total control over it. See Alexey Golubev and Olga Smolyak, "Making Selves through Making Things: Soviet Do-It-Yourself Culture and Practices of Late Soviet Subjectivation," *Cahiers du monde russe* 54, no. 3–4 (July–December 2013): 517–41.

66. Golubev and Smolyak, "Making Selves through Making Things," 526–33.

67. Katerina Clark, *The Soviet Novel: History as Ritual* (Bloomington: Indiana University Press, 2000), 100–41, 225; Emma Widdis, *Visions of a New Land: Soviet Film from the Revolution to the Second World War* (New Haven: Yale University Press, 2003); John McCannon, "Tabula Rasa in the North: The Soviet Arctic and Mythic Landscapes in Stalinist Popular Culture," in *The Landscape of Stalinism: The Art and Ideology of Soviet Space*, ed. Evgeny Dobrenko, Eric Naiman (Seattle: University of Washington Press, 2005), 241–60; Lilya Kaganovsky, *How the Soviet Man Was Unmade: Cultural Fantasy and Male Subjectivity under Stalin* (Pittsburgh: University of Pittsburgh Press, 2008), 111–18.

68. "Avtofestival-82," *Modelist-Konstruktor*, no. 12 (1982), inlet between 16 and 17; "V nebe Tushino—SLA," *Modelist-Konstruktor*, nos. 3, 4, 5 (1988).

69. *Katera i yakhty*, no. 2 (1975): 30; V. Kondratiev "Idei novye, problemy starye," *Modelist-Konstruktor*, no. 2 (1990): 3.

70. Lewis H. Siegelbaum, *Cars for Comrades: The Life of the Soviet Automobile* (Ithaca, NY: Cornell University Press, 2008), 244.

71. Vasilii Zakharchenko, "Molodoe dykhaniie veka," *Nauka i zhizn'*, no. 5 (1978): 79.

72. See, e.g., Michel Foucault, *The History of Sexuality. Vol.1: An Introduction* (New York: Vintage Books, 1976), esp. the part "Scientia Sexualis," 53–73.

73. Readers of Soviet technical magazines were also offered to conquer the outer space, although in an indirect manner: by observing the night sky, playing space-related games, or constructing replicas of spaceships, both existing and from the imagined future. See *Modelist-Konstructor*, no. 10 (1973): 30–31, 41; *Modelist-Konstructor*, no. 4 (1974): 46; *Modelist-Konstructor*, no. 7 (1974): 18–19.

74. On the role of travel in the transformation of nature into a landscape, see Christof Mauch and Thomas Zeller, eds., *The World beyond the Windshield: Roads and Landscapes in the United States and Europe* (Athens: Ohio University Press, 2008), esp. "Introduction" by Christof Mauch and Thomas Zeller, 1–13.

75. Peter Kenez, *Cinema and Soviet Society, 1917–1953* (Cambridge: Cambridge University Press, 1992), 157.

76. See, e.g., V. Kopyev, "Paradoksy uspekha," *Tekhnika—Molodezhi*, no. 5 (1989): 2–4.

77. For the articles and forum threads related to a popular myth that the Japanese and South Korean technological advances were based on solutions from *Modelist-Konstruktor* and other Soviet technical journals, see K. Moldavskaia, "Dobit' rossiiskuiu nauku?" *Newsland*, http://www.newsland.ru/news/detail/id/530110/; "Subaru Outback 2008," Drom.ru, http://news.drom.ru/Subaru-Outback-2008-9338.html; "Copy/Paste po-sovetski," Noname.ru, http://aligency.ru/blogs/NoNaMe-Y/copy-paste-po-sovetski/page8/.

78. A comment by a user Rumato to the article by Ievgeniia Shtefan, "Iaponiia gotova mirno dogovoritsia s RF to Kurilam," *Newsland*, September 24, 2009, http://www.newsland.ru/news/detail/id/414574.

79. Genrikh Altshuller et al., *Teoriia i praktika resheniia izobretatel'skikh zadach* (Kishinev: Vsesoiuznyi institut TRIZ, 1989), 56.

80. Interview with Alexander Seliutskii and Alla Nesterenko by Aleksandr Osipov. Petrozavodsk, July 15, 2016.

81. Shklovsky, "Zoo, ili Pisma ne o liubvi," 130–31.

82. Aleksei Tarasov, "Inzhener ne dolzhen presmykatsia pered finansistom," *Novaya gazeta*, October 7, 2009, http://www.novayagazeta.ru/politics/43216.html.

83. Yulia Latynina, "Kod dostupa," *Ekho Moskvy*, broadcast on June 19, 2010, a transcript http://echo.msk.ru/programs/code/688747-echo/.

Chapter 2. Time in 1:72 Scale

1. M. B. Koval, "Stanovleniie i razvitie sistemy vospitatel'noi deiatel'nosti vneshkol'nykh ob'iedinenii" (Doctor of Sciences in Education diss., Moscow, 1991); M. A. Zaitseva, "K voprosu o roli uchrezhdenii vneshkol'noi raboty v vospitanii

sotsial'noi aktivnosti starsheklassnikov v 50–80-e gg. XX veka," *Yaroslavskii pedagogicheskii vestnik* 1 (2009): 90–94.

2. A. A. Romanov and A. I. Shuvalov, "Genezis klubno-kruzhkovoi raboty v pedagogicheskoi praktike Rossii," *Psikhologo-pedagogicheskii poisk* 1 (2007): 117.

3. *Itogi Vsesoiuznoi perepisi naseleniia 1989 goda. Tom 2. Vozrast i sostoianiie v brake. Chast' 1* (Minneapolis: East View Publications, 1992), 11.

4. Ye. N. Medynskii, *Vneshkol'noe obrazovanie, ego znachenie, organizatsiia i tekhnika*, 4th ed. (Moscow: Nauka, [1913]1918). See esp. chap. 1 on the general importance of extracurricular education and chap. 13 on museums and technical exhibitions.

5. For the discussion of the propaganda of aviation in the early USSR, see Scott W. Palmer, *Dictatorship of the Air: Aviation Culture and the Fate of Modern Russia* (Cambridge: Cambridge University Press, 2006), 103–24. Lev Kassil and Maks Polianovskii's *Ulitsa mladshego syna* (The street of the younger son) (awarded the State Stalin Prize of the 3rd Degree in 1950) explicitly linked its protagonist's hobby activities in aircraft modeling and his wartime heroism: Lev Kassil and Maks Polianovskii, *Ulitsa mladshego syna* (Moscow: Detskaia literatura, 1949).

6. The specialized journal *Politekhnicheskoe obuchenie* (Polytechnic education) was established in 1957 and renamed *Shkola i proizvodstvo* (School and industry) in 1960. Yuri Stoliarov, whose pedagogical theory I discussed in chapter 1, was its regular contributor.

7. In Vitalii Melentiev's futurist *33 marta. 2005 god* (March 33rd, 2005) (Moscow: Gos. izd-vo det. lit-ry, 1957), Soviet high school students from 2005 operate advanced agricultural equipment, and in Kir Bulychev's series of novels, the protagonist, a teenage girl from the communist Earth of the late twenty-first century, works on cutting-edge scientific experiments. Kir Bulychev, *Sto let tomu vpered* (Moscow: Det. lit-ra, 1978).

8. "V nogu so vremenem," *Modelist-Konstruktor* 3 (1988): 2–3; "Fakel gorit . . . no kakim plamenem?," *Tekhnika—Molodezhi*, no. 3 (1990): 2–3; A. M. Koshev, *Istoriia i problemy kul'turno-tekhnicheskogo razvitiia rabochikh kadrov narodov Severnogo Kavkaza v 60-e—nachale 80-kh godov* (Maikop: [n.p.], 1994), 91.

9. N. Bulatov, "Sozdaniie detskikh tekhnicheskikh stantsii," in *Smena komsomola: Dokumenty, vospominaniia, materiialy po istorii VPO (1917–1962 gg.)*, ed. V. Iakovlev (Moscow: Molodaia gvardiia, 1964), 134–35.

10. V. Bezrodnyi, "Imia emu—pedagog," *Modelist-Konstruktor*, no. 3 (1970): 7.

11. Vladimir Gurin, "Tvorcheskii trud kak sredstvo formirovaniia nravstvennogo soznaniia i povedeniia starsheklassnikov," *Sovetskaia Pedagogika*, no. 7 (1980): 54.

12. Gabrielle Hecht, "Introduction," in *Entangled Geographies: Empires and Technopolitics in the Global Cold War*, ed. Gabrielle Hecht (Cambridge: MIT Press, 2011), 3. For a more detailed discussion of technopolitics as a strategic usage of technologies to reach certain political goals, see Hecht, *The Radiance of France*, 15–17.

13. N. Babaev and S. Kudriavtsev, *Letaiushchiie igrushki i modeli* (Moscow: Oborongiz, 1946).

14. David Brandenberger and Kevin M. F. Platt, "Introduction: Tsarist-Era Heroes in Stalinist Mass Culture and Propaganda," in *Epic Revisionism: Russian History and Literature as Stalinist Propaganda*, ed. Kevin M. F. Platt and David Brandenberger (Madison: University of Wisconsin Press, 2006), 3–16; David Brandenberger, *National*

Bolshevism: Stalinist Mass Culture and the Formation of Modern Russian National Identity, 1931–1956 (Cambridge: Harvard University Press, 2002).

15. Richard Stites, "Soviet Russian Wartime Culture: Freedom and Control, Spontaneity and Consciousness," in *The People's War: Responses to World War II in the Soviet Union*, ed. Robert W. Thurston and Bernd Bonwetsch (Urbana: University of Illinois Press, 2000), 171–86.

16. It was not much different in this respect from other modern cultures of the Global North: see Michael Adas, *Machines as the Measure of Men: Science, Technology, and Ideologies of Western Dominance* (Ithaca, NY: Cornell University Press, 1989).

17. Industrially produced scale model kits appeared with the introduction of plastic injection technologies in model making in the mid-1930s and, after World War II, enjoyed steady growth; prior to this all models were custom built. See Brett Green, *Modelling Scale Aircraft* (Oxford: Osprey, 2012), 4–6.

18. A. Tarasenko, "Relikviia trudovogo podviga," *Modelist-Konstruktor*, no. 5 (1969): 4.

19. NARK, f. R-2323, op. 1, d. 63a, l. 27–28; d. 162, l. 74.

20. Richard Lines and Leif Hellström, *Frog Model Aircraft, 1932–1976: The Complete History of the Flying Aircraft & the Plastic Kits* (London: New Cavendish, 1989), 126–27, 195–97, 206–9; Sergey Svinkov, "Neizvestnaia Novo," *M-Hobbi*, no. 4 (1995): 44–46.

21. Until the summer of 2018, Russian enthusiasts of the USSR-produced ex-Frog scale models maintained an online encyclopedia Novokits.Ru which provides detailed information on all models purchased by the Soviet Union from Frog and their production and marketing in the USSR: http://www.novokits.ru/.

22. The kit is identical to the kit in figure 2.1.

23. This was a tendency rather than a strict rule. Both Spitfires and Hurricanes, for example, were supplied to the USSR under the lend-lease agreement, but their models were produced anonymously. By contrast, the Avro Lancaster, which was not imported to the USSR, was sold under its own name.

24. An excerpt from the *Daily Telegraph*, April 13, 1985, reproduced in Lines and Hellström, *Frog Model Aircraft*, 135.

25. Letter from Oleg Kasatkin to the author, September 9, 2014.

26. Sergey Luchininov, *Iunyi korablestroitel'* (Moscow: Molodaia gvardiia, 1955), 4.

27. Sergei Malik, "Bol'shoi smotr aviamodelizma," *Modelist-Konstruktor*, no. 1 (1975): 47.

28. Luchininov, *Iunyi korablestroitel'*, 4. The author refers to the Russian circumnavigation of 1819–21, the participants of which were among the first explorers to sight the ice shelf of Antarctica; this sighting was framed in terms of the "discovery" of the Antarctic continent by later Russian and Soviet historians.

29. Luchinov, *Iunyi korablestroitel'*, 7–47; I. A. Maksimikhin, *Kak postriot' model' korablia: Posobiie dlia uchashchikhsia* (Leningrad: Gosuchpedgiz, 1956), 5–16; A. I. Dremliuga and L. P. Dubinina, *Iunomu sudomodelistu* (Kiev: Radianska shkola, 1983), 3–9, 21–37.

30. My discussion of the fetishism of detail in modeling hobby is inspired by the debates about the fetishization of facts and documents in the discipline of history, such as: Edward H. Carr, *What Is History?* (London: Palgrave Macmillan, 2001); Alun Munslow, *Deconstructing History* (London: Routledge, 2006).

31. Oleg Lagutin, *Samolet na stole* (Moscow: Izd-vo DOSAAF SSSR, 1988), 5.

32. NARK, f. R-2323, op. 1, d. 63a, l. 68–69; d. 126, l. 75, 87.

33. A. M. Pankratova, ed., *Istoriia SSSR: Uchebnik dlia 10 klassa srednei shkoly* (Moscow: Uchpedgiz, 1952), 138–74; S. A. Seraev, ed., *Istoriia SSSR: Epokha sotsializma* (Moscow: Prosveshcheniie, 1973), 11–13, 32–35; A. P. Averianov et al., *Novaia istoriia, 1871–1917: Uchebnik dlia 9 klassa srednei shkoly* (Moscow: Prosveshcheniie, 1987), 228.

34. NARK, f. R-2323, op. 1, d. 162, l. 74.

35. Luchinov, *Iunyi korablestroitel'*, 7; Dremliuga and Dubinina, *Iunomu sudomodelistu*, 21.

36. V. N. Krasnov, "Sudostroienie i morekhodstvo v dopetrovskoi Rusi," in *Institut istorii estestvoznaniia i tekhniki im. S. I. Vavilova. Godichnaia nauchnaia konferentsiia. 2010*, ed. Yu.M. Baturin et al. (Moscow: Ianus-K, 2010), 482.

37. Krasnov, "Sudostroienie i morekhodstvo."

38. Ethan Pollock, *Stalin and the Soviet Science Wars* (Princeton, NJ: Princeton University Press, 2006), 7; Palmer, *Dictatorship of the Air*, 32–36.

39. NARK, f. R-2323, op. 1, d. 162, l. 86.

40. See, e.g., R. M. Melnikov, *Kreiser Variag* (Leningrad: Sudostroenie, 1983).

41. Compare with Gabrielle Hecht's discussion of the historical discourse produced by French technocrats: Hecht, *The Radiance of France*, 21–22.

42. Walter Benjamin, *The Arcades Project* (Cambridge, MA: Belknap Press, 1999), 204–5. See also Susan Stewart, *On Longing: Narratives of the Miniature, the Gigantic, the Souvenir, the Collection* (Durham, NC: Duke University Press, 1993), 151–66; James Clifford, *The Predicament of Culture: Twentieth-Century Ethnography, Literature, and Art* (Cambridge: Harvard University Press, 1988), 215–51; Susan Pearce, ed., *Interpreting Objects and Collections* (London: Routledge, 1994); Kevin M. Moist and David C. Banash, *Contemporary Collecting: Objects, Practices, and the Fate of Things* (Lanham, MD: Scarecrow Press, 2013).

43. See the discussion of late Soviet-era personal experiences in collecting scale models: "Kto kak nachinal: Istoriia hobbi," Diarama.ru, http://www.diorama.ru/forum/viewtopic.php?t=4220.

44. Interview with Igor Zhmurin, Petrozavodsk, June 27, 014, author's personal archive; letter from Oleg Kasatkin to the author, October 25, 2014; letter from Andrei Krumkach to the author, October 28, 2014.

45. NARK, f. R-2323, op. 1, d. 63a, l. 28; "Zapishite moi adres," *Modelist-Konstruktor*, no. 6 (1969): 13.

46. Letter from Oleg Kasatkin to the author, October 25, 2014; letter from Andrei Krumkach to the author, October 28, 2014.

47. For examples of such classified, see *Modelist-Konstruktor*, no. 6 (1969): 13; *Modelist-Konstruktor*, no. 2 (1970): 19, 27; *Modelist-Konstruktor*, no. 2 (1973): 32.

48. S. Pavlov, "Uvlechenie na vsiu zhizn'," *Kryl'ia rodiny*, no. 12 (1970): 26.

49. Jean Baudrillard, *The System of Objects* (London: Verso, 1996), 87–89; Stewart, *On Longing*, 161–63.

50. The author refers to an electric motor built in 1834 by Moritz von Jacobi, a German physicist and engineer, in Königsberg. Von Jacobi was later employed by the Russian Academy of Sciences, while Königsberg became Kaliningrad after 1945, which gave Soviet historians of science and technology a justification to regard this invention as belonging to the history of Russia.

51. *Modelist-Konstruktor*, no. 1 (1989): 2.

52. Jean Baudrillard argues that this is typical for any collectible object: "This is why owning absolutely any object is always so satisfying and so disappointing at the same time: a whole series lies behind any single object, and makes it into a source of anxiety." Baudrillard, *The System of Objects*, 86.

53. Susan M. Pearce, "Objects as Meaning; or Narrating the Past," in *Interpreting Objects and Collections*, 19–29.

54. Interview with Igor Zhmurin, Petrozavodsk, June 7, 2014; "Kto kak nachinal."

55. Baudrillard, *The System of Objects*, 86.

56. Baudrillard, *The System of Objects*.

57. Tony Bennett, "The Exhibitionary Complex," *New Formations* 4 (Spring 1988): 96.

58. Mark Kabakov, "Put' na moria," in *Radi zhizni na zemle*, ed. Viktor Oliinik (Moscow: DOSAAF, 1988), 433.

59. Clifford, *The Predicament of Culture*, 218.

60. *Modelist-Konstruktor*, no. 7 (1981): back cover.

61. Clifford, *The Predicament of Culture*, 218–19.

62. "Editorial," *M-Hobbi*, no. 3 (1996): 1.

63. Slavoj Žižek, *The Sublime Object of Ideology* (London: Verso, 2008), 34.

64. A. M. Sevastianov, *Volshebstvo modelei: Posobie dlia sudomodelistov* (Nizhny Novgorod: Nizhpoligraf, 1997); Nikolai Polikarpov, *Model'nye khitrosti: Posobie dlia modelistov* (Moscow: Tseikhgauz, 2006).

65. Aleksandr Leontovich and Boris Rudenko, "Vozrozhdenie NTTM prikhodit v shkolu," *Nauka i zhizn'*, no. 6 (2004): 40–41; Boris Rudenko, "Krug chistoi vody," *Nauka i zhizn'*, no. 10 (2006): 49–51.

Chapter 3. History in Wood

1. Victor Buchli, *An Archaeology of Socialism* (Oxford: Berg, 2000), 64–76.

2. On the regulation of architectural preservation in Soviet legislation, see L. I. Livshits, "Istoriia zakonodatel'stva v oblasti okhrany i restavratsii pamiatnikov kul'tury," in *Restavratsiia pamiatnikov istorii i iskusstva v Rossii v XIX–XX vekakh. Istoriia, problemy: Uchebnoe posobie*, ed. L. I. Livshits and A. V. Trezvov (Moscow: Alma Mater, 2008), 51–72. See also Catriona Kelly, "From 'Counter-Revolutionary Monuments' to 'National Heritage,'" *Cahiers du monde russe* 54, no. 1 (2014): 131–64.

3. "Postanovlenie SM RSFSR ot 30 avgusta 1960 g. No. 1327 'O dal'neishem uluchshenii dela okhrany pamiatnikov kul'tury v RSFSR,'" http://base.consultant.ru/cons/cgi/online.cgi?req=doc;base=ESU;n=3268.

4. The official register of "objects of the historical and cultural heritage" of the Russian Federation currently includes over 140,000 items: https://opendata.mkrf.ru/opendata/7705851331-egrkn/.

5. Jerzy Czajkowski, "Muzeiam pod otkrytym nebom—100 let," in *Muzeevedenie: Muzei-zapovedniki*, N. A. Nikishin and O. G. Sevan, eds. (Moscow: NII Kul'tury, 1991), 10–26.

6. Rolf Hellebust, *Flesh to Metal: Soviet Literature and the Alchemy of Revolution* (Ithaca, NY: Cornell University Press, 2003); Eli Rubin, *Synthetic Socialism: Plastics and Dictatorship in the German Democratic Republic* (Chapel Hill: University of North Carolina Press, 2012); Krisztina Fehérváry, *Politics in Color and Concrete: Socialist*

Materialities and the Middle Class in Hungary (Bloomington: Indiana University Press, 2013); Julia Bekman Chadaga, *Optical Play: Glass, Vision, and Spectacle in Russian Culture* (Chicago: Northwestern University Press, 2014).

7. Moisei Ginzburg, "Novye metody arkhitekturnogo myshlenia," *Sovremennaia arkhitektura* no. 1 (1926): 3.

8. Opolovnikov, *Muzei dereviannogo zodchestva* (Moscow: Stroiizdat, 1968), 9.

9. Bittner, *The Many Lives of Khrushchev's Thaw*; Catriona Kelly, "Socialist Churches: Heritage Preservation and 'Cultic Buildings' in Leningrad, 1924–1940," *Slavic Review* 71, no. 4 (December 1, 2012): 792–823; Kelly, "From 'Counter-Revolutionary Monuments.'"

10. Irina Pokrovskaia, *Naseleniie Karelii* (Petrozavodsk: Karelia, 1978), 50.

11. György Lukács, *Soul and Form*, trans. Anna Bostock (Cambridge: MIT Press, 1974), 91–92.

12. See, for example, Christopher Ely, *This Meager Nature: Landscape and National Identity in Imperial Russia* (DeKalb: Northern Illinois University Press, 2009); Tricia Cusack, *Riverscapes and National Identities* (Syracuse, NY: Syracuse University Press, 2010).

13. John Urry, *The Tourist Gaze: Leisure and Travel in Contemporary Societies* (London: Sage, 1990); Thomas Greider and Lorraine Garkovich, "Landscapes: The Social Construction of Nature and the Environment," *Rural Sociology* 59, no. 1 (1994): 1–24.

14. Lars Elenius et al., eds., *The Barents Region: A Transnational History of Subarctic Northern Europe* (Oslo: PAX, 2015), 183–86.

15. Nick Baron, *Soviet Karelia: Politics, Planning and Terror in Stalin's Russia, 1920–1939* (London: Routledge, 2012).

16. Pokrovskaia, *Naselenie Karelii*, 59.

17. Viktor Vanslov, ed., *Izobrazitel'noe iskusstvo avtonomnykh respublik RSFSR: Al'bom* (Moscow: Khudozhnik RSFSR, 1973), 156.

18. NARK, f. R-785, op. 1, d. 94a/529v, l. 1.

19. George Liber, *Alexander Dovzhenko: A Life in Soviet Film* (London: British Film Institute, 2002), 106–13.

20. NARK, f. R-785, op. 1, d. 94a/529v, l. 25.

21. NARK, f. R-785, op. 1, d. 94a/529v, l. 34–35.

22. The population figures are from the 1970 USSR Census,http://demoscope.ru/weekly/ssp/rus70_reg1.php. The editorial script is stored in the National Archive of the Republic of Karelia: NARK, f. R-785, op. 1, d. 94a/529v, l. 32–41.

23. The areal perspective was also characteristic of much of Karelian landscape painting, for example, Boris Pomotsev's 1975 *Nad Onego* (Above Lake Onega).

24. William E. Connolly, "The Order of Modernity," in *Democracy, Pluralism and Political Theory*, ed. Samuel A. Chambers and Terrell Carver (London, New York: Routledge, 2008), 281.

25. For authenticity as a form of political and colonial domination, see Paige Raibmon, *Authentic Indians: Episodes of Encounter from the Late-Nineteenth-Century Northwest Coast* (Durham: Duke University Press, 2005); Michelle Mawhinney, "Marx, Nature, and the Ethics of Nonidentity," *Rethinking Marxism* 12, no. 1 (2000): 47–64.

26. Vyacheslav Orfinskii, *V mire skazochnoi real'nosti: Dereviannaia arkhitektura Karelii* (Petrozavodsk: Karelia, 1972), esp. the chapter "Unity"; A.T. Belyaev, B. A. Gushchin and V. A. Gushchina, *Gosudarstvennyi istoriko-arkhitekturnyi i etnograficheskii muzei-zapovednik Kizhi: Putevoditel'* (Petrozavodsk: Karelia, 1973), 8, 16.

27. NARK, f. R-2916, op. 1, d. 1/10, l. 2; d 5/47, l. 99; d. 7/60, l. 43, 47. Another prominent example was the Finnish epos Kalevala by Elias Lönnrot. It was largely based on folklore of northern Karelian areas, and in the postwar period the government of the Karelian-Finnish SSR used its genealogy to claim Kalevala as a common Karelian-Finnish epos: Takehiro Okabe, "Negotiating Elias Lönnrot: Shared Soviet-Finnish National Symbol Articulated and Blurred, 1945–1952," *Nordic Historical Review*, no. 2 (2015): 129–49. On the educational use of heritage objects in Soviet postwar tourism, see Anne E. Gorsuch, *All This Is Your World: Soviet Tourism at Home and Abroad after Stalin* (Oxford: Oxford University Press, 2011), 26–48; Diane P. Koenker, *Club Red: Vacation Travel and the Soviet Dream* (Ithaca, NY: Cornell University Press, 2013), 128–66.

28. NARK, f. R-2916, op. 1, d. 1/10, l. 2; d. 1/16, l. 30; Aleksandr Opolovnikov, *Restavratsiia pamiatnikov narodnogo zodchestva* (Moscow: Stroiizdat, 1974), 19.

29. Leo Suni, "Ingermanlandskie finny: Istoricheskii ocherk," in *Finny v Rossii: Istoriia, kul'tura, sud'ba*, ed. Eino Kiuru (Petrozavodsk: Izd-vo PetrGU, 1998), 4–25.

30. Museum of Kizhi, KP-2670. Buildings plans and sketches from this expedition are also stored in the archive of the museum: KP-314; KP-5992/1-3; KP-5993/1-3; KP-274/1-30.

31. Museum of Kizhi, KP-5713/1, 2; KP-5714.

32. Museum of Kizhi, KP-271/1.

33. Opolovnikov, *Restavratsiia pamiatnikov*, 202; emphasis added.

34. Opolovnikov, *Muzei dereviannogo zodchestrva*, 6.

35. NARK, f. R-2916, op. 1, d. 5/47, l. 57.

36. Aleksandr Opolovnikov, *Kizhi*, 2nd ed. (Moscow: Stroiizdat, 1976), 10.

37. Igor Melnikov, ed., *Muzei-zapovednik Kizhi. 40 let* (Petrozavodsk: Scandinavia, 2006), 48.

38. NARK, f. R-2916, op. 1, d. 5/47, l. 99; d. 7/60, l. 43.

39. Opolovnikov, *Kizhi*, 100.

40. Opolovnikov, *Kizhi*, 101.

41. Moisei Ginzburg, *Style and Epoch*, trans. Anatole Senkevitch, Jr. (Cambridge: MIT Press, 1982), 114.

42. On Opolovnikov's contribution to his discipline, see his entry at the Russian Society for Preservation of Historical and Cultural Monuments (VOOPIK): http://www.voopik.ru/keeper/detail.php?ELEMENT_ID=2129.

43. Opolovnikov, *Restavratsiia pamiatnikov*, 62.

44. Ginzburg, *Style and Epoch*, 113; for the section on industrial design, see 76–93.

45. Opolovnikov, *Kizhi*, 87.

46. Opolovnikov, *Kizhi*, 88.

47. Opolovnikov, *Restavratsiia pamiatnikov*, 51–52; Svetlana Vorobyeva, "Ne utratit' pamiat'," *Kizhi*, no. 6 (2011): 4.

48. Bittner, *The Many Lives of Khrushchev's Thaw*, 140.

49. Catriona Kelly, *St. Petersburg: Shadows of the Past* (New Haven, CT: Yale University Press, 2014), 288–89.

50. Opolovnikov, *Restavratsiia pamiatnikov*, 27.

51. Ginzburg's first book was titled *"Ritm v arkhitekture* (Rhythms in Architecture) (Moscow: Sredi kollektsionerov, 1923).

52. Kristin Romberg, *Gan's Constructivism: Aesthetic Theory for an Embedded Modernism* (Berkeley: University of California Press, 2018), 77–105.

53. Aleksei Gan, "Konstruktivism," in *Formalnyi metod: Antologiia russkogo modernizma*, ed. Serguei Oushakine (Moscow: Kabinetnyi uchenyi, 2016), 1:852.

54. Opolovnikov, *Muzei dereviannogo zodchestva*, 16.

55. Opolovnikov, *Kizhi*, 14.

56. NARK, f. R-2916, op. 1, d. 3/32, l. 54.

57. NARK, f. R-2916, op. 1, d. 1/16, l. 25.

58. NARK, f. R-2916, op. 1, d. 3/32, l. 63.

59. Olga Ilyukha and Yuri Shikalov, "Kartina mira na stranitsakh uchebnikov finskogo iazyka dlia nachal'nykh klassov karelskikh shkol 1920–1940-kh godov," *Vestnik filiala Severo-Zapadnoi akademii Gosudarstvennoi sluzhby v Vyborge* (Vyborg: Filial SZAGS v Vyborge, 2010): 267–95; Victoria Donovan, " 'Going Backwards, We Stride Forwards': Kraevedenie Museums and the Making of Local Memory in North West Russia, 1956–1981," *Forum for Anthropology and Culture*, no. 7 (2012): 211–30; Victoria Donovan, " 'How Well Do You Know Your Krai?' The Kraevedenie Revival and Patriotic Politics in Late Khrushchev-Era Russia," *Slavic Review* 74, no. 3 (2015): 464–83.

60. NARK, f. R-2916, op. 1, d. 3/32, l. 63.

61. In Soviet literature, this search for historical authenticity—often at the price of a conflict with official authorities—became the main motif of Vladimir Soloukhin's 1968 novel *Chernye doski* (Black boards), published in English with a different title: *Searching for Icons in Russia* (New York: Harcourt Brace Jovanovich, 1972).

62. Vera Taroeva, *Material'naia kul'tura karel (Karel'skaia ASSR)* (Leningrad: Nauka, 1965), 195–98.

63. Alexander Opolovnikov, *Rus' dereviannaia: Obrazy russkogo dereviannogo zodchestva* (Moscow: Detlit, 1981), 31.

64. Orfinskii, *V mire skazochnoi real'nosti*, 5–6.

65. Some scholars contest this interpretation of new tendencies in the vernacular architecture of North Russia in the late nineteenth and early twentieth centuries as a "decline." See, e.g., Olga Sevan, *"Malye Korely": Arkhangel'skii muzei dereviannogo zodchestva* (Moscow: Progress-Traditsiia, 2011), 152–53.

66. Irina Ye. Grishina, "Etnoarkhitektura: Printsipy issledovaniia," *Uchenye zapiski Petrozavodskogo gosudarstvennogo universiteta*, no. 5 (March 2009): 7–13.

67. "Polozheniie o nauchno-issledovatel'skom institute istoriko-teoreticheskikh problem narodnogo zodchestva," a bylaw of Petrozavodsk State University, Petrozavodsk, 1997.

68. Roza F. Nikolskaia, *Karel'skaia kukhnia* (Petrozavodsk: Karelia, 1986), 4, 13–36.

69. NARK, f. R-785, op. 1, d. 94a/529v, l. 38–39.

70. Fehérváry, *Politics in Color and Concrete*, 142.

71. Quoted in David Pearson, *New Organic Architecture: The Breaking Wave* (Berkeley: University of California Press, 2001), 137.

72. Interview with Viktor Dmitriev taken by the author, June 7, 2014, Petrozavodsk.

73. Pomors is a name for the Russian population of the White Sea coast that had lived there continuously since the twelfth century. Their traditional economic activities were fishing, sea mammal hunting, sea trade with Norway, and boatbuilding.

74. Interview with Viktor Dmitriev.

75. Stanislav Zaitsev, "Kak otkryt' Ameriku," in *Tot'ma: Istoriko-kraevedcheskii al'manakh, Vyp. 1* (Vologda: Rus', 1995), 334–72. The author of the article was a member of the 1991 expedition of the Pomor; in 1992, the expedition reached Vancouver, B.C., where he tragically drowned while the ship was moored near the Vancouver Maritime Museum.

76. Interview with Viktor Dmitriev.

77. "Dmitriev Viktor Leonidovich," *Club Polar Odyssey*, http://polar-odyssey.org/sea-club/prezident.html.

78. Viktor Georgi, "Belomorskaia petlia," *Vokrug sveta*, no. 6 (1989): 20.

79. Natalia Meshkova, "Soversheno prestuplenie," *Internet-Journal Litsei*, June 16, 2013, http://gazeta-licey.ru/culture/5662-soversheno-prestuplenie-video, accessed December 10, 2015.

80. Yulia Karpova, *Comradely Objects: Design and Material Culture in Soviet Russia, 1960s–80s* (Manchester: Manchester University Press, 2020), 65–88.

81. Markku Nieminen, "Mezhdu proshlym i budushchim," in *Panozero: Serdtse Belomorskoi Karelii*, ed. Aleksei Konkka and Vyacheslav Orfinskii (Petrozavodsk: Izdatel'stvo PetrGU, 2003), 6–18; Aleksandr Yaskeliainen, "Predposylki vozrozhdeniia derevni: Plotnitskie kursy i kontseptsii restavratsii panozerskikh domov," in Konkka and Orfinskii, *Panozero*, 291–308.

82. *Vesti. Karelia*, aired June 27, 2006 on GTRK Karelia.

83. Vyacheslav Orfinskii, "Rodnik karel'skoi kul'tury," in Konkka and Orfinskii, *Panozero*, 313.

84. Sergei Kulikov, "Komu nuzhny karely?" *Stolitsa na Onego*, http://www.stolica.onego.ru/articles/168616.html.

85. "Pamiatniki istorii i kul'tury—vsenarodnoe dostoianie," *Leninskaia Pravda* (Petrozavoodsk), April 17 (1980): 3; "Perspektivy 'neperspektivnoi' derevni," *Leninskaia Pravda*, July 6 (1980): 2; *Vesti. Karelia*, aired September 4, 2015 on GTRK Karelia.

86. "V kraiu pogibshikh vepsskikh dereven,'" Finugor.ru, October 12, 2011, http://finugor.ru/news/v-krayu-pogibshih-vepsskih-dereven,; "Politsiia predpolagaet, chto istoricheskoe zdanie v Sortavala podozhgli," Karelinform.ru, January 17, 2014, http://karelinform.ru/news/society/44859/politsiya_predpolagaet_chto_istoricheskoe_zdanie_v_sortavala_podojgli.

87. "'Ozhivshaia ekspozitsiia' muzeia Kizhi: Delo mastera boitsia," *Kizhi*, no. 10 (2013): 7.

88. Interview with Viktor Dmitriev.

89. Alexander Pasechnik, dir., *Kovcheg* (Obshchee delo, 2014).

Chapter 4. When Spaces of Transit Fail Their Designers

1. On Soviet communal apartments, see Svetlana Boym, *Common Places: Mythologies of Everyday Life in Russia* (Cambridge, MA: Harvard University Press, 1994); Ilia Utekhin, *Ocherki kommunal'nogo byta* (Moscow: O.G.I., 2001). On the most up-to-date research on Soviet modernist housing in the post-Stalinist era, including a detailed historiography, see Harris, *Communism on Tomorrow Street*; Varga-Harris, *Stories of House and Home*.

2. A. S. Senyavskii, *Rossiiskii gorod v 1960-e–1980-e gg.* (Moscow: Izd-vo MGU, 1995), 204.

3. German scholars have done remarkable research on Soviet garrisons stationed in East Germany. Still, their focus has been on interpreting the repressive aspects of the Soviet military presence in Eastern Europe as occupation. A social history of Soviet garrison towns has yet to be written. See Silke Satjukow, *Besatzer: "Die Russen" in Deutschland 1945–1994* (Göttingen: Vandenhoeck & Ruprecht, 2008); Ilko-Sascha Kowalczuk and Stefan Wolle, *Roter Stern über Deutschland: Sowjetische Truppen in der DDR* (Berlin: Ch. Links Verlag, 2010).

4. Kharkhordin, *The Collective and the Individual in Russia*, 279–354; Susan E. Reid, "The Meaning of Home: 'The Only Bit of the World You Can Have to Yourself,'" in *Borders of Socialism: Private Spheres of Soviet Russia*, ed. Lewis Siegelbaum (New York: Palgrave Macmillan, 2006), 145–70; Brian LaPierre, *Hooligans in Khrushchev's Russia: Defining, Policing, and Producing Deviance during the Thaw* (Madison: University of Wisconsin Press, 2012), 59–95.

5. Andrei Konchalovsky, *Vozvyshaiushchii obman* (Moscow: Sovershenno sekretno, 1999), 62–63.

6. See Nigel Thrift's discussion of how affects are an integral part of urban landscapes and politics: Nigel Thrift, "Intensities of Feeling: Towards a Spatial Politics of Affect," *Geografiska Annaler. Series B, Human Geography* 86, no. 1 (January 1, 2004): 57–78.

7. Noam Chomsky and Michel Foucault, *The Chomsky-Foucault Debate: On Human Nature* (New York: New Press, 2006), 40.

8. N. P. Bylinkin and A. V. Riabushin, eds., *Sovremennaia sovetskaia arkhitektura* (Moscow: Stroiizdat, 1985), 77–108.

9. "Direktivy XXIII s'ezda KPSS po piatiletnemu planu razvitiia narodnogo khoziaistva SSSR na 1966–1970 gody," *XXIII s'ezd Kommunisticheskoi partii Sovetskogo Soiuza, 26 marta–8 aprelia 1966 goda* (Moscow: Politizdat, 1966), 324.

10. V. A. Golikov, ed., *Sovetskii Soiuz: Politiko-ekonomicheskii spravochnik* (Moscow: Politizdat, 1982), 223. Not all of them moved to khrushchevki—there were other, although less widespread, types of new housing, which included elite housing (*obkomovskiie doma*), cooperative housing, and detached houses in rural areas.

11. Natan Osterman, "O zhilishche budushchego," *Sovetskaia arkhitektura* 19 (1970): 68–79; Stephen E. Harris, "Soviet Mass Housing and the Communist Way of Life," in *Everyday Life in Russia: Past and Present*, ed. Choi Chatterjee et al. (Bloomington: Indiana University Press, 2015), 184–85.

12. The connection between the concepts of early Soviet "commune houses" and microdistricts is particularly visible in the bold and ambitious, albeit not realized, Arctic architecture projects of 1960s–1980s of Aleksandr Shipkov who envisioned apartment complexes the size of entire town districts: Rena Sheiko, "Dom v Zapoliar'e," *Iunost'*, no. 7 (1976): 90–94. Stephen Harris discusses this connection in his book on Soviet mass housing: Harris, *Communism on Tomorrow Street*, 192–208.

13. Zhan Toshchenko, *Sotsial'naia infrastruktura: Sushchnost' i puti razvitiia* (Moscow: Mysl', 1980), 22–25, 100–119.

14. See a contemporary representation of this logic in Chelkash, "Novaia statuiia v Moskve," *Krokodil*, no. 36 (1957): 7.

15. Kharkhordin, *The Collective and the Individual in Russia*, 279–303; Reid, "Cold War in the Kitchen"; Reid, "The Meaning of Home"; Deborah A. Field, *Private Life and Communist Morality in Khrushchev's Russia* (New York: Peter Lang, 2007); LaPierre, *Hooligans in Khrushchev's Russia*, 59–95.

16. Galina Shilova, "Ideino-vospitatel'naia rabota po mestu zhitel'stva v sovremennykh usloviiakh i puti ee sovershenstvovanii," (Dr. Sc. in history thesis, Academy of Social Sciences of the CPSU Central Committee, 1984).

17. Postanovleniie Sovmina SSSR ot 25.03.1959 No. 322 "O merakh po uluchsheniiu ekspluatatsii i sokhraneniiu gosudarstvennogo zhilishchnogo fonda," in *Sobranie postanovlenii SSSR*, no. 11 (1960), article 75.

18. Smith, *Property of Communists*, 116–21.

19. Vladimir Ladygin, *Prostoi sovetskii chelovek (vospominaniia spetsialista)* (Tula: OOO TRK "Arsenal," 2001), 201.

20. Postanovleniie prezidiuma VTsSPS ot 16.10.1959 "Ob obshchestvennykh domovykh komitetakh v gosudarstvennom zhilishchnom fonde RSFSR" (Moscow: Izd-vo VTsSPS, 1959).

21. Postanovleniie Sovmina RSFSR, VTsSPS ot 9.08.1968 No. 548 "Ob usilenii roli domovykh komitetov v upravlenii gosudarstvennym zhilishchnym fondom," in *Sobranie postanovlenii RSFSR*, no. 15 (1968), article 75.

22. As judged by the transcripts of the TV program Evening Petrozavodsk (Vechernii Petrozavodsk) and several local radio programs: NARK, f. R-785, op. 1, d. 53/287, ll. 8–11; NARK, f. R-785, op. 1, d. 53/293, ll. 94, 206.

23. The Leningrad obkom of the Komsomol, in particular, promoted it through its movement Komsomol Projector (Komsomol'skii prozhektor). Central State Archive of Historical and Political Documents of St. Petersburg (TsGAIPD SPb), f. K-598, op. 25, d. 49, ll. 117–18; f. K-598, op. 25, d. 64, ll. 1–4.

24. K. Barykin, "Zelenye Cheremushki," *Ogoniok*, no. 40 (1973): 14–15; "Na strazhe obshchestvennogo poriadka," *Novosti dnia* (newsreel), no. 3 (January 1973).

25. Reproduced in Viktor Kanetskii, "Vampuka. Nekotorym obrazom drama," *Zvezda*, no. 3 (1989): 12.

26. Reproduced in Viktor Kanetskii, "Vampuka. Nekotorym obrazom drama," *Zvezda*, no. 3 (1989): 12.

27. A website specializing in humor dates it as the early 2000s: http://www.anekdot.ru/id/-10018836/. The plot, however, does not differ much from Soviet-era jokes.

28. NARK, f. R-1799, op. 8, d. 3/16, ll. 43–44.

29. Harris, *Communism on Tomorrow Street*, 205.

30. Adrian Geiges and Tatiana Suvorova wrote a separate chapter "Intimate relationships . . . Where?" on topographies of Soviet sexual life in their book: Adrian Geiges and Tatiana Suvorova, *Liubov—vne plana: (sex & perestroika): intimnaia zhizn' i polozhenie zhenshchin v SSSR* (Moscow: Sobesednik, 1990), 77–86. Igor Kon had a similar chapter, "Housing question," in his monograph on the history of sex in Russia: Igor Kon, *Seksual'naia kul'tura v Rossii: Klubnichka na berezke*, 3rd ed. (Moscow: Vremia, 2010), 268–71. See also Anna Rotkirch, *The Man Question: Loves and Lives in Late 20th Century Russia* (Helsinki: University of Helsinki—Department of Social Policy, 2000), 261; Natalia Lebina, *Muzhchina i zhenshchina: Telo, moda, kul'tura. SSSR—ottepel'* (Moscow: NLO, 2015), 115.

31. Mark Popovsky, *Tretii lishnii: On, ona i sovetskii rezhim* (London: Overseas Publications, 1985), 129. The unnamed respondent rephrased Guy de Maupassant's famous saying about the bed: "The bed comprehends our whole life; for we were born in it, we live in it, and we shall die in it" (from the short story "The Bed"): Guy de Maupassant, *Complete Short Stories* (New York: Walter J. Black Inc., 1903), 681.

32. Tatiana Akhmetova, ed., *Russkii mat: Tolkovyi slovar'*, 2nd ed. (Moscow: Kolokol-press, 1997), 14, 112.

33. George Chauncey, *Gay New York: Gender, Urban Culture, and the Makings of the Gay Male World, 1890–1940* (New York: Basic Books, 1994), 131–267; James N. Green, *Beyond Carnival: Male Homosexuality in Twentieth-Century Brazil* (Chicago: University of Chicago Press, 2001).

34. Kon, *Seksual'naia kul'tura v Rossii*, 297–321.

35. D. N. Isaev and V. E. Kagan, *Polovoe vospitanie i psikhogigiena pola u detei* (Moscow: Meditsina, 1979), 78–79.

36. Isaev and Kagan, *Polovoe vospitanie*.

37. Vladimir Vysotsky, *Sochineniia* (Moscow: Lokid, 1999), 473–44.

38. Rotkirch, *The Man Question*, 211.

39. Rotkirch, *The Man Question*, 213–14.

40. V. F. Pirozhkov, *Zakony prestupnogo mira molodezhi: Kriminal'naia subkul'tura* (Tver: Priz, 1994), 10.

41. D. N. Isaev, B. Ye. Mikirtumov, and Ye. I. Bogdanova, "Seksual'nye proiavleniia v klinicheskoi kartine pogranichnykh nervno-psikhicheskikh rasstroistv v detskom i podrostkovom vozraste," *Pediatriia*, no. 3 (1979): 42.

42. Tatiana Vasilieva, dir., *Pod'ezd*, a special issue of the newsreel *Sovetskii Ural*, no. 5 (1990).

43. LaPierre, *Hooligans in Khrushchev's Russia*, 9.

44. LaPierre, *Hooligans in Khrushchev's Russia*, 19–20. For primary sources, see N. A. Belyaev and M. D. Shargorodskii, eds., *Kurs sovetskogo ugolovnogo prava (chast' obshchaia)* (Leningrad: Izd-vo LGU, 1968), 1:192–96.

45. Russian archives store an innumerable number of residents' complaints that linked disorderly urban space and juvenile delinquency. For example, the executive committee of the Vyborgsky district council in Leningrad collected hundreds of complaints each year. For complaints of 1967, see TsGA SPb, f. 148, op. 7, d. 555a. For complaints of 1979, see TsGA SPb, f. 148, op. 9, d. 435.

46. TsGA SPb, f. 148, op. 7, d. 647, l. 28.

47. NARK, f. P-3, op. 26, d. 56, ll. 1–7.

48. NARK, f. P-3, op. 26, d. 56, ll. 58–61.

49. NARK, f. P-779, op. 62, d. 107, l. 33.

50. Koenker, *Club Red*, 54–59.

51. For Soviet theory on "education through space," see, for example, Pavel Istomin, "Turistskaia deiatel'nost kak sredstvo vospitaniia sotsial'noi aktivnosti starsheklassnikov" (Cand. Sc. dissertation in education, Research Institute of General Problems of Education of the USSR Academy of Pedagogical Sciences, 1978). For practice, see NARK, f. R-1799, op. 8, d. 3/19, ll. 74–80; NARK, f. R-3665, op. 1, d. 3/75, ll. 1–4; NARK, f. R-2032, op. 2, d. 26/298, ll. 15–16.

52. Gilbert Ryle, *The Concept of Mind* (London: Routledge, 2009), 38.

53. Stanislav Rodionov, "Kriminal'nyi talant," in *Kriminal'nyi talent: Povesti* (St. Petersburg: Interlast, 1994), 387–590.

54. Sergei Muratov, "Soviet Television and the Structure of Broadcasting Authority," *Journal of Communication* 41, no. 2 (1991): 172.

55. Juris Podnieks, dir., *Vai viegli būt jaunam??* (Rīgas kinostudija, 1986).

56. TsGA SPb, f. 148, op. 7, d. 647, l. 31.

57. Andrei Troitskii, "Sud'ba pochina," *Sovety narodnykh deputatov*, no. 5 (1987): 61. The author later became a well-known writer in the genre of criminal novel, actively exploiting the imagery of marginal socialist and postsocialist urban spaces in his writing.

58. On the history of Soviet graffiti, see John Bushnell, *Moscow Graffiti: Language and Subculture* (London: Unwin Hyman, 1990).

59. Unpublished diary of Rostislav Rokitianskii, entry 3311. I am grateful to Vladimir Rokitianskii for sharing his father's diary.

60. Reproduced in *The Current Digest of Soviet Press* 35, no. 33 (1983): 16.

61. TsGA SPb, f. 148, op. 9, d. 435, ll. 54–55.

62. TsGA SPb, f. 148, op. 9, d. 435, l. 55.

63. Tricia Starks, *The Body Soviet Propaganda, Hygiene, and the Revolutionary State* (Madison: University of Wisconsin Press, 2008). Alaina Lemon also discusses the dirt as a category of Russian modernity in relation to another marginalized group—Russian Roma people. Alaina Lemon, *Between Two Fires: Gypsy Performance and Romani Memory from Pushkin to Post-Socialism* (Durham: Duke University Press, 2000).

64. Interview with V. G. by the author, June 19, 2014.

65. Vladimir Amlinsky, "Response to Sergei Mikhalkov's speech," *Detskaia literatura*, no. 12 (1977): 36.

66. Amlinsky, "Response to Sergei Mikhalkov's speech."

67. Sergei Mikhalkov, "Podrostki: Problemy vospitaniia i literatura," *Detskaia literatura*, no. 12 (1977): 21.

68. John Bushnell, for example, interprets Soviet graffiti as a product of new social stratification in post-Stalinist culture, through which new groups sought to announce their existence and to claim social space: Bushnell, *Moscow Graffiti*, 40.

69. Ditmar Rozental, *Upravleniie v russkom iazyke* (Moscow: Nauka, 1981), 14.

70. TsGA SPb, f. 148, op. 7, d. 647, l. 28.

71. Writing in 1987, the authors of sociological research on Soviet workers noted that children of the latter fell notably behind children from "white collar" families (sem'i sluzhashchikh-spetsialistov) in rates of attendance of extracurricular activities, especially in music: A. K. Nazimova, ed., *Sovetskie rabochie v usloviiakh uskoreniia sotsial'no-ekonomicheskogo razvitiia* (Moscow: Nauka, 1987), 158.

72. L. A. Krapivina, "Pionerskii otriad 'Karavella': Vzgliad skvoz' prizmu desiatiletiia," *Obrazovaniie i nauka*, no. 4 (2012): 128–43.

73. Aleksandr Razumikhin, "Pravilo bez iskliuchenii, ili Prozrachnaia zlost' i intelligentnye mal'chiki Vladislava Krapivina," *Ural*, no. 8 (1988): 149–52. For a response to Razumikhin by an advocate of Krapivin's juvenile fiction, see Valentin Luk'ianin, "Schast'e byt' chelovekom," *Ural*, no. 8 (1988): 152–56.

74. Caroline Humphrey, *The Unmaking of Soviet Life: Everyday Economies after Socialism* (Ithaca, NY: Cornell University Press, 2002), 212.

75. Arkady and Boris Strugatsky, *Prisoners of Power* (New York: Macmillan, 1977), 43.

76. E.g., Evgeny Sukhov, the author of the popular book series *Ia—vor v zakone*, is a Candidate of Sciences in geology and an associate professor at Kazan State University. Andrei Konstantinov (Bakonin), the screenwriter of the famous TV series *Banditskii Peterburg*, is a graduate of the Faculty of Oriental Studies of Leningrad State University and a professional interpreter and translator from the Arabic language. Vladimir Kolychev, another popular author of this genre, received a degree in engineering from a military academy and served as a military engineer in the Soviet and later Russian Army.

77. Chomsky and Foucault, *The Chomsky-Foucault Debate*, 40.

78. Sergei Mikhalkov, "Podrostki: Problemy vospitaniia i literatura," *Detskaia literatura*, no. 12 (1977): 21.

79. See, e.g., Rosa Vihavainen, "Common and Dividing Things in Homeowners' Associations," in *Political Theory and Community Building in Post-Soviet Russia*, ed. Oleg Kharkhordin and Risto Alapuro (London: Routledge, 2010), 139–63.

Chapter 5. The Men of Steel

1. Vladimir Iakovlev, "Kontora liuberov," *Ogoniok*, no. 5 (1987): 20–21; Aleksandr Kupriianov, "Liubertsy pri svete fonarei, ili Pasynki stolitsy," *Sobesednik*, no. 7 (1987): 10–15.

2. Iakovlev, "Kontora liuberov," 20.

3. Quoted in Dilan Troi, Viktor Troiegubov, and Margarita Pushkina, *"Ariia": Legenda o dinozavre (s iskopaiemykh vremen)* (Moscow: Nota-R, 2005), 14.

4. See a historical discussions of the contemporary public reaction to these publications in terms of a "moral panic": Anna Rudnitskaia, "Kuda ukhodiat liubera," *Ogoniok*, no. 46 (2005): 24–25; Hilary Pilkington, *Russia's Youth and Its Culture: A Nation's Constructors and Constructed* (London: Routledge, 1994), 141–60; Dmitry Gromov, "'Moral'naia panika' kak mekhanizm razvitiia riada molodezhnykh soobshchestv Sovetskogo Soiuza i Rossii," *Istoricheskaia psikhologiia i sotsiologiia istorii 5*, no. 1 (2012): 164–78.

5. Gromov, "Moral'naia panika kak mekhanizm," 169.

6. Iakovlev, "Kontora liuberov," 21; N. Ivanov, "Vorkuta—stolitsa razdorov?" *Detskaia literatura*, no. 10 (1988): 16–18. It was the time when Soviet television stations broadcast the Italian TV series *La piovra* (Octopus) about the Italian mafia, which became an immediate hit in the USSR, so the Soviet public already possessed the cultural expertise to recognize these conspiratorial implications: Leonid Parfionov, *Namedni. Nasha era. 1981–1990* (Moscow: Kolibri, 2010), 169. For a critique of these views, see Pilkington, *Russia's Youth and Its Culture*, 147–48; Gromov, "Moral'naia panika kak mekhanizm," 169.

7. Leonid Chuiko and Sergey Metelitsa, "Parni iz Liuberets," *Nedelia*, no. 27 (1987): 17.

8. Olga Bobrova, "Sportpodvaly v Liubertsakh," *Tekhnika—Molodezhi*, no. 4 (1988): 19–21.

9. Yuri Sorokin, *Atleticheskaia podgotovka doprizyvnika, ili tel'niashka v podarok* (Moscow: Sovetskii sport, 1990).

10. Rolf Hellebust, *Flesh to Metal: Soviet Literature and the Alchemy of Revolution* (Ithaca, NY: Cornell University Press, 2003). See also Katerina Clark, *The Soviet Novel: History as Ritual* (Bloomington: Indiana University Press, 2000), 93–113; Evgeny Dobrenko, *Political Economy of Socialist Realism* (New Haven: Yale University Press, 2007), 151–77.

11. Sara Ahmed, *The Cultural Politics of Emotion* (New York: Routledge, 2004); Judy Wajcman, *TechnoFeminism* (Cambridge, MA: Polity, 2004).

12. Boris Nuvakhov, *Doktor Ilizarov* (Moscow: Progress, 1987).

13. Oleg Baraev, dir., *Gavriil Ilizarov—Kudesnik iz Kurgana*, episode 87 of the TV series *Genii i zlodei* (Tsivilizatsiia, 2013).

14. E. Battaloglu and D. Bose, "The History of Ilizarov," *Trauma* 15, no. 3 (July 1, 2013): 257–62.

15. Valery Brumel, *Vysota* (Moscow: Molodaia gvardiia, 1971), 39.

16. Nuvakhov, *Doktor Ilizarov*.

17. S. I. Bunkov, *Khirurg Ilizarov* (Chelyabinsk: Iuzh.-Ural. kn. izd-vo, 1972); Ye. Legat, dir., *Pozovite menia, doctor* (TsSDF, 1973); L. Fisher, dir., *Apparat Ilizarova* (Tsentrnauchfilm, 1979); Gavriil Ilizarov, "Zhit' bez upreka," *Komsomolskaya pravda*, September 1, 1983; Gavriil Ilizarov, "Po real'nomu vkladu," *Sovetskaia kul'tura*, February 25, 1986, 3; Gavriil Ilizarov, "Obyknovennoe chudo," *Ogoniok*, no. 5 (1986): 14–15.

18. Nuvakhov, *Doktor Ilizarov*.

19. Valery Brumel and Aleksandr Lapshin, *Ne izmeni sebe* (Moscow: Molodaia gvardiia, 1980), 249.

20. L. Grafova, "Interview: Khirurg G. A. Ilizarov," *Nauka i zhizn'*, no. 8 (1982): 36–41, photo on 37.

21. Valentin Dikul and Alexandr Eliseikin, *Razorvannyi krug* (Moscow: Sovetskii sport, 1993).

22. Ie. Velichko, "Preodoleniie," *Sportivnaia zhizn' Rossii*, no. 6 (1983): 30.

23. Velichko, "Preodoliniie"; M. Zalesskii, "Silach nomer odin," *Znanie—sila*, no. 8 (1983): 140–44; M. Zalesskii, "Novaia vstrecha s Dikulem," *Znanie—sila*, no. 3 (1986): 58–63; D. Likhanov, "Fenomen Dikulia," *Ogoniok*, no. 41 (1986): 18–20; D. Likhanov, "I snova Dikul," *Ogoniok*, no. 18 (1987): 18. A correspondent of the Soviet health magazine *Zdorov'e* witnessed in 1989 that postal workers delivered letters to Dikul in large paper bags because of the large quantity: P. Smol'nikov, "Poverit' v sebia," *Zdorov'e*, no. 6 (1989): 24.

24. A. Ivankin, dir., *Piramida* (TsSDF, 1985).

25. Aleksandr Lavrin, *Kto est kto v perestroike* (Berlin: Blaue Hörner Verlag, 1990), 55–56, 68–69.

26. Nuvakhov, *Doktor Ilizarov*.

27. M. Zalesskii, "Novaia vstrecha s Dikulem," *Nauka i zhizn'*, no. 3 (1986): 58.

28. See, for example, the blueprints of Dikul's equipment published in *Zdorov'e*, no. 5–8 (1989).

29. Dikul and Eliseikin, *Razorvannyi krug*, 36.

30. Tomas Matza, *Shock Therapy: Psychology, Precarity, and Well-Being in Postsocialist Russia* (Durham: Duke University Press, 2018), 104–9, 214–16. Matza argues that self-help advice was "for ideological reasons . . . rare to nonexistent" in the USSR (p. 16). This claim omits the fact that self-help literature as a separate genre emerged and became popular in the USSR at least in the early 1970s: Vladimir Levi, *Iskusstvo*

byt" soboi (Moscow: Znanie, 1973); Iakov Kolominskii, *Psikhologiia obshcheniia* (Moscow: Znanie, 1974).

31. Michele Rivkin-Fish, *Women's Health in Post-Soviet Russia: The Politics of Intervention* (Bloomington: Indiana University Press, 2005); Suvi Salmenniemi, "Post-Soviet Khoziain: Class, Self and Morality in Russian Self-Help Literature," in *Rethinking Class in Russia*, ed. Suvi Salmenniemi (London: Routledge, 2012): 67–84.

32. Soviet popular psychotherapy literature, especially the books by Vladimir Levi, is another Soviet-era cultural phenomenon that represents a focus on individual autonomy and self-development.

33. Beate Fieseler, "The Bitter Legacy of the 'Great Patriotic War': Red Army Disabled Soldiers under Late Stalinism," in *Late Stalinist Russia: Society between Reconstruction and Reinvention*, ed. Juliane Fürst (London: Routledge, 2005), 46–61. For a personal account of disability as social alienation in the USSR, see Ruben Gallego's memoir of his childhood in Soviet orphanages for disabled children: Ruben Gallego, *White on Black* (Orlando: Harcourt, 2006).

34. Nuvakhov, *Doktor Ilizarov*.

35. Shishanov, "O razvitii atleticheskoi gimnastiki," 52; Sheiko, "Kratkii ocherk," 242; Mikhail Bokov, "Kak v Sovetskom Soiuze poiavilis' kachki," Furfur, http://www.furfur.me/furfur/all/culture/176291-istoriya-kulturizma-v-sssr.

36. Igor Kon, *The Sexual Revolution in Russia: From the Age of the Czars to Today*, trans. James Riordan (New York: Free Press, 1995), 85–90; Debora A. Field, *Private Life and Communist Morality in Khrushchev's Russia* (New York: Peter Lang, 2007): 51–65; Natalia Lebina, *Muzhchina i zhenshchina: Telo, moda, odezhda. SSSR—ottepel'* (Moscow: NLO, 2014).

37. Joe Weider and Ben Weider, *Brothers of Iron* (Champaign, IL: Sports Publishing, 2006), 144–49.

38. Roman Moroz, "Ia—za!" *Sportivnaia zhizn' Rossii*, no. 1 (1962): 19; Anatoly Zilberborg, "Sila, zdorov'e, krasota: Pogovorim o 'kul'turizme,'" *Smena*, no. 12 (1962): 30–31; Yuri Sorokin and Georgi Tenno, "Vaiateli tela," *Nash sovremennik*, no. 10 (1964): 109–11; Georgi Tenno, "Ne kul't, a kul'tura: Zametki o kul'turizme," *Iunost'*, no. 5 (1966): 103; Georgi Tenno, "Osnovnoi kurs atleticheskoi trenirovki," *Tekhnika—Molodezhi*, no. 8 (1966): 16–17.

39. M. L. Ukran, V. M. Smolevskii, and A. M. Shlemin, *Atleticheskaia gimnastika: Dlia iunoshei* (Moscow: Fizkul'tura i sport, 1965); Georgii Tenno and Yuri Sorokin, *Atletizm* (Moscow: Molodaia gvardiia, 1968). References to Tenno and Sorokin's *Atletizm* as an informal bodybuilding textbook repeatedly occur in interviews and memoirs of Soviet-era bodybuilders.

40. Shishanov, "O razvitii atleticheskoi gimnastiki," 52.

41. Aleksandr Solzhenitsyn, *The Gulag Archipelago, 1918–1956: An Experiment in Literary Investigation*, V–VII, trans. Harry Willetts (New York: Harper & Row, 1979), chapters 5 "The Committed Escaper" and 6 "The White Kitten (Georgi Tenno's Tale)."

42. M. L. Aptekar, *Tiazhelaia atletika. Spravochnik* (Moscow: Fizkul'tura i sport, 1983), 410. Ben Weider recalled in his memoir how surprised he was during his visit to the USSR in 1955 when he saw a collection of bodybuilding magazines published by his brother Joe Weider at one of Moscow's sport-related institutions: Weider and Weider, *Brothers of Iron*, 145.

43. A. A. Volkov, "Kul'turizm ili atleticheskaia gimnastika?," *Teoriia i praktika fizkul'tury*, no. 1 (1966): 56; Dmitry Ivanov, "Doroga k sile—doroga truda: Po povodu uvlecheniia kul'turizmom," *Sovetskii sport*, March 16, 1966, 4–5; K. S. Tsvetkov, "O kul'turizme i atletizme," *Teoriia i praktika fizkul'tury*, no. 12 (1966): 66.

44. Tenno, "Ne kul't, a kul'tura"; Kostiv, "Chelovek-motor," 12; Dmitry Murzin, *Bibliia bodibildinga* (Moscow: Eksmo, 2011), 211.

45. Yuri Sorokin, "Myshtsy—chto ty znaesh' o nikh?," *Tekhnika—Moloiozhi*, no. 8 (1965): 14–15; Georgi Tenno and Yuri Sorokin, "Atletizm—sila, zdorov'e, krasota," *Tekhnika—Molodezhi*, no. 2 (1966): 26–27; Anatoly Golubev, "Formula krasoty," *Molodoi kommunist*, no. 3 (1968): 122–27.

46. Tenno and Sorokin, *Atletizm*, 283.

47. V. Zatsiorskii, "Nam chuzhd kul'turizm," *Sovetskii sport*, March 23, 1963, 3; Volkov, "Kul'turizm ili atleticheskaia gimnastika?"; Ivanov, "Doroga k sile—doroga truda"; Tsvetkov, "O kul'turizme i atletizme."

48. Tenno, "Ne kul't, a kul'tura," 105.

49. "Repei v konfetnoi obertke," *Sovetskii sport*, April 15, 1969, 4; Dmitry Ivanov, "Troianskii kon' kul'turizma," *Sovetskii sport*, September 28 1969, 3 and September 29, 1969, 3.

50. Quoted in Dmitry Ivanov, "Izlom," *Sovetskii sport*, September 11, 1977, 3.

51. Ivanov, "Izlom," *Sovetskii sport*, September 11, 1977, 3; September 13, 1977, 3; September 14, 1977, 3. *Sovetskii sport* also published follow-up articles: "Stolknoveniie v pol'zu razumnogo," *Sovetskii sport*, December 14, 1977, 3; "Polozhit' konets nezdorovym iavleniiam," *Sovetskii sport*, December 27, 1977: 2.

52. Quoted in "Polozhit' konets."

53. Dimitrios Liokaftos, "From 'Classical' To 'Freaky': An Exploration of the Development of Dominant, Organised, Male Bodybuilding Culture" (PhD diss., Goldsmiths, University of London, 2012), 19–122.

54. Liokaftos, "From 'Classical' To 'Freaky,'" 111.

55. Wolfgang Welsch, "Sport Viewed Aesthetically, and Even as Art?," in *The Aesthetics of Everyday Life*, ed. Andrew Light and Jonathan Smith (New York: Columbia University Press, 2005), 135–55.

56. Tsvetkov, "O kul'turizme i atletizme," 64.

57. Ivanov, "Izlom," *Sovetskii sport*, September 13, 1977, 3.

58. Volkov, "Kul'turizm ili atleticheskaia gimnastika?," 53.

59. Alan M. Klein, *Little Big Men: Bodybuilding Subculture and Gender Construction* (Albany: State University of New York Press, 1993); Liokaftos, "From 'Classical' to 'Freaky,'" 104–33.

60. Aleksei Gan, "Bor'ba za 'massovoe deistvie,'" *O teatre* (Tver': 2-ia gostipografiia, 1922), 49–80; Pat Simpson, "Parading Myths: Imaging New Soviet Woman on Fizkul'turnik's Day, July 1944," *Russian Review* 63, no. 2 (2004): 187–211.

61. See, e.g., Tenno, "Ne kul't, a kul'tura," 101.

62. Ivanov, "Troianskii kon' kul'turizma."

63. Interview with Andrei Zhukov, November 2016, taken by Alexander Osipov.

64. Sergei Pakhotin, "Fenomen Evgeniia Koltuna, ili 'Wundermann Anteievskoi zakalki,'" *Zheleznyi mir*, no. 1 (2005): 40–41.

65. Natalia Kuksanova, *Sotsial'no-bytovaia infrastruktura Sibiri (1956–1980-e gg.)* (Novosibirsk: Izd-vo NGU, 1993), 29, 139; Timothy J. Colton, *Moscow: Governing the Socialist Metropolis* (Cambridge, MA: Harvard University Press, 1998), 331.

66. Interview with Sergey B., October 2016, taken by Alexander Osipov.

67. Interview with Aleksandr Cherepanov, July 2016, taken by Alexander Osipov.

68. Bobrova, "Sportpodvaly v Liubertsakh," 21.

69. B. I. Sheiko, "Kratkii ocherk razvitiia pauerliftinga v Rossii," *Zheleznyi mir*, 4 (2004): 242; Yuri Smolyakov, "Sportu nuzhno otdavat' dushu," *Zheleznyi mir*, 6 (2005): 32; Zinovii Kostiv, "Chelovek-motor," *Zheleznyi mir*, 1 (2006): 11; Aleksandr Vishnevskii, "Bodibilding—eto ne stydno," *Zheleznyi mir*, 3 (2013): 65–66.

70. Gromov, "Liubera," 182–83.

71. Interview with Aleksandr Cherepanov.

72. Nikolai Yasinovsky, *Zheleznaia pravda "Russkogo koshmara" II* (Moscow: Veche, 2011), 20.

73. *Leninskaia pravda* (Petrozavodsk), April 15, 1987, 4.

74. Interview with Sergey B.

75. Olga Smolyak, "'Rabota na sebia': Ispol'zovanie resursov promyshlennogo predpriiatiia v lichnykh tseliakh v pozdniuiu sovetskuiu epokhu," *Laboratorium: Russian Review of Social Research* 6, no. 2 (2014): 21–57; Xenia Cherkaev, "Self-Made Boats and Social Self-Management," *Cahiers du monde russe* 59, no. 2 (2018): 289–310.

76. Interview with Aleksandr Cherepanov.

77. Interview with Aleksandr Cherepanov.

78. Yasinovsky, *Zheleznaia pravda*, 19.

79. Interview with Andrei Zhukov.

80. Tenno and Sorokin, *Atletizm*, 71–82.

81. Gromov, "Liubera," 187.

82. Yasinovsky, *Zheleznaia pravda*, 29; interview with Aleksandr Cherepanov.

83. Sergei Pakhotin, "Fenomen Evgeniia Koltuna," 40–41; interview with Aleksandr Cherepanov.

84. Ivanov, "Izlom," 3.

85. Mary Douglas, *Purity and Danger: An Analysis of Concepts of Pollution and Taboo* (London: Routledge, 2003), 36.

86. Bobrova, "Sportpodvaly v Liubertsakh," 21.

87. I. Iu. Sundiiev, "Anatomiia neformal'nykh ob'iedinenii (tipologiia i kharakteristika)," in *Po nepisannym zakonam ulitsy . . .*, ed. Iu. M. Kotchenkov (Moscow: Iuridicheskaia literatura, 1991), 50.

88. Iakovlev, "Kontora liuberov."

89. Dmitry Gromov, "Liuberetskiie ulichnye molodezhnye kompanii 1980-kh godov: Subkul'tura na pereput'e istorii," *Etnograficheskoe obozrenie*, no. 4 (2006): 28.

90. Mikhail Bokov, "'Zagasit' nefera s vertushki bylo verkhom krutizny': Anonimnoe interview s byvshim liuberom," Furfur, http://www.furfur.me/furfur/all/culture/176477-intervyu-s-kachkom.

91. Valeriy Rybarev, dir., *Menia zovut Arlekino* (Belarusfilm, 1988).

92. Starks, *The Body Soviet*; David Hoffmann, *Cultivating the Masses: Modern State Practices and Soviet Socialism, 1914–1939* (Ithaca, NY: Cornell University Press, 2011).

93. Alexei Kozlov, *Kozel na sakse* (Moscow: Vagrius, 1998), 81–82, 106–8, 219–20; Mark Edele, "Strange Young Men in Stalin's Moscow: The Birth and Life of the Stiliagi, 1945–1953," *Jahrbücher für Geschichte Osteuropas* 50, no. 1 (January 1, 2002): 42–43.

94. Bobrova, "Sportpodvaly v Liubertsakh"; Sorokin, *Atleticheskaia podgotovka doprizyvnika*.

95. Efim Berezner, "Matchi veka: SSSR–SShA," *Kul'tura tela*, no. 1 (1999): 59–61.

96. Aleksandr Ivanitskii, "Shestoe chuvstvo: Razmyshleniia ob atleticheskoi gimnastike," *Smena*, no. 14 (1971): 20.

97. Ivanitskii, "Shestoe chuvstvo," 20–21.

98. Dmitry Kononov, "Ne boites' bol'shikh doz I . . . malen'kikh vesov," *Zheleznyi mir*, no. 1 (2004): 154.

99. Bokov, " 'Zagasit' nefera s vertushki bylo verkhom krutizny.' "

100. Vladimir Kozlov, *Real'naia kul'tura: Ot al'ternativy do emo* (Moscow: Amfora, 2008), 123.

101. Georgi Tenno and Anatoly Zilberbort, "Sputnitsa rekordov: Snova ob atleticheskoi gimnastike," *Smena*, no. 3 (1965): 26–27; Tenno, "Ne kul't, a kul'tura," 103.

102. Tenno and Sorokin, *Atletizm*, 13, 20, 54, 81, 173.

103. Tenno and Sorokin, *Atletizm*, 25.

104. Ivanov, "Izlom."

105. Klein, *Little Big Men*.

106. Klein, *Little Big Men*, 3, see also quote on 203: "The biographical and observational data strongly point to the widespread (although not universal) feeling [among bodybuilders] . . . that they are psychologically insignificant."

107. Vladimir Pisarev, "Pionery podzemel'ia," *Zheleznyi mir*, no. 2 (2004): 54.

108. Susan Grant, *Physical Culture and Sport in Soviet Society: Propaganda, Acculturation, and Transformation in the 1920s and 1930s* (London: Routledge, 2013), 37–44.

109. Tenno and Sorokin, *Atletizm*, 282. On bodies as instruments, see Michael A. Messner, "When Bodies Are Weapons: Masculinity and Violence in Sport," *International Review for the Sociology of Sport* 25, no. 3 (September 1, 1990): 203–20.

110. Kharkhordin, *The Collective and the Individual in Russia*, 300.

111. Volkov, "Kul'turizm ili atleticheskaia gimnastika?," 54; Bokov, " 'Zagasit' nefera s vertushki bylo verkhom krutizny' "; Gromov, "Liuberetskiie ulichinyie molodezhnye kompanii," 29; Gromov: "Liubera," 197.

112. Bokov, " 'Zagasit' nefera s vertushki bylo verkhom krutizny.' "

113. Tenno and Sorokin, *Atletizm*, 42.

114. Michel Foucault, *Security, Territory, Population: Lectures at the Collège de France 1977–1978*, ed. Michel Senellart, trans. Graham Burchell (New York: Picador, 2009); George Stocking, *Victorian Anthropology* (New York: Free Press, 1987); Marina Mogilner, *Homo Imperii: A History of Physical Anthropology in Russia* (Lincoln: University of Nebraska Press, 2013).

115. Tenno and Sorokin, *Atletizm*, 45–46.

116. Allan Sekula, "The Body and the Archive," *October* 39 (December 1, 1986): 3–64.

117. Tenno and Sorokin, *Atletizm*, 56.

118. Hellbeck, *Revolution on My Mind*; Pinsky, "The Diaristic Form and Subjectivity under Khrushchev."

119. Tenno and Sorokin, *Atletizm*, 282.

120. Tenno, "Ne kul't, a kul'tura," 105; Tenno and Sorokin, *Atletizm*, 13, 47.

121. Gromov, "Liubera"; Mikhail Bokov, "Chem i kak kachalis' v SSSR: Rel'sy, utiugi i drugoi samodel'nyi inventar'," Furfur, http://www.furfur.me/furfur/all/culture/176313-chem-i-kak-kachalis-v-sssr.

Chapter 6. Ordinary and Paranormal

1. L. Artsimovich, "Mif o 'letaiushchikh tarelkakh,'" *Pravda*, January 8, 1961; A. Mikirov, "Est' li 'letaiushchiie tarelki'?" *Komsomolskaya pravda*, January 8, 1961.

2. TASS, "Proisshestvie v parke," *Komsomolskaya pravda*, October 11, 1989. For official reporting of earlier cases of alleged UFO sightings, see B. Kotov, "Snova 'letaiushchiie tarelki,'" *Pravda*, July 21, 1967; Ye. Tsvetkov, "Kto vidit marsian," *Znanie-sila*, no. 10 (1972): 63; Ye. Parnov, "Tekhnologiia mifa," *Komsomolskaya Pravda*, November 28, 1976; N. Milov, "Neopoznannoe iavlenie prirody," *Izvestia*, September 23, 1977; S. Korepanov, "NLO: Abonentnyi iashchik 664," *Sovetskaia Rossia*, July 12, 1984. See also Sabrina P. Ramet, "UFOs over Russia and Eastern Europe," *Journal of Popular Culture* 32, no. 3 (1998): 81–99.

3. Sergei Obruchev, "Sovremennoe sostoianie problemy o snezhnom cheloveke," *Priroda*, no. 10 (1959): 60–66.

4. Kirill Staniukovich, *Po sledam udivitel'noi zagadki* (Moscow: Molodaia gvardiia, 1965); Nikolai Nepomniashchii, "Na poroge nevedomogo (Tri vstrechi s zagadochnym neznakomtsem)," in *Vremia iskat'*, ed. V. D. Zakharchenko (Moscow: Molodaia gvardiia, 1990), 23–30.

5. A. A. Gorbovskii, *Nezvanye gosti? Poltergeist vchera i segodnia* (Moscow: Znanie, 1990), the story of Barabashka is on 36–38.

6. Boris Sokolov, *Wolf Messing* (Moscow: Molodaia gvardiia, 2010), 13–14.

7. Oleg Moroz, *Ot imeni nauki: O sueveriiakh XX veka* (Moscow: Politizdat, 1989), 116–27.

8. Ye. T. Faddeev, "Tak chto zhe takoe telepatiia?" *Nauka i zhizn'*, no. 6 (1961): 60–63; V. P. Zinchenko et al., "Parapsikhologiia: Fiktsiia ili real'nost'?" *Voprosy filosofii*, no. 9 (1973): 128–36; V. P. Zinchenko and A. N. Leontiev, "Parapsikhologiia," in *Bol'shaia sovetskaia entsiklopediia*, 3rd ed. (Moscow: Sovetskaia entsiklopediia, 1975), 19:192193.

9. Yu. V. Guliaev and E. E. Godik, "Fizicheskiie polia biologicheskikh ob'ektov," *Vestnik AN SSSR*, no. 8 (1983): 118–25; Yu. V. Guliaev and E. E. Godik, "Raduga fizicheskikh polei cheloveka," *Tekhnika—molodezhi*, no. 12 (1986): 12–15. The concept of human energy was also extrapolated to entire social groups, such as nations, giving rise to popular and scholarly theories of ethnic vitalities, such as in Lev Gumelev. See Serguei Oushakine, *The Patriotism of Despair: Nation, War, and Loss in Russia* (Ithaca, NY: Cornell University Press, 2009), 79–129.

10. Eduard Godik, *Zagadka ekstrasensov: Chto uvideli fiziki* (Moscow: AST-Press Kniga, 2010), 7–12.

11. Paragraph 43 of the Federal Law No. 5487-1 "Osnovy zakonodatel'stva RF ob okhrane zdorov'ia grazhdan" of July 22, 1993.

12. Archival footage of Soviet audiences watching these séances was featured in the following documentary film: Andrei Solonevich, dir., *Kashpirovskii protiv Chumaka* (Profi-TV, 2008).

13. Vera Nikitina, "God za godom: 1990 g.," *Monitoring obshchestvennogo mneniia: Ekonomicheskiie i sotsial'nye peremeny*, no. 5 (1997): 43.

14. *Kashpirovskii protiv Chumaka*.

15. David Remnick, *Lenin's Tomb: The Last Days of the Soviet Empire* (New York: Vintage Books, 1994), 256–63.

16. The minutes of the conference were published in Aleksandr Perevozchikov, *Fenomen? Sindrom? Ili . . .* (Moscow: Znanie, 1990), 19–47.

17. Yuri Bogomolov, *Igry v liudei po-krupnomu i na interes: Iz dembel'skogo al'ma teleobozrevatelia* (Moscow: MIK, 2010), 27.

18. Eduard Limonov, *Inostranets: Smutnoe vremia* (Novosibirsk: Sibirskiie ogni, 1992), 60–63; Vladimir Solovev, *1001 vopros o proshlom, nastoiashchem i budushchem Rossii* (Moscow: Eksmo, 2010), 175–77; author's interview with G. S., Vancouver, July 2014.

19. Perevozchikov, *Fenomen? Sindrom? Ili . . .*, 28–29.

20. Sergei Muratov, *Televidenie v poiskakh televideniia: Khronika avtorskikh nabliudenii* (Moscow: Izd-vo MGU, 2009), 79 (originally published as "Kino kak raznovidnost' televideniia," *Radio i televideniie*, no. 24 and 25 (1967)); Anne Friedberg, "The Virtual Window," in *Rethinking Media Change: The Aesthetics of Transition*, ed. David Thorburn and Henry Jenkins (Cambridge: MIT Press, 2003), 338.

21. Boris Firsov, *Televideniie glazami sotsiologa* (Moscow: Iskusstvo, 1971), 51–59; A. A. Ksenofontov, *A esli v sem'e televizor . . . i deti?* (Moscow: Znanie, 1973).

22. A. Ivanitskii, "Esli khochesh byt' zdorov: O sportivnykh programmakh Tsentral'nogo Televideniia," *Televideniie. Radioveshchaniie*, no. 8 (1985): 1–3, 33–34; my interview with Natalia Korkh (Efremova), West Vancouver, April 2015.

23. Iraklii Andronikov, "Okno v mir," *Ogoniok*, no. 9 (1962): 26; Margarita Khemlin, "Pro kota i pro molniiu," *Televidenie i radioveshchanie*, no. 8 (1990): 43–45. For a deconstruction and critical analysis to the vernacular link between the TV set and family, see Roger Silverstone, *Television and Everyday Life* (London: Routledge, 1994), 32–43.

24. Muratov, *Televidenie v poiskakh televideniia*, 48.

25. Boris Firsov, *Televideniie glazami sotsiologa* (Moscow: Iskusstvo, 1971), 141–57.

26. Muratov, *Televidenie v poiskakh televideniia*, 46.

27. For general English-language works on Soviet television, including its historiography, see Ellen Propper Mickiewicz, *Split Signals: Television and Politics in the Soviet Union* (New York: Oxford University Press, 1988); Kristin Roth-Ey, *Moscow Prime Time: How the Soviet Union Built the Media Empire That Lost the Cultural Cold War* (Ithaca, NY: Cornell University Press, 2011); Christine Evans, *Between Truth and Time: A History of Soviet Central Television* (New Haven: Yale University Press, 2017). For an annotated bibliography of Russian-language scholarship, see TVMuseum.ru: http://www.tvmuseum.ru/catalog.asp?ob_no=7253.

28. Mihaly Csikszentmihalyi and Eugene Rochberg-Halton, *The Meaning of Things: Domestic Symbols and the Self* (Cambridge: Cambridge University Press, 1981), 47.

29. Andronikov, "Okno v mir," 25–29; Vladimir Sappak, *Televidenie i my: Chetyre besedy* (Moscow: Iskusstvo, 1963).

30. Muratov, *Televidenie v poiskakh televideniia*, 48, 88; Sappak, *Televidenie i my*, 13.

31. Marshall McLuhan, *Understanding Media: The Extensions of Man* (New York: McGraw-Hill, 1964).

32. Friedrich A. Kittler, *Gramophone, Film, Typewriter*, trans. Geoffrey Winthrop-Young and Michael Wutz (Stanford, CA: Stanford University Press, 1999).

33. John Armitage, "From Discourse Networks to Cultural Mathematics: An Interview with Friedrich A. Kittler," *Theory, Culture & Society* 23, no. 7–8 (December 1, 2006): 36.

34. *Torgovlia SSSR: Statisticheskii sbornik* (Moscow: Finansy i statistika, 1989), 32.

35. R. N. Musina, "Sotsial'no-etnicheskie aspekty sovremennoi dukhovnoi kul'tury sel'skikh tatar," *Etnograficheskoie obozreniie* 5 (1983): 90.

36. Lynn Spigel, *Make Room for TV: Television and the Family Ideal in Postwar America* (Chicago: University of Chicago Press, 1992), 36–40.

37. Ethnographic research of Russian regions noted that TV sets were often installed in the former icon corner: A. S. Kuchumova, "Krasnyi ugol. Polozheniie v prostranstve (location) kak semanticheskii priznak veshchi," Folk.ru, http://www.folk.ru/Research/kuchumova_krasny_ugol.php. See also Andrei Stepanov, "Severnorusskaia izba: Dinamika prostranstva i povsednevnyi opyt (2-ia polovina XX–nachalo XXI v.)," *Antropologicheskii forum*, no. 16 (2012): 77.

38. Leonid Parfionov, *Namedni, 1971–1980* (Moscow: KoLibri, 2010), 156–57.

39. Susan Reid, "Everyday Aesthetics in the Khrushchev-era Standard Apartment," in *Everyday Life in Russia: Past and Present*, ed. Choi Chatterjee et al. (Bloomington: Indiana University Press, 2015), 215.

40. Serguei Oushakine, "Mnogo khleba i mnogo roz: O krasote i pol'ze sovetkogo veshchizma," an unpublished paper.

41. Gorsuch, *All This Is Your World*, 93–97.

42. Dunham, *In Stalin's Time*, 43.

43. Reid, "Cold War in the Kitchen"; Reid, "Khrushchev Modern"; Harris, *Communism on Tomorrow Street*.

44. I. A. Kriukova, "Dekorativno-prikladnoie iskusstvo," in *Ocherki sovremennogo sovetskogo iskusstva*, ed. I. A. Kriukova et al. (Moscow: Nauka, 1975), 91–92.

45. L. A. Gordon and E. V. Klopov, *Man after Work: Social Problems of Daily Life and Leisure Time, Based on the Surveys of Workers' Time Budgets in Major Cities of the European Part of the USSR* (Moscow: Progress Publishers, 1975), 131.

46. "Rech' A. T. Tvardovskogo," in *Vneocherednoi XXI S'ezd Kommunisticheskoi partii Sovetskogo Soiuza: Stenograficheskii otchet* (Moscow: Politizdat, 1959), 1:562; see also Catriona Kelly, "'Thank-You for the Wonderful Book': Soviet Child Readers and the Management of Children's Reading, 1950–1975," *Kritika: Explorations in Russian and Eurasian History* 6, no. 4 (2005): 717–53.

47. T. Simonova, "Kopit' znaniia, a ne izdaniia," *V mire knig*, no. 9 (September 1985): 56.

48. Sappak, *Televidenie i my*, 91.

49. G. I. Kositskii, *Tsivilizatsiia i serdtse* (Moscow: Nauka, 1977), 94.

50. Ivanitskii, "Esli khochesh byt' zdorov."

51. A. V. Ivanitskii et al., *Ritmicheskaia gimnastika na TV* (Moscow: Sovetskii sport, 1989), 3–4.

52. Many of these episodes are currently available on YouTube and similar streaming services. In particular, the official YouTube channel of the Russian State Fund of Television and Radio programs (Gosteleradiofond) published several episodes of *Ritmicheskaia gimnastika* with the hashtag #ритмика; see, e.g., https://www.youtube.com/watch?v=PG3oLeB9PiI.

53. Olga Pautova, dir., *Zariadka v stile disko* (1 Kanal, 2015). See also Leonid Parfionov, dir., *Namedni. 1985* (NTV, 1998).

54. Ivanitskii et al., *Ritmicheskaia gimnastika na TV*, 3.

55. Interview with Natalia Korkh.

56. It has been subject to multiple speculations ever since, most recently in *Kashpirovskii protiv Chumaka*.

57. V. Shcherbachev, "Vnusheniie vmesto narkoza," *Trud*, April 8, 1988; L. Rodina, "Bez boli, bez narkoza," *Sovetskaia Rossiia*, April 10, 1988; S. Tutorskaia, "Gipnoz bez chudes," *Izvestia*, April 16, 1988.

58. Anton Morgovskii, *Anatolii Kashpirovskii . . . Vchera, segodnia, zavtra . . .* (Kiev: Molod', 1990), 6–8.

59. V. Vrublevskaia, "Vnushaiu vam tol'ko dobro," *Pravda Ukrainy*, March 25, 1989; Stanislav Kalinichev, " 'Ia umeiu dat' komandu,' " *Smena* 14 (1989): 14–16.

60. Author's transcript of the TV show.

61. Author's transcript of the TV show.

62. Remnick, *Lenin's Tomb*, 258–61.

63. For example, A. Medelianovskii, "Sharlatanstvo ili panatseiia?," *Argumenty i fakty*, no. 35 (September 1989): 5–6; " 'Fenomen Kashpirovskogo': Chto govoriat uchenye?" *Sovetskaia kul'tura*, November 28, 1989; I. Kharitonov, "Glaza v glaza," *Sovetskaia Rossiia*, November 26, 1989.

64. I observed the audiences of their live performances available in video records, as well as noted the gender of the authors of laudatory and critical responses.

65. Perevozchikov, *Fenomen? Sindrom? Ili . . .*, 42.

66. Perevozchikov, *Fenomen? Sindrom? Ili . . .*, 30. Some of these letters were reproduced in Morgovskii, *Anatolii Kashpirovskii*.

67. Perevozchikov, *Fenomen? Sindrom? Ili . . .*, 32–34.

68. Limonov, *Inostranets*, 60–63.

69. Eve Kosofsky Sedgwick, *Touching Feeling: Affect, Pedagogy, Performativity* (Durham: Duke University Press, 2003), 37.

70. Muratov, *Televidenie v poiskakh televideniia*, 79, 88.

71. Perevozchikov, *Fenomen? Sindrom? Ili . . .*, 32–34.

72. Brian McNair, *Glasnost, Perestroika and the Soviet Media* (London: Routledge, 2006).

73. Irakly Andronikov, "Okno v mir," *Ogoniok*, no. 9 (1962): 26.

74. Alaina Lemon, in particular, emphasized the communicative function of television, its ability to connect audiences with celebrities, in her analysis of Chumak's séances: Alaina Lemon, *Technologies for Intuition: Cold War Circles and Telepathic Rays* (Oakland: University of California Press, 2018), 99–103.

75. Kaganovsky, *How the Soviet Man Was Unmade*.

Conclusions

1. For example, Michel de Certeau begins his *The Practice of Everyday Life* with an "invention" of a new language for social description, as his main claim is that the dominant analytical language cannot describe, but only "capture" the "the fleeting and massive reality of a social activity at play with the order that contains it." Michel de Certeau, *The Practice of Everyday Life* (Berkeley: University of California Press, 1984), xxiv. On the emancipatory political potential of materiality and material culture, see also Miller, *Material Culture and Mass Consumption*, especially the chapters "Object Domains, Ideology and Interests" and "Towards a Theory of Consumption," 158–217.

2. Coole and Frost, *New Materialism*; Bennett, *Vibrant Matter*; Brown, "Thing Theory."

3. Shklovsky, "Art as Technique," 12.

4. Langdon Winner, "Do Artifacts Have Politics?" *Daedalus* 109, no. 1 (1980): 121–36.

5. For a detailed discussion of the problem of the Soviet Union and modernity, see Michael David-Fox, *Crossing Borders: Modernity, Ideology, and Culture in Russia and the Soviet Union* (Pittsburgh: University of Pittsburgh Press, 2015), 1–7, 21–47; special issue "Sporia o modernosti," in *Novoe literaturnoe obozrenie*, no. 4 (2016): 16–91.

6. Göran Therborn, "Entangled Modernities," *European Journal of Social Theory* 6, no. 3 (2003): 293–305. See also David-Fox, *Crossing Border*, 47.

SELECTED BIBLIOGRAPHY

Adas, Michael. *Machines as the Measure of Men: Science, Technology, and Ideologies of Western Dominance*. Ithaca, NY: Cornell University Press, 1989.

Ahmed, Sara. *The Cultural Politics of Emotion*. New York: Routledge, 2004.

Althusser, Louis. "Ideology and Ideological State Apparatuses (Notes towards an Investigation)." In *Lenin and Philosophy, and Other Essays*, 127–93. New York: Monthly Review Press, 1974.

Altov, Genrikh. "Tret'e tysiacheletie." In *NF: Sbornik nauchnoi fantastiki*, 14:3–52. Moscow: Znanie, 1974.

Altshuller, Genrikh. *Algoritm izobreteniia*. Moscow: Moskovskii rabochii, 1973.

——. *Naiti ideiu*. Novosibirsk: Nauka, 1984.

——. *TRIZ Keys to Technical Innovation*. Translated and edited by Lev Shulyak and Steven Rodman. Worcester, MA: Technical Innovation Center, 2002.

Altshuller, Genrikh S., and Aleksandr B. Seliutskii. *Kryl'ia dlia Ikara: Kak reshat' izobretatel'skie zadachi*. Petrozavodsk: Karelia, 1980.

Altshuller, Genrikh S., and Igor M. Viortkin. *Kak stat' geniem*. Minsk: Belarus, 1994.

Altshuller, Genrikh, B. L. Zlotin, and A. V. Zusman, eds. *Teoriia i praktika resheniia izobretatel'skikh zadach*. Kishinev: Vsesoiuznyi institut TRIZ, 1989.

Ananieva, M. I. et al., eds. *Dialekticheskii materialism*. Moscow: Mysl', 1989.

Andrews, James T., and Asif A. Siddiqi, eds. *Into the Cosmos: Space Exploration and Soviet Culture*. Pittsburgh: University of Pittsburgh Press, 2011.

Aptekar, M. L. *Tiazheaia atletika. Spravochnik*. Moscow: Fizkul'tura i sport, 1983.

Aptekman, D. M. *Formirovanie ateisticheskoi ubezhdennosti rabochego klassa v razvitom sotsialiticheskom obshchestve*. Leningrad: Izd-vo LGU, 1979.

Armitage, John. "From Discourse Networks to Cultural Mathematics: An Interview with Friedrich A. Kittler." *Theory, Culture & Society* 23, no. 7–8 (2006): 17–38.

Arvatov, Boris. "Everyday Life and the Culture of the Thing (Toward the Formulation of the Question)." Translated by Christina Kiaer. *October* 81 (1997): 119–28.

Attwood, Lynne. *Gender and Housing in Soviet Russia: Private Life in a Public Space*. Manchester: Manchester University Press, 2010.

Auslander, Leora, Amy Bentley, Halevi Leor, H. Otto Sibum, and Christopher Witmore. "AHR Conversation: Historians and the Study of Material Culture." *American Historical Review* 114, no. 5 (2009): 1355–404.

Austin, J. L. *How to Do Things with Words*. Oxford: Clarendon Press, 1962.

Babaev, N., and S. Kudriavtsev. *Letaiushchiie igrushki i modeli*. Moscow: Oborongiz, 1946.

Balzer, Harley. "Education, Science and Technology." In *The Soviet Union Today: An Interpretive Guide*, edited by James Cracraft, 233–43. Chicago: University of Chicago Press, 1988.

Baron, Nick. *Soviet Karelia: Politics, Planning and Terror in Stalin's Russia, 1920–1939*. London: Routledge, 2012.

Barthes, Roland. "Death of the Author." In *Image, Music, Text*, 142–48. Translated by Stephen Heath. New York: Hill and Wang, 1977.

Battaloglu, E., and D. Bose. "The History of Ilizarov." *Trauma* 15, no. 3 (2013): 257–62.

Baudrillard, Jean. *The System of Objects*. London: Verso, 1996.

Belyaev, A.T., B. A. Gushchin, and V. A. Gushchina. *Gosudarstvennyi istoriko-arkhitekturnyi i etnograficheskii muzei-zapovednik Kizhi: Putevoditel'*. Petrozavodsk: Karelia, 1973.

Belyaev, N. A., and M. D. Shargorodskii, eds. *Kurs sovetskogo ugolovnogo prava (chast obshchaia)*. Vol. 1. Leningrad: Izd-vo LGU, 1968.

Benjamin, Walter. *The Arcades Project*. Cambridge, MA: Belknap Press, 1999.

Bennett, Jane. *Vibrant Matter: A Political Ecology of Things*. Durham: Duke University Press, 2010.

Bennett, Tony. "The Exhibitionary Complex." *New Formations* 4 (1988): 73–102.

Bittner, Stephen. *The Many Lives of Khrushchev's Thaw: Experience and Memory in Moscow's Arbat*. Ithaca, NY: Cornell University Press, 2008.

Bogdanov, Alexander. *Vseobshchaia organizatsionnaia nauka (tektologiia)*. 2 vols. Moscow: Ekonomika, 1989.

Bogoliubov, K. M., and F. P. Petrov, eds. *KPSS o formirovanii novogo cheloveka: Sbornik dokumentov i materialov, 1965–1981*. Moskva: Politizdat, 1982.

Bogomolov, Yuri. *Igry v liudei po-krupnomu i na interes: Iz dembel'skogo al'boma teleobozrevatelia*. Moscow: MIK, 2010.

Bondarenko, Svetlana, and Viktor Kurilskii, eds. *Neizvestnye Strugatskie. Pis'ma. Rabochie dnevniki. 1963–1966 gg*. Moscow: AST, 2009.

Bourdieu, Pierre. *Distinction: A Social Critique of the Judgement of Taste*. Cambridge, MA: Harvard University Press, 1984.

Boym, Svetlana. *Common Places: Mythologies of Everyday Life in Russia*. Cambridge, MA: Harvard University Press, 1994.

Brandenberger, David. *National Bolshevism: Stalinist Mass Culture and the Formation of Modern Russian National Identity, 1931–1956*. Cambridge, MA: Harvard University Press, 2002.

Brandenberger, David, and Kevin M. F. Platt. "Introduction: Tsarist-Era Heroes in Stalinist Mass Culture and Propaganda." In *Epic Revisionism: Russian History and Literature as Stalinist Propaganda*, edited by Kevin M. F. Platt and David Brandenberger, 3–16. Madison: University of Wisconsin Press, 2006.

Brezhnev, Leonid. "Otchetnyi doklad TsK KPSS XXIV s'ezdu KPSS." In *XXIV s'ezd KPSS. Stenogr. otchet*, vol. 1, 26–131. Moscow: Politizdat, 1971.

Brown, Bill. "Thing Theory." *Critical Inquiry* 28, no. 1 (2001): 1–22.

Brumel, Valery. *Vysota*. Moscow: Molodaia gvardiia, 1971.

Brumel, Valery, and Aleksandr Lapshin. *Ne izmeni sebe*. Moscow: Molodaia gvardiia, 1980.

Buchli, Victor. *An Archaeology of Socialism*. Oxford: Berg, 2000.

Bulatov, N. "Sozdanie detskikh tekhnicheskikh stantsii." In *Smena komsomola: Dokumenty, vospominaniia, materiialy po istorii VPO (1917–1962 gg.)*, edited by V. Iakovlev 134–35. Moscow: Molodaia gvardiia, 1964.

Bulychev, Kir. *Sto let tomu vpered*. Moscow: Det. lit-ra, 1978.

Bunkov, S. I. *Khirurg Ilizarov*. Chelyabinsk: Iuzh.-Ural. kn. izd-vo, 1972.

Bushnell, John. *Moscow Graffiti: Language and Subculture*. London: Unwin Hyman, 1990.

Butler, Judith. *Excitable Speech: A Politics of the Performative*. New York: Routledge, 1997.

Bylinkin, N. P., and A. V. Riabushin, eds. *Sovremennaia sovetskaia arkhitektura*. Moscow: Stroiizdat, 1985.

Bylov, V. G., and I. G. Minervin, eds. *Molodezh' i nauchno-tekhnicheskii progress*. Moscow: INION RAN, 1985.

Carr, Edward. *What Is History?* London: Palgrave Macmillan, 2001.

Certeau, Michel de. *The Practice of Everyday Life*. Berkeley: University of California Press, 1984.

Chadaga, Julia Bekman. *Optical Play: Glass, Vision, and Spectacle in Russian Culture*. Chicago: Northwestern University Press, 2014.

Chatterjee, Choi, and Karen Petrone. "Models of Selfhood and Subjectivity: The Soviet Case in Historical Perspective." *Slavic Review* 67, no. 4 (2008): 967–86.

Chauncey, George. *Gay New York: Gender, Urban Culture, and the Makings of the Gay Male World, 1890–1940*. New York: Basic Books, 1994.

Cherkaev, Xenia. "Self-Made Boats and Social Self-Management." *Cahiers du monde russe* 59, no. 2 (2018): 289–310.

Chernyshova, Natalya. *Soviet Consumer Culture in the Brezhnev Era*. London: Routledge, 2013.

Chomsky, Noam, and Michel Foucault. *The Chomsky-Foucault Debate: On Human Nature*. New York: New Press, 2006.

Clark, Katerina. *Moscow, the Fourth Rome: Stalinism, Cosmopolitanism, and the Evolution of Soviet Culture, 1931–1941*. Cambridge, MA: Harvard University Press, 2011.

———. *The Soviet Novel: History as Ritual*. Bloomington: Indiana University Press, 2000.

Clifford, James. *The Predicament of Culture: Twentieth-Century Ethnography, Literature, and Art*. Cambridge, MA: Harvard University Press, 1988.

Colton, Timothy. *Moscow: Governing the Socialist Metropolis*. Cambridge, MA: Harvard University Press, 1988.

Connolly, William E. "The Order of Modernity." In *Democracy, Pluralism and Political Theory*, edited by Samuel A. Chambers and Terrell Carver, 280–93. London: Routledge, 2008.

Coole, Diana H., and Samantha Frost, eds. *New Materialisms: Ontology, Agency, and Politics*. Durham: Duke University Press, 2010.

Cooper, Julian. "The Scientific and Technical Revolution in Soviet Theory." In *Technology and Communist Culture: The Socio-Cultural Impact of Technology under Socialism*, edited by Frederic Fleron, 146–79. New York: Praeger, 1977.

Csikszentmihalyi, Mihaly, and Eugene Rochberg-Halton. *The Meaning of Things: Domestic Symbols and the Self*. Cambridge: Cambridge University Press, 1981.

Cusack, Tricia. *Riverscapes and National Identities*. Syracuse, NY: Syracuse University Press, 2010.

Czajkowski, Jerzy. "Muzeiam pod otkrytym nebom—100 let." In *Muzeevedenie: Muzei-zapovedniki*, edited by N. A. Nikishin and O. G. Sevan, 10–26. Moscow: NII Kul'tury, 1991.

David-Fox, Michael. *Crossing Borders: Modernity, Ideology, and Culture in Russia and the Soviet Union*. Pittsburgh: University of Pittsburgh Press, 2015.

De Maupassant, Guy. *Complete Short Stories*. New York: Walter J. Black Inc., 1903.

Derrida, Jacques. " 'To Do Justice to Freud': The History of Madness in the Age of Psychoanalysis." Translated by Pascale-Anne Brault and Michael Naas. *Critical Inquiry* 20, no. 2 (1994): 227–66.

Dikul, Valentin, and Alexandr Eliseikin. *Razorvannyi krug*. Moscow: Sovetskii sport, 1993.

"Direktivy XXIII s'ezda KPSS po piatiletnemu planu razvitiia narodnogo khoziaistva SSSR na 1966–1970 gody." In *XXIII s'ezd Kommunisticheskoi partii Sovetskogo Soiuza, 26 marta—8 aprelia 1966 goda*, 321–82. Moscow: Politizdat, 1966.

Dobrenko, Evgeny. *The Making of the State Reader: Social and Aesthetic Contexts of the Reception of Soviet Literature*. Stanford, CA: Stanford University Press, 1997.

Dobrenko, Evgeny, and Eric Naiman, eds. *The Landscape of Stalinism the Art and Ideology of Soviet Space*. Seattle: University of Washington Press, 2003.

Donovan, Victoria. " 'Going Backwards, We Stride Forwards': Kraevedenie Museums and the Making of Local Memory in North West Russia, 1956–1981." *Forum for Anthropology and Culture* 7 (2012): 211–30.

——. " 'How Well Do You Know Your Krai?' The Kraevedenie Revival and Patriotic Politics in Late Khrushchev-Era Russia." *Slavic Review* 74, no. 3 (2015): 464–83.

Douglas, Mary. *Purity and Danger: An Analysis of Concepts of Pollution and Taboo*. London and New York: Routledge, 2003.

Dremliuga, A. I., and L. P. Dubinina. *Iunomu sudomodelistu*. Kiev: Radianska shkola, 1983.

Dunham, Vera. *In Stalin's Time: Middleclass Values in Soviet Fiction*. Cambridge: Cambridge University Press, 1976.

Edele, Mark. "Strange Young Men in Stalin's Moscow: The Birth and Life of the Stiliagi, 1945–1953." *Jahrbücher Für Geschichte Osteuropas* 50, no. 1 (2002): 37–61.

Elenius, Lars, Hallvard Tjelmeland, Maria Lähteenmäki, and Alexey Golubev, eds. *The Barents Region: A Transnational History of Subarctic Northern Europe*. Oslo: PAX, 2015.

Ely, Christopher. *This Meager Nature: Landscape and National Identity in Imperial Russia*. DeKalb: Northern Illinois University Press, 2009.

Evans, Christine. *Between Truth and Time: A History of Soviet Central Television*. New Haven: Yale University Press, 2017.

Fehérváry, Krisztina. *Politics in Color and Concrete: Socialist Materialities and the Middle Class in Hungary*. Bloomington: Indiana University Press, 2013.

Field, Deborah. *Private Life and Communist Morality in Khrushchev's Russia*. New York: Peter Lang, 2007.

Fieseler, Beate. "The Bitter Legacy of the 'Great Patriotic War': Red Army Disabled Soldiers under Late Stalinism." In *Late Stalinist Russia: Society between Reconstruction and Reinvention*, edited by Juliane Fürst, 46–61. London: Routledge, 2005.

Firsov, Boris. *Televidenie glazami sotsiologa*. Moscow: Iskusstvo, 1971.

——. *Raznomyslie v SSSR i Rossii (1945–2008): Istoriia, teoriia i praktiki*. St. Petersburg: EU SPb Press, 2008.

Foucault, Michel. *Discipline and Punish: The Birth of the Prison*. New York: Pantheon Books, 1977.

——. *The History of Sexuality*. Vol. 1. New York: Pantheon Books, 1978.

——. *Security, Territory, Population: Lectures at the Collège de France 1977–1978*. Edited by Michel Senellart. Translated by Graham Burchell. New York: Picador, 2009.

Friedberg, Anne. "The Virtual Window." In *Rethinking Media Change the Aesthetics of Transition*, edited by David Thorburn and Henry Jenkins, 337–53. Cambridge, MA: MIT Press, 2003.

Gallego, Ruben. *White on Black*. Orlando: Harcourt, 2006.

Gan, Aleksei. "Konstruktivism." In *Formal'nyi metod: Antologiia russkogo modernizma*, edited by Serguei Oushakine, vol. 1, 818–58. Yekaterinburg: Kabinetnyi uchenyi, 2016.

Gastev, Aleksei. *Kak nado rabotat'*. Moscow: Ekonomika, 1972.

Geiges, Adrian, and Tatiana Suvorova. *Liubov'—vne plana: (sex & perestroika): Intimnaia zhizn' i polozhenie zhenshchin v SSSR*. Moscow: Sobesednik, 1990.

Gesler, V. M. *Avtomobil' svoimi rukami*. Moscow: DOSAAF, 1970.

Ginzburg, Carlo. "Morelli, Freud and Sherlock Holmes: Clues and Scientific Method." Translated by Anna Davin. *History Workshop* 9 (1980): 5–36.

Ginzburg, Moisei. *Style and Epoch*. Translated by Anatole Senkevitch Jr. Cambridge: MIT Press, 1982.

Godik, Eduard. *Zagadka ekstrasensov: Chto uvideli fiziki*. Moscow: AST-Press Kniga, 2010.

Golikov, V. A., ed. *Sovetskii Soiuz: Politiko-ekonomicheskii spravochnik*. Moscow: Politizdat, 1982.

Golubev, Alexey. "Affective Machines or the Inner Self? Drawing the Boundaries of the Female Body in the Socialist Romantic Imagination." *Canadian Slavonic Papers/Revue canadienne des slavistes* 58, no. 2 (2013): 141–59.

Golubev, Alexey, and Olga Smolyak. "Making Selves through Making Things: Soviet Do-It-Yourself Culture and Practices of Late Soviet Subjectivation." *Cahiers du monde russe* 54, no. 3/4 (2013): 517–41.

Gombrich, Ernst. *Art and Illusion: A Study in the Psychology of Pictorial Representation*. London: Phaidon Press, 1977.

Gorbovskii, A. A. *Nezvanyie gosti? Poltergeist vchera i segodnia*. Moscow: Znaniie, 1990.

Gordon, L. A., and E. V. Klopov. *Man after Work: Social Problems of Daily Life and Leisure Time, Based on the Surveys of Workers' Time Budgets in Major Cities of the European Part of the USSR*. Moscow: Progress Publishers, 1975.

Gorsuch, Anne. *All This Is Your World: Soviet Tourism at Home and Abroad after Stalin*. Oxford: Oxford University Press, 2011.

Gramsci, Antonio. *Prison Notebooks*. Vol. II. New York: Columbia University Press, 1996.

Grant, Susan. *Physical Culture and Sport in Soviet Society: Propaganda, Acculturation, and Transformation in the 1920s and 1930s*. London: Routledge, 2013.

Green, Brett. *Modelling Scale Aircraft*. Oxford: Osprey, 2012.

Green, James. *Beyond Carnival: Male Homosexuality in Twentieth-Century Brazil*. Chicago: University of Chicago Press, 2001.

Greider, Thomas, and Lorraine Garkovich. "Landscapes: The Social Construction of Nature and the Environment." *Rural Sociology* 59, no. 1 (1994): 1–24.

Grishina, Irina Ye. "Etnoarkhitektura: Printsipy issledovaniia." *Uchenye zapiski Petrozavodskogo gosudarstvennogo universiteta* 5 (2009): 7–13.

Gromeka, Vasilii. *Nauchno-tekhnicheskaia revoliutsiia i sovremennyi kapitalizm*. Moscow: Politizdat, 1976.

Gromov, Dmitry. "Liuberetskie ulichinye molodezhnye kompanii 1980-kh godov: Subkul'tura na pereput'e istorii." *Etnograficheskoie obozreniie* 4 (2006): 23–38.

——. "'Moral'naia panika' kak mekhanizm razvitiia riada molodezhnykh soob-shchestv Sovetskogo Soiuza i Rossii." *Istoricheskaia psikhologiia i sotsiologiia istorii* 5, no. 1 (2012): 164–78.

Groys, Boris. *The Total Art of Stalinism*. London: Verso, 2011.

Guliaev, Yu. V., and E. E. Godik. "Fizicheskie polia biologicheskikh ob'ektov." *Vestnik AN SSSR* 8 (1983): 118–25.

Halfin, Igal. *Terror in My Soul: Communist Autobiographies on Trial*. Cambridge, MA: Harvard University Press, 2002.

——. *Red Autobiographies: Initiating the Bolshevik Self*. Seattle: University of Washington Press, 2011.

Halfin, Igal, and Jochen Hellbeck. "Rethinking the Stalinist Subject: Stephen Kotkin's 'Magnetic Mountain' and the State of Soviet Historical Studies." *Jahrbücher Für Geschichte Osteuropas* 44, no. 3 (1996): 456–63.

Harris, Stephen E. *Communism on Tomorrow Street: Mass Housing and Everyday Life after Stalin*. Washington, DC: Johns Hopkins University Press, 2013.

——. "Soviet Mass Housing and the Communist Way of Life." In *Everyday Life in Russia: Past and Present*, edited by Choi Chatterjee, David L. Ransel, Mary Cavender, and Karen Petrone, 181–202. Bloomington: Indiana University Press, 2015.

Hartman, Andrew. *Education and the Cold War: The Battle for the American School*. New York: Palgrave Macmillan, 2008.

Hecht, Gabrielle, ed. *Entangled Geographies: Empires and Technopolitics in the Global Cold War*. Cambridge: MIT Press, 2011.

——. *The Radiance of France: Nuclear Power and National Identity after World War II*. Cambridge: MIT Press, 1998.

Hellbeck, Jochen. *Revolution on My Mind: Writing a Diary under Stalin*. Cambridge, MA: Harvard University Press, 2006.

Hellebust, Rolf. *Flesh to Metal: Soviet Literature and the Alchemy of Revolution*. Ithaca, NY: Cornell University Press, 2003.

Heller, Mikhail. *Cogs in the Wheel: The Formation of Soviet Man*. New York: Knopf, 1988.

Hill, Ronald J., and Peter Frank. *The Soviet Communist Party*. London: Allen and Unwin, 1986.

Hoffmann, David. *Cultivating the Masses Modern State Practices and Soviet Socialism, 1914–1939*. Ithaca, NY: Cornell University Press, 2011.

Horn, Eva. *The Secret War: Treason, Espionage, and Modern Fiction*. Translated by Geoffrey Winthrop-Young. Evanston, IL: Northwestern University Press, 2013.

Hornborg, Alf. "Technology as Fetish: Marx, Latour, and the Cultural Foundations of Capitalism." *Theory, Culture & Society* 31, no. 4 (2014): 119–40.

Humphrey, Caroline. *The Unmaking of Soviet Life: Everyday Economies after Socialism*. Ithaca, NY: Cornell University Press, 2002.

Ilyukha, Olga, and Yuri Shikalov. "Kartina mira na stranitsakh uchebnikov finskogo iazyka dlia nachal'nykh klassov karel'skikh shkol 1920–1940-kh godov." *Vestnik filiala Severo-Zapadnoi akademii Gosudarstvennoi sluzhby v Vyborge*. Vyborg: Filial SZAGS v Vyborge, 2010.

Intimnye anekdoty. St. Petersburg: OOO Diamant, 1996.

Isaev, D. N., and V. E. Kagan. *Polovoe vospitanie i psikhogigiena pola u detei.* Moscow: Meditsina, 1979.

Isaev, D. N., B. Ye. Mikirtumov, and Ye. I. Bogdanova. "Seksual'nye proiavleniia v klinicheskoi kartine pogranichnykh nervno-psikhicheskikh rasstroistv v detskom i podrostkovom vozraste." *Pediatriia* 3 (1979): 39–43.

Istomin, Pavel. "Turistskaia deiatel'nost' kak sredstvo vospitaniia sotsial'noi aktivnosti starsheklassnikov." Cand. Sc. dissertation in education, Research Institute of General Problems of Education of the USSR Academy of Pedagogical Sciences, 1978.

Itogi Vsesoiuznoi perepisi naseleniia 1989 goda. Tom 2. Vozrast i sostoianiie v brake. Chast 1. Minneapolis: East View Publications, 1992.

Ivanitskii, A. V., V. V. Matov, O. A. Ivanova, and I. N. Sharabarova. *Ritmicheskaia gimnastika na TV.* Moscow: Sovetskii sport, 1989.

Ivanov, B. S. *Elektronika svoimi rukami.* Moscow: Molodaia gvardiia, 1964.

Joerges, Bernward. "Technology in Everyday Life: Conceptual Queries." *Journal for the Theory of Social Behaviour* 18, no. 2 (1988): 219–37.

Kabakov, Mark. "Put' na moria." In *Radi zhizni na zemle*, ed. Viktor Oliinik, 345–445. Moscow: DOSAAF, 1988.

Kaganovsky, Lilya. *How the Soviet Man Was Unmade: Cultural Fantasy and Male Subjectivity under Stalin.* Pittsburgh: University of Pittsburgh Press, 2008.

Karpova, Yulia. *Comradely Objects: Design and Material Culture in Soviet Russia, 1960s–80s.* Manchester: Manchester University Press, 2020.

Kassil, Lev, and Maks Polianovskii. *Ulitsa mladshego syna.* Moscow: Detskaia literatura, 1949.

Kelly, Catriona. "'Thank-You for the Wonderful Book': Soviet Child Readers and the Management of Children's Reading, 1950–1975." *Kritika: Explorations in Russian and Eurasian History* 6, no. 4 (2005): 717–53.

——. "Socialist Churches: Heritage Preservation and 'Cultic Buildings' in Leningrad, 1924–1940." *Slavic Review* 71, no. 4 (2012): 792–823.

——. "From 'Counter-Revolutionary Monuments' to 'National Heritage.'" *Cahiers du monde russe* 54, no. 1 (2014): 131–64.

——. *St. Petersburg: Shadows of the Past.* New Haven: Yale University Press, 2014.

Kenez, Peter. *Cinema and Soviet Society, 1917–1953.* Cambridge: Cambridge University Press, 1992.

Kharkhordin, Oleg. *The Collective and the Individual in Russia: A Study of Practices.* Berkeley: University of California Press, 1999.

Khrushchev, Nikita. "Otchetnyi doklad TsK KPSS XX s'ezdu partii." In *XX s'ezd KPSS. 14–25 fevralia 1956 g. Stenograficheskii otchet*, 9–120. Moscow: Politizdat, 1956.

Kiaer, Christina. *Imagine No Possessions: The Socialist Objects of Russian Constructivism.* Cambridge, MA: MIT Press, 2008.

Kittler, Friedrich. *Gramophone, Film, Typewriter.* Translated by Geoffrey Winthrop-Young and Michael Wutz. Stanford: Stanford University Press, 1999.

Klein, Alan M. *Little Big Men: Bodybuilding Subculture and Gender Construction.* Albany: State University of New York Press, 1993.

Koenker, Diane P. *Club Red: Vacation Travel and the Soviet Dream.* Ithaca, NY: Cornell University Press, 2013.

Kojevnikov, Alexei. "Science as Co-Producer of Soviet Polity." *Historia Scientiarum* 22, no. 3 (2010): 161–80.

Kolominskii, Iakov. *Psikhologiia obshcheniia*. Moscow: Znanie, 1974.

Kon, Igor. *The Sexual Revolution in Russia: From the Age of the Czars to Today* Translated by James Riordan. New York: Free Press, 1995.

——. *Seksual'naia kul'tura v Rossii: Klubnichka na berezke*. 3rd ed. Moscow: Vremia, 2010.

Konchalovsky, Andrei. *Vozvyshaiushchii obman*. Moscow: Sovershenno sekretno, 1999.

Konkka, Aleksei, and Vyacheslav Orfinskii, eds. *Panozero: Serdtse Belomorskoi Karelii*. Petrozavodsk: Izdatel'stvo PetrGU, 2003.

Kopytoff, Igor. "The Cultural Biography of Things: Commoditization as Process." In *The Social Life of Things*, edited by Arjun Appadurai, 64–91. Cambridge: Cambridge University Press, 1986.

Koselleck, Reinhart. *Futures Past: On the Semantics of Historical Time*. New York: Columbia University Press, 2004.

Koshev, M. A. *Istoriia i problemy kul'turno-tekhnicheskogo razvitiia rabochikh kadrov narodov Severnogo Kavkaza v 60-e—nachale 80-kh godov*. Maikop: [n.p.], 1994.

Kositskii, G. I. *Tsivilizatsiia i serdtse*. Moscow: Nauka, 1977.

Kotkin, Stephen. *Magnetic Mountain: Stalinism as a Civilization*. Berkeley: University of California Press, 1995.

Koval, M. B. "Stanovlenie i razvitie sistemy vospitatel'noi deiatel'nosti vneshkol'nykh ob'edinenii." Doctor of Sciences dissertation in education, Moscow, 1991.

Kowalczuk, Ilko-Sascha, and Stefan Wolle. *Roter Stern über Deutschland: Sowjetische Truppen in der DDR*. Berlin: Ch. Links Verlag, 2010.

Kozlov, Aleksei. *Kozel na sakse*. Moscow: Vagrius, 1998.

Kozlov, G. A., ed. *Politicheskaia ekonomiia: Sotsializm—pervaia faza kommunisticheskogo sposoba proizvodstva*. Moscow: Mysl', 1975.

Kozlov, Vladimir. *Realnaia kultura: Ot alternativy do emo*. Moscow: Amfora, 2008.

Kozulin, Alex. "The Concept of Activity in Soviet Psychology: Vygotsky, His Disciples and Critics." *American Psychologist* 41, no. 3 (1986): 264–74.

Krapivina, L. A. "Pionerskii otriad 'Karavella': Vzgliad skvoz' prizmu desiatiletiia." *Obrazovanie i nauka* 4 (2012): 128–43.

Kriukova, I. A. "Dekorativno-prikladnoie iskusstvo." In *Ocherki sovremennogo sovetskogo iskusstva*, edited by I. A. Kriukova, G. A. Nedoshivin, G. Iu. Sternin, A. G. Khalturin, and O. A. Shvidkovskii, 87–104. Moscow: Nauka, 1975.

Ksenofontov, A. A. 1973. *A esli v sem'ie televizor . . . i deti?* Moscow: Znanie.

Kuksanova, Natalia. *Sotsial'no-bytovaia infrastruktura Sibiri (1956–1980-e gg.)*. Novosibirsk: Izd-vo NGU, 1993.

Kukulin, Ilya. "Prodistsiplinarnye i antidistsiplinarnye seti v pozdnesovetskom obshchestve." *Sotsiologicheskoe obozrenie* 16, no. 3 (2017): 136–73.

Kurdenkov, K. N. *Suda: Stroim sami*. Moscow: Sudostroieniie, 1964.

Lacan, Jacques. *The Four Fundamental Concepts of Psycho-Analysis*. Edited by Jacques-Alain Miller. Translated by Alan Sheridan. London: Hogarth Press, 1977.

Ladygin, Vladimir. *Prostoi sovetskii chelovek (vospominaniia spetsialista)*. Tula: OOO TRK "Arsenal," 2001.

Lagutin, Oleg. *Samolet na stole*. Moscow: Izd-vo DOSAAF SSSR, 1988.

LaPierre, Brian. *Hooligans in Khrushchev's Russia: Defining, Policing, and Producing Deviance during the Thaw*. Madison: University of Wisconsin Press, 2012.

Latour, Bruno, and Stève Woolgar. *Laboratory Life: The Social Construction of Scientific Facts*. Princeton: Princeton University Press, 1986.

Lavrin, Aleksandr. *Kto est' kto v perestroike*. Berlin: Blaue Hörner Verlag, 1990.

Lebina, Natalia. *Muzhchina i zhenshchina: Telo, moda, kul'tura. SSSR—ottepel'*. Moscow: NLO, 2015.

Lemon, Alaina. *Between Two Fires: Gypsy Performance and Romani Memory from Pushkin to Post-Socialism*. Durham: Duke University Press, 2000.

——. *Technologies for Intuition: Cold War Circles and Telepathic Rays*. Oakland: University of California Press, 2018.

Lenin, V. I. *Collected Works*. Vol. 14. London: Lawrence & Wishart, 1962.

——. *Polnoe sobranie sochinenii*. Vol. 35. Moscow: Politizdat, 1962.

——. *Selected Works*. Vol. 3. Moscow: Progress Publishers, 1971.

Levi, Vladimir. *Iskusstvo byt' soboi*. Moscow: Znanie, 1973.

Liber, George. *Alexander Dovzhenko: A Life in Soviet Film*. London: British Film Institute, 2002.

Limonov, Eduard. *Inostranets: Smutnoe vremia*. Novosibirsk: Sibirskiie ogni, 1992.

Lines, Richard, and Leif Hellström. *Frog Model Aircraft, 1932–1976: The Complete History of the Flying Aircraft & the Plastic Kits*. London: New Cavendish, 1989.

Liokaftos, Dimitrios. "From 'Classical' To 'Freaky': An Exploration of the Development of Dominant, Organised, Male Bodybuilding Culture." PhD diss., Goldsmiths, University of London, 2012.

Lipovetsky, Mark. "Traektorii ITR-diskursa." *Neprikosnovennyi zapas*, no. 6 (2010): 213–30.

Livshits, L. I. "Istoriia zakonodatel'stva v oblasti okhrany i restavratsii pamiatnikov kul'tury." In *Restavratsiia pamiatnikov istorii i iskusstva v Rossii v XIX–XX vekakh. Istoriia, problemy: Uchebnoe posobie*, edited by L. I. Livshits and A. V. Trezvov, 51–72. Moscow: Alma Mater, 2008.

Luchininov, Sergey. *Iunyi korablestroitel'*. Moscow: Molodaia gvardiia, 1955.

Lukács, György. *Soul and Form*. Translated by Anna Bostock. Cambridge, MA: MIT Press, 1974.

Maksimikhin, I. A. *Kak postriot' model' korablia: Posobie dlia uchashchikhsia*. Leningrad: Gosuchpedgiz, 1956.

Malinowski, Bronislaw. *Argonauts of the Western Pacific: An Account of Native Enterprise and Adventure in the Archipelagoes of Melanesian New Guinea*. LaVergne, TN: Malinowski Press, [1922] 2008.

Martin, Terry Dean. *The Affirmative Action Empire: Nations and Nationalism in the Soviet Union, 1923–1939*. Ithaca, NY: Cornell University Press, 2001.

Marx, Karl. *The Eighteenth Brumaire of Louis Bonaparte*. New York: International Publishers, 1981.

Marx, Karl, and Friedrich Engels. *Collected Works*. Vol. 25. New York: International Publishers, 1987.

Matza, Tomas. *Shock Therapy: Psychology, Precarity, and Well-Being in Postsocialist Russia*. Durham: Duke University Press, 2018.

Mauch, Christof, and Thomas Zeller, eds. *The World Beyond the Windshield: Roads and Landscapes in the United States and Europe*. Athens: Ohio University Press, 2008.

Mauer, Eva, Julia Richers, Monica Rüthers, and Carmen Scheide, eds. *Soviet Space Culture: Cosmic Enthusiasm in Socialist Societies*. Basingstoke: Palgrave Macmillan, 2011.

Mawhinney, Michelle. "Marx, Nature, and the Ethics of Nonidentity." *Rethinking Marxism* 12, no. 1 (2000): 47–64.

McCannon, John. "Tabula Rasa in the North: The Soviet Arctic and Mythic Landscapes in Stalinist Popular Culture," in *The Landscape of Stalinism: The Art and Ideology of Soviet Space*, ed. Evgeny Dobrenko and Eric Naiman, eds., 241–60. Seattle: University of Washington Press, 2005.

McLuhan, Marshall. *Understanding Media: The Extensions of Man*. New York: McGraw-Hill, 1964.

Medynskii, Ye. N. *Vneshkol'noe obrazovanie, ego znachenie, organizatsiia i tekhnika* 4th ed. Moscow: Nauka, 1918.

Melentiev, Vitalii. *33 marta. 2005 god*. Moscow: Gos. izd-vo det. lit-ry, 1957.

Melnikov, Igor, ed. *Muzei-zapovednik Kizhi. 40 let*. Petrozavodsk: Scandinavia, 2006.

Messner, Michael A. "When Bodies Are Weapons: Masculinity and Violence in Sport." *International Review for the Sociology of Sport* 25, no. 3 (September 1, 1990): 203–20.

Mickiewicz, Ellen Propper. *Split Signals: Television and Politics in the Soviet Union*. New York: Oxford University Press, 1988.

Miller, Daniel. *Material Culture and Mass Consumption. Social Archaeology*. Oxford: Blackwell, 1987.

Mogilner, Marina. *Homo Imperii: A History of Physical Anthropology in Russia*. Lincoln: University of Nebraska Press, 2013.

Morgovskii, Anton. *Anatolii Kashpirovskii . . . Vchera, segodnia, zavtra . . .* Kiev: Molod', 1990.

Moroz, Oleg. *Ot imeni nauki: O sueveriiakh XX veka*. Moscow: Politizdat, 1989.

Muratov, Sergei. "Soviet Television and the Structure of Broadcasting Authority." *Journal of Communication* 41, no. 2 (1991): 172–84.

——. *Televidenie v poiskakh televideniia: Khronika avtorskikh nabliudenii*. Moscow: Izd-vo MGU, 2009.

Murzin, Dmitry. *Bibliia bodibildinga*. Moscow: Eksmo, 2011.

Musina, R. N. "Sotsial'no-etnicheskie aspekty sovremennoi dukhovnoi kul'tury sel'skikh tatar." *Etnograficheskoe obozrenie*, 5 (1983): 88–97.

Nazimova, A. K., ed. *Sovetskie rabochie v usloviiakh uskoreniia sotsial'no-ekonomicheskogo razvitiia*. Moscow: Nauka, 1987.

Nepomniashchii, Nikolai. "Na poroge nevedomogo (Tri vstrechi s zagadochnym neznakomtsem)." In *Vremia iskat'*, edited by V. D. Zakharchenko, 23–30. Moscow: Molodaia gvardiia, 1990.

Nikitina, Vera. "God za godom: 1990 g." *Monitoring obshchestvennogo mneniia: Ekonomicheskiie i sotsial'nye peremeny*, no. 5 (1997): 42–44.

Nikolskaia, Roza F. *Karel'skaia kukhnia*. Petrozavodsk: Karelia, 1986.

Novak, G. M. *Katera, lodki i motory v voprosakh i otvetakh: Spravochnik*. Moscow: Sudostroienie, 1977.

Nuvakhov, Boris. *Doktor Ilizarov*. Moscow: Progress, 1987.

Obruchev, Sergei. "Sovremennoe sostoianie problemy o snezhnom cheloveke." *Priroda*, no. 10 (1959): 60–66.

Okabe, Takehiro. "Negotiating Elias Lönnrot: Shared Soviet-Finnish National Symbol Articulated and Blurred, 1945–1952." *Nordic Historical Review*, special issue "Language and Border between Scandinavia and Russia," edited by Alexey Golubev, Antti Räihä and Aleksandr Tolstikov, no. 2 (2015): 129–49.

Opolovnikov, Aleksandr. *Muzei dereviannogo zodchestva*. Moscow: Stroiizdat, 1968.

———. *Restavratsiia pamiatnikov narodnogo zodchestva*. Moscow: Stroiizdat, 1974.

———. *Kizhi*. 2nd ed. Moscow: Stroiizdat, 1976.

———. *Rus' dereviannaia: Obrazy russkogo dereviannogo zodchestva*. Moscow: Detlit, 1981.

Orfinskii, Vyacheslav. *V mire skazochnoi real'nosti: Dereviannaia arkhitektura Karelii*. Petrozavodsk: Karelia, 1972.

Orlova, Galina. "Fiziki-iadershchiki v bor'be za kosmos. Apokrif." *Vestnik PNIPU*, no. 2 (2018): 108–26

Oushakine, Serguei. "The Terrifying Mimicry of Samizdat." *Public Culture* 13, no. 2 (2001): 191–214.

———. "'Chelovek roda on': Znaki otsutstviia," in *O muzhe(n)stvennosti*, edited by Serguei Oushakine, 7–40. Moscow: NLO, 2002.

———. *The Patriotism of Despair: Nation, War, and Loss in Russia*. Ithaca, NY: Cornell University Press, 2009.

———. "'Against the Cult of Things': On Soviet Productivism, Storage Economy, and Commodities with No Destination." *Russian Review* 73, no. 2 (2014): 198–236.

———. "'Ne vzletevshiie samolioty mechty': O pokolenii formal'nogo metoda." In *Formal'nyi metod: Antologiia russkogo modernizma*. Edited by Serguei Oushakine, vol. 1, 1–14. Moscow: Kabinetnyi uchenyi, 2016.

———. "Mnogo khleba i mnogo roz: O krasote i pol'ze sovetkogo veshchizma." Unpublished paper.

Palmer, Scott W. *Dictatorship of the Air: Aviation Culture and the Fate of Modern Russia*. Cambridge: Cambridge University Press, 2006.

Paretskaya, Anna. "A Middle Class without Capitalism? Socialist Ideology and Post-Collectivist Discourse in the Late-Soviet Era." In *Soviet Society in the Era of Late Socialism, 1964–1985*, edited by Neringa Klumbytė and Gulnaz Sharafutdinova, 43–66. New York: Lexington Books, 2013.

Parfionov, Leonid. *Namedni. Nasha era. 1971–1980*. Moscow: KoLibri, 2010.

———. *Namedni. Nasha era. 1981–1990*. Moscow: KoLibri, 2010.

Pearson, David. *New Organic Architecture: The Breaking Wave*. Berkeley: University of California Press, 2001.

Perevozchikov, Aleksandr. *Fenomen? Sindrom? Ili . . .* Moscow: Znanie, 1990.

Pilkington, Hilary. *Russia's Youth and Its Culture: A Nation's Constructors and Constructed*. London: Routledge, 1994.

Pinsky, Anatoly. "The Diaristic Form and Subjectivity under Khrushchev." *Slavic Review* 73, no. 4 (December 1, 2014): 805–27.

Pirozhkov, V. F. *Zakony prestupnogo mira molodezhi: Kriminal'naia subkul'tura*. Tver: Priz, 1994.

Pokrovskaia, Irina. *Naselenie Karelii*. Petrozavodsk: Karelia, 1978.

Polikarpov, Nikolai. *Model'nye khitrosti: Posobie dlia modelistov*. Moscow: Tseikhgauz, 2006.

"Polozheniie o nauchno-issledovatel'skom institute istoriko-teoreticheskikh problem narodnogo zodchestva," a bylaw of Petrozavodsk State University, Petrozavodsk, 1997.

Popovsky, Mark. *Tretii lishnii: On, ona i sovetskii rezhim*. London: Overseas Publications, 1985.

Prezidium VTsSPS. *Postanovlenie ot 16.10.1959 "Ob obshchestvennykh domovykh komitetakh v gosudarstvennom zhilishchnom fonde RSFSR."* Moscow: Izd-vo VTsSPS, 1959.

Raibmon, Paige. *Authentic Indians: Episodes of Encounter from the Late-Nineteenth-Century Northwest Coast*. Durham: Duke University Press, 2005.

Raleigh, Donald. *Russia's Sputnik Generation: Soviet Baby Boomers Talk about Their Lives*. Bloomington: Indiana University Press, 2006.

Ramet, Sabrina P. "UFOs over Russia and Eastern Europe." *Journal of Popular Culture* 32, no. 3 (1998): 81–99.

Razumikhin, Aleksandr. "Pravilo bez iskliuchenii, ili Prozrachnaia zlost' i intelligentnye mal'chiki Vladislava Krapivina." *Ural*, no. 8 (1988): 149–52.

Reid, Susan E. "Cold War in the Kitchen: Gender and the De-Stalinization of Consumer Taste in the Soviet Union under Khrushchev." *Slavic Review* 61, no. 2 (2002): 211–52.

——. "Khrushchev Modern: Agency and Modernization in the Soviet Home." *Cahiers Du Monde Russe* 47, no. 1/2 (January 1, 2006): 227–68.

——. "The Meaning of Home: 'The Only Bit of the World You Can Have to Yourself.'" In *Borders of Socialism: Private Spheres of Soviet Russia*, edited by Lewis Siegelbaum, 145–70. New York: Palgrave Macmillan, 2006.

——. "Who Will Beat Whom? Soviet Popular Reception of the American National Exhibition in Moscow, 1959." *Kritika: Explorations in Russian and Eurasian History* 9, no. 4 (Fall 2008): 855–904.

——. "Everyday Aesthetics in the Khrushchev-era Standard Apartment." In *Everyday Life in Russia: Past and Present*, edited by Choi Chatterjee, David L. Ransel, Mary Cavender and Karen Petrone, 203–33. Bloomington: Indiana University Press, 2015.

Remnick, David. *Lenin's Tomb: The Last Days of the Soviet Empire*. New York: Vintage Books, 1994.

Rivkin-Fish, Michele. *Women's Health in Post-Soviet Russia: The Politics of Intervention*. Bloomington: Indiana University Press, 2005.

Rodionov, Stanislav. *Kriminal'nyi talant: Povesti*. St. Petersburg: Interlast, 1994.

Rolf, Malte. *Soviet Mass Festivals, 1917–1991*. Pittsburgh: University of Pittsburgh Press, 2013.

Romanov, A. A., and A. I. Shuvalov, "Genezis klubno-kruzhkovoi raboty v pedagogicheskoi praktike Rossii." *Psikhologo-pedagogicheskii poisk* 1 (2007): 109–19.

Romberg, Kristin. *Gan's Constructivism: Aesthetic Theory for an Embedded Modernism*. Berkeley: University of California Press, 2018.

Roth-Ey, Kristin. *Moscow Prime Time: How the Soviet Union Built the Media Empire That Lost the Cultural Cold War*. Ithaca, NY: Cornell University Press, 2011.

Rotkirch, Anna. *The Man Question: Loves and Lives in Late 20th Century Russia*. Helsinki: University of Helsinki—Department of Social Policy, 2000.

Rozental, Ditmar. *Upravlenie v russkom iazyke*. Moscow: Nauka, 1981.

Rubin, Eli. *Synthetic Socialism: Plastics and Dictatorship in the German Democratic Republic*. Chapel Hill: University of North Carolina Press, 2012.

Ryle, Gilbert. *The Concept of Mind*. London: Routledge, 2009.

Salmenniemi, Suvi. "Post-Soviet Khoziain: Class, Self and Morality in Russian Self-Help Literature." In *Rethinking class in Russia*, ed. Suvi Salmenniemi, 67–84. London: Routledge, 2012.

Sappak, Vladimir. *Televidenie i my: Chetyre besedy*. Moscow: Iskusstvo, 1963.

Satjukow, Silke. *Besatzer: "Die Russen" in Deutschland 1945–1994*. Göttingen: Vandenhoeck & Ruprecht, 2008.

Schechter, Brandon. *The Stuff of Soldiers: A History of the Red Army in World War II through Objects*. Ithaca, NY: Cornell University Press, 2019.

Sedgwick, Eve Kosofsky. *Touching Feeling: Affect, Pedagogy, Performativity*. Durham: Duke University Press, 2003.

Sekula, Allan. "The Body and the Archive." *October* 39 (December 1, 1986): 3–64.

Seliutskii, Aleksandr, ed. *Derzkie formuly tvorchestva*. Petrozavodsk: Karelia, 1987.

——, ed. *Pravila igry bez pravil*. Petrozavodsk: Karelia, 1989.

Senyavskii, A. S. *Rossiiskii gorod v 1960-e–1980-e gg*. Moscow: Izd-vo MGU, 1995.

Sevan, Olga. *"Malye Korely": Arkhangel'skii muzei dereviannogo zodchestva*. Moscow: Progress-Traditsiia, 2011.

Sevastianov, A. M. *Volshebstvo modelei: Posobie dlia sudomodelistov*. Nizhny Novgorod: Nizhpoligraf, 1997.

Sherstennikov, Lev. *Ostalis' za kadrom*. Moscow: Muzei organicheskoi kul'tury, 2013.

Shilova, Galina. "Ideino-vospitatel'naia rabota po mestu zhitel'stva v sovremennykh usloviiakh i puti ee sovershenstvovanii." Dr. Sc. in History thesis, Academy of Social Sciences of the CPSU Central Committee, 1984.

Shklovsky, Viktor. "Zoo, ili Pis'ma ne o liubvi." In *Zhili-byli*, 119–208. Moscow: Sovetskii pisatel', 1964.

——. "Art as Technique." In *Russian Formalist Criticism: Four Essays*, edited by Lee T. Lemon and Marion J. Reis, 3–24. Lincoln: University of Nebraska Press, 1965.

——. "Kuda shagaet Dziga Vertov?" in *Formal'nyi metod: Antologiia russkogo modernizma*, edited by Serguei Oushakine, vol. 1, 192–94. Moscow: Kabinetnyi uchenyi, 2016.

Shvartsman, Klara. *Etika . . . bez morali (kritika sovremennykh burzhuaznykh eticheskikh teorii)*. Moscow: Mysl', 1964.

Siegelbaum, Lewis. *Cars for Comrades: The Life of the Soviet Automobile*. Ithaca, NY: Cornell University Press, 2008.

Silverstone, Roger. *Television and Everyday Life*. London: Routledge, 1994.

Simpson, Pat. "Parading Myths: Imaging New Soviet Woman on Fizkul'turnik's Day, July 1944." *Russian Review* 63, no. 2 (2004): 187–211.

Smith, Mark B. *Property of Communists: The Urban Housing Program from Stalin to Khrushchev*. DeKalb: Northern Illinois University Press, 2010.

Smolyak, Olga. " 'Rabota na sebia': Ispol'zovanie resursov promyshlennogo predpriiatiia v lichnykh tseliakh v pozdniuiu sovetskuiu epokhu." *Laboratorium: Russian Review of Social Research* 6, no. 2 (2014): 21–57.

Snegiriova, T. I. *Dukhovnaia kul'tura razvitogo sotsialisticheskogo obshchestva*. Moscow: Nauka, 1981.

Sokolov, Boris. *Wolf Messing*. Moscow: Molodaia gvardiia, 2010.

Soloukhin, Vladimir. *Searching for Icons in Russia*. New York: Harcourt Brace Jovanovich, 1972.

Solovyov, Vladimir. *1001 vopros o proshlom, nastoiashchem i budushchem Rossii*. Moscow: Eksmo, 2010.

Solzhenitsyn, Aleksandr. *The Gulag Archipelago, 1918–1956: An Experiment in Literary Investigation, V–VII*. Translated by Harry Willetts. New York: Harper & Row, 1979.

Sorokin, Yuri. *Atleticheskaia podgotovka doprizyvnika, ili tel'niashka v podarok.* Moscow: Sovetskii sport, 1990.

Spigel, Lynn. *Make Room for TV: Television and the Family Ideal in Postwar America.* Chicago: University of Chicago Press, 1992.

Stalin, Joseph. *Sochineniia. Works.* Vol. 6. Moscow: Foreign Languages Publishing House, 1953.

——. Vol. 15. Moscow: Pisatel', 1997.

Staniukovich, Kirill. *Po sledam udivitel'noi zagadki.* Moscow: Molodaia gvardiia, 1965.

Starks, Tricia. *The Body Soviet Propaganda, Hygiene, and the Revolutionary State.* Madison: University of Wisconsin Press, 2008.

Steiner, Evgeny. *Stories for Little Comrades: Revolutionary Artists and the Making of Early Soviet Children's Books.* Seattle: University of Washington Press, 1999.

Stepanov, Andrei. "Severnorusskaia izba: Dinamika prostranstva i povsednevnyi opyt (2-ia polovina XX–nachalo XXI v.)." *Antropologicheskii forum* 16 (2012): 72–105."

Stewart, Susan. *On Longing: Narratives of the Miniature, the Gigantic, the Souvenir, the Collection.* Durham: Duke University Press, 1993.

Stites, Richard. "Soviet Russian Wartime Culture: Freedom and Control, Spontaneity and Consciousness." In *The People's War: Responses to World War II in the Soviet Union,* edited by Robert W. Thurston and Bernd Bonwetsch, 171–86. Urbana: University of Illinois Press, 2000.

Stocking, George. *Victorian Anthropology.* New York: Free Press, 1987.

Stoliarov, Iu. S. *Iunye konstruktory i tekhnicheskoe tvorchestvo.* Moscow: Izd-vo DOSAAF, 1966.

Stoliarov, Iu. S., B. P. Iusov, and V. I. Leibson. "Child Creativity." In *The Great Soviet Encyclopedia,* vol. 8, 19–22. New York: Macmillan, 1975.

Strugatsky, Arkady, and Boris Strugatsky. *Prisoners of Power.* New York: Macmillan, 1977.

Sundiiev, I. Iu. "Anatomiia neformal'nykh ob'iedinenii (tipologiia i kharakteristika)." In *Po nepisannym zakonam ulitsy . . . ,* edited by Iu. M. Kotchenkov, 46–55. Moscow: Iuridicheskaia literatura, 1991.

Suni, Leo. "Ingermanlandskie finny: Istoricheskii ocherk." In *Finny v Rossii: Istoriia, kul'tura, sud'ba,* edited by Eino Kiuru, 4–25. Petrozavodsk: Izd-vo PetrGU, 1998.

Taroeva, Vera. *Material'naia kul'tura karel (Karel'skaia ASSR).* Leningrad: Nauka, 1965.

Tenno, Georgii, and Yuri Sorokin. *Atletizm.* Moscow: Molodaia gvardiia, 1968.

Thrift, Nigel. "Intensities of Feeling: Towards a Spatial Politics of Affect." *Geografiska Annaler. Series B, Human Geography* 86, no. 1 (2004): 57–78.

Torgovlia SSSR: Statisticheskii sbornik. Moscow: Finansy i statistika, 1989.

Toshchenko, Zhan. *Sotsial'naia infrastruktura: Sushchnost' i puti razvitiia.* Moscow: Mysl', 1980.

Tretiakov, Sergei. "The Biography of the Object." *October* 118 (2006): 57–62.

Troi, Dilan, Viktor Troiegubov, and Margarita Pushkina. *"Ariia": Legenda o dinozavre (s iskopaiemykh vremion).* Moscow: Nota-R, 2005.

Tvardovsky, Aleksandr. "Rech' A. T. Tvardovskogo." In *Vneocherednoi XXI S'ezd Kommunistichekoi partii Sovetskogo Soiuza: Stenograficheskii otchet,* vol. 1, 558–65. Moscow: Politizdat, 1959.

Ukran, M. L., V. M. Smolevskii, and A. M. Shlemin. *Atleticheskaia gimnastika: Dlia iunoshei*. Moscow: Fizkul'tura i sport, 1965.

Urry, John. *The Tourist Gaze: Leisure and Travel in Contemporary Societies*. London: Sage, 1990.

Utekhin, Ilia. *Ocherki kommunal'nogo byta*. Moscow: O.G.I., 2001.

Vanslov, Viktor. *Izobrazitel'noe iskusstvo avtonomnykh respublik RSFSR: Al'bom*. Moscow: Khudozhnik RSFSR, 1973.

Varga-Harris, Christine. *Stories of House and Home: Soviet Apartment Life during the Khrushchev Years*. Ithaca, NY: Cornell University Press, 2015.

Vasilyeva, Zinaida. "Soobshchestvo TRIZ: Logika i etika sovetskogo izobretatelia." *Etnograficheskoe obozrenie* 3 (2012): 29–46.

Vertov, Dziga. *Kino-Eye: The Writings of Dziga Vertov*. Edited by Annette Michelson. Translated by Kevin O'Brien. Berkeley: University of California Press, 1984.

Vihavainen, Rosa. "Common and Dividing Things in Homeowners' Associations." In *Political Theory and Community Building in Post-Soviet Russia*, edited by Oleg Kharkhordin and Risto Alapuro, 139–63. London: Routledge, 2010.

Vihavainen, Timo. *The Inner Adversary: The Struggle against Philistinism as the Moral Mission of the Russian Intelligentsia*. Washington, DC: New Academia Publishing, 2006.

Vysotsky, Vladimir. *Sochineniia*. Vol. 2. Moscow: Lokid, 1999.

Wajcman, Judy. *TechnoFeminism*. Cambridge: Polity, 2004.

Weider, Joe, and Ben Weider. *Brothers of Iron*. Champaign, IL: Sports Publishing, 2006.

Welsch, Wolfgang. "Sport Viewed Aesthetically, and Even as Art?" In *The Aesthetics of Everyday Life*, edited by Andrew Light and Jonathan Smith, 135–55. New York: Columbia University Press, 2005.

Werneke, Jessica. "The Boundaries of Art: Soviet Photography from 1956 to 1970." PhD diss., University of Texas at Austin, 2015.

Widdis, Emma. "Faktura: Depth and Surface in Early Soviet Set Design." *Studies in Russian and Soviet Cinema* 3, no. 3 (2009): 5–32.

——. "Sew Yourself Soviet: The Pleasures of Texture in the Machine Age." In *Petrified Utopia: Happiness Soviet Style*, edited by Marina Balina and Evgeny Dobrenko, 115–32. London: Anthem Press, 2011.

——. *Socialist Senses: Film, Feeling, and the Soviet Subject, 1917–1940*. Bloomington: Indiana University Press, 2017.

Wierzbicka, Anna. "Antitotalitarian Language in Poland: Some Mechanisms of Linguistic Self-Defense." *Language in Society* 19, no. 1 (1990): 1–59.

Winner, Langdon. "Do Artifacts Have Politics?" *Daedalus* 109, no. 1 (1980): 121–36.

Wise, M. Norton. "Mediating Machines," *Science in Context* 2 (1988): 77–113.

Yasinovsky, Nikolai. *Zheleznaia pravda "Russkogo koshmara" II*. Moscow: Veche, 2011.

Yurchak, Alexei. *Everything Was Forever, until It Was No More: The Last Soviet Generation*. Princeton, NJ: Princeton University Press, 2006.

Zaitsev, Stanislav. "Kak otkryt' Ameriku." In *Tot'ma: Istoriko-kraevedcheskii al'manakh*. Vyp. 1, edited by M. A. Beznin, 334–72. Vologda: Rus', 1995.

Zaitseva, M. A. "K voprosu o roli uchrezhdenii vneshkol'noi raboty v vospitanii sotsial'noi aktivnosti starsheklassnikov v 50–80-e gg. XX veka." *Yaroslavskii pedagogicheskii vestnik* 1 (2009): 90–94.

Zinchenko, V. P., and A. N. Leontiev. "Parapsikhologiia." *Bol'shaia sovetskaia entsiklopedia*, 3rd ed., vol. 19, 192–93. Moscow: Sovetskaia entsiklopediia, 1975.

Zinchenko, V. P., A. N. Leontiev, B. V. Lomov, and A. P. Luriia. 1973. "Parapsikhologiia: Fiktsiia ili real'nost'?" *Voprosy filosofii* 9 (1973): 128–36.

Žižek, Slavoj. *The Sublime Object of Ideology*. London: Verso, 2008.

Zlotin, B., and A. Zusman. *Mesiats pod zvezdami fantazii*. Kishinev: Lumina, 1988.

Zubok, Vladislav. *A Failed Empire: The Soviet Union in the Cold War from Stalin to Gorbachev*. Chapel Hill: University of North Carolina Press, 2007.

——. *Zhivago's Children: The Last Russian Intelligentsia*. Cambridge: Harvard University Press, 2009.

Index

accretions, 64, 74–78, 134. *See also* icons, Orthodox; Opolovnikov, Aleksandr; wood

adults and adulthood, 43, 45, 53, 93, 97, 103, 107–8, 114, 157

aesthetics; avant-gardist, 22–23, 87; of the body, 122, 124–25, 134, 138; politics of, 91, 107, 111; post-Stalinist, 24, 38; Stalinist, 24

affect, 9, 13, 15, 108. *See also* emotions

affective objects, 13, 15–16, 38–40, 44, 160–61, 82, 91–92, 107–9, 118, 146, 158, 165. *See also* things: assemblages of bodies and

Altshuller, Genrikh, 28, 29, 30, 31, 34, 35, 37, 165. *See also* TRIZ (Theory of Inventive Problem Solving)

Andronikov, Iraklii, 148, 159

apartment blocks, 92–93, 185n10; doors, 90–91, 112; interior design, 146, 148–51. *See also* basements; stairwells; urban space

architectural preservation, 62–65, 70–82, 85–88, 116, 134, 165; politics of, 82, 87–89. *See also* cultural heritage; Kizhi (museum); Opolovnikov, Aleksandr

architecture: Constructivist, 61–63, 75, 77, 80, 87, 93; of Northern Romanticism, 86; as "social condenser," 61; vernacular, 61–65, 67–68, 70–81. *See also* Ginzburg, Moisei; Narkomfin House

archive. *See* knowledge: archive of

authenticity, 16, 53, 56, 58, 63–65, 68–71, 74–82, 85–87, 89, 181n25

basements, 2, 8, 13, 91, 97, 99, 103, 105, 109, 113–15, 126–41. *See also* apartment blocks

Benjamin, Walter, 41, 53

biopolitics, 25, 134, 137

boats and boatbuilding, 32–33, 35–36, 67, 69, 72, 81–85, 88, 165

body, 1, 4, 32, 100, 121–22, 124, 140–41, 143, 152–53, 155, 159, 161; aggressive, 105, 114; classical, 134–35; exercising, 152–53; inner reserves of, 116, 120–21, 143–44; materiality of, 8; muscular, 16, 115, 124–25, 131, 134–38; national, 8, 39–40, 89, 157–59, 162, 166; teenage, 105; as spectacle, 119, 124, 137, 139, 153

bodybuilding, 2, 16–18, 113–16, 121–41, 165–66; magazines, 122–24, 130, 135; moral panic about, 113–14; nutrition, 129–30; opposition to, 123–26, 131–32, 136–37

Briusova, Vera, 78, 79. *See also* icons, Orthodox

Brumel, Valery, 118, 190, 202

children and childhood, 34, 41–47, 54–55, 58–60, 97, 99, 102, 107, 109–110, 118, 127, 131, 154, 157. *See also* teenagers; youth

Chumak, Alan, 9, 143–48, 156–59. *See also* Kashpirovsky, Anatoly; paranormal; television set

citizenship, 8, 11, 30, 34, 43, 58, 102, 110, 113–15, 133–34, 137, 141, 158

class, 8, 43, 50–51, 73–75, 90, 92, 166; antagonism and conflicts, 8, 69, 92, 111, 160; educated, 16–17, 30, 33, 64, 88, 90–91, 103, 110, 145, 157, 160; working, 25, 91, 105, 115, 133

collections, 8, 41, 44–45, 53–60, 166. *See also* scale models

community-building, 2, 59, 148, 164–65

concrete, 62–63, 82

consumption, 2, 10–11, 33, 37, 53, 164

creativity, 15, 27, 30, 47

cultural heritage, 76, 83, 85; buildings as, 15–16, 63–65, 72, 76–81; UNESCO monuments of, 61–62. *See also* architecture: vernacular; Opolovnikov, Aleksandr